Food and Beverage Management

For the hospitality, tourism and event industries

The third edition

John Cousins, David Foskett and Andrew Pennington

The Food and Beverage Training Company, London

The London School of Tourism, Hospitality and Leisure, University of West London

(G) **Goodfellow Publishers Ltd**

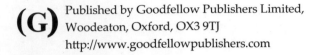 Published by Goodfellow Publishers Limited,
Woodeaton, Oxford, OX3 9TJ
http://www.goodfellowpublishers.com

British Library Cataloguing in Publication Data: a catalogue record for this title is available from the British Library.

Library of Congress Catalog Card Number: on file.

ISBN: 978-1-906884-26-0

Design and typesetting by P.K. McBride, www.macbride.org.uk

Printed by Marston Book Services, www.marston.co.uk

Cover design by Cylinder, www.cylindermedia.com

Contents

Preface

Modern day food and beverage (or foodservice) operations are continuing to improve in the quality of food, beverages and the service on offer. Professionalism is increasing, through better training and development, and there is a much greater understanding of customer needs. Additionally the quality of service is now becoming the principal differentiating factor when customers are choosing between different establishments. It is against this background that this text has been revised.

The content of this book is intended to be reflective of current industrial practice but this does not mean that it should be seen as a prescriptive book. It provides information and viewpoints on a variety of aspects of food and beverage management and considers various approaches which students and food and beverage practitioners will find useful. The book will also be of value to those in the hospitality, tourism and events industries who are responsible for purchasing food and beverage services.

The aims of the book are to:

- provide supporting information for those involved or likely to be involved, at a variety of levels, in food and beverage management;
- meet the needs of students and practitioners who want to acquire underpinning knowledge and skills in order for them to achieve competence in industry at the equivalent of up to level 4 NVQ;
- meet the broader needs of students studying for a range of qualifications including Higher Diplomas, Institute of Hospitality and foundation and undergraduate degrees;.
- provide support for in-company training programmes, and
- provide a framework for the achievement of higher levels knowledge and skills.

The book covers aspects of the management of food and beverage (or foodservice) operations that are applicable to a wide variety of industrial sectors. We have also assumed that those using this text will have already acquired knowledge and skills in food and beverage operations.

The underlying thinking behind this text relies on the application of a systems approach to the management of operations. The text therefore proposes systematic approaches to the design, planning and control of food and beverage operations, and also recognises the need to manage foodservice operations as operating systems. The book considers a food and beverage operation as comprising four distinct but interlinked operating systems: food production; beverage provision; food and beverage service as a delivery system, and food and beverage service as a customer process system. The component parts of the four systems are examined, as well as the linkages between them, and how these together create a food and beverage operation.

The orientation of the text is to set the consideration of the management of food and beverage operations within a broader business framework. Operations are not an end in themselves and food and beverage management is as much about the management of the business as it is about specific aspects of the food and beverage product.

This approach is reflected throughout the book, with the structure of the book being based on an adaptation of the foodservice cycle in order to provide for a logical presentation of the material (see Chapter 1 page 3). The user is led from consideration of food and beverage operations and the business environment, in Chapter 1, to the relationship between the consumer and the food and beverage product, in Chapters 2 and 3; the operational areas, equipment and staffing considerations in Chapter 4; the management of food production in Chapter 5; beverage provision in Chapter 6, and food and beverage service in Chapter 7. Chapter 8 considers events management in more detail and the book culminates with performance appraisal in Chapter 9 and strategic decision making in Chapter 10.

Learning is supported through the provision of an aim and objectives being identified for each of the chapters. These indicate the learning outcomes that may be achieved and they can also be mapped against the learning outcome requirements of different education programmes, or in-company training courses. In addition, three appendices are provided, which detail particular approaches: an operational calculations exercise is at Appendix A; a listing and explanation of operational and other financial ratios is provided in Appendix B, and an exercise on budget and trading results comparison and evaluation is set out at Appendix C. Teaching and learning is also supported through the provision of PowerPoint presentations available from the publisher's web site.

The main focus of the material is directly relevant to the management of food and beverage operations. For the business management areas such as marketing, personnel and finance there is already a range of well-established resources to support those areas. Although some applications are covered within the book there are also specific references given to other information sources and further reading. Additionally high-level craft in the culinary arts is beyond the scope of the book.

Overall our view remains that successful foodservice operations are those that have a clear understanding of their customers' needs, which they continually seek to meet.

John Cousins, David Foskett and Andrew Pennington,

September 2011

Acknowledgements

The preparation of this text has drawn upon a variety of research and experience. We would like to express our grateful thanks to all the organisations and individuals who gave us assistance and support and especially those who have provided feedback on the previous editions.

In particular we would like to thank:

Academy of Culinary Arts, UK; Academy of Food and Wine Service, UK; Mathew Alexander, lecturer in Marketing, Strathclyde Business School, University of Strathclyde, Glasgow; Foodservice Consultants Society International, UK&I; Croner's Catering, Croner Publications, London; Andrew Durkan, independent food and wine consultant; Institute of Hospitality; IFS Publications, Bedford; Dennis Lillicrap, consultant, author and trainer in food and beverage service; Kevin O'Gorman, Associate Dean, Strathclyde Business School, University of Strathclyde, Glasgow; Conor O'Leary, Director of Food and Beverage, Hyatt Regency London – The Churchill; the Restaurant Association of Great Britain; Carole Rodger, principal lecturer, Leeds Metropolitan University; Ashley Shaw, House Manager, The Westbury Hotel, London; Suzanne Weeks, senior lecturer in Hospitality Management and Licensing Law at University of West London, and Linden Wilkie, Managing Director, the Fine Wine Experience Ltd, London and Hong Kong.

A special thank-you goes to Cailein Gillespie, formerly of the Scottish Hotel School, who was co-author of the second edition.

1 Food and beverage operations and management

Aim

This chapter aims to set the scene for the rest of the text.

Objectives

This chapter is intended to support you in:

- Identifying the foodservice cycle as a tool for the systematic examination of foodservice operations
- Establishing the relationship between the foodservice cycle and the content and structure of this book
- identifying and applying a systems approach to foodservice operations
- Categorising the industry sectors
- Exploring the nature of the foodservice product
- Identifying the nature of customer demand
- Analysing the business environment in order to identify factors which may affect the success of a foodservice organisation
- Identifying the legal framework in which the foodservice industry operates.

1.1   Food and beverage operations

Food and beverage (or foodservice) operations are concerned with the provision of food and a variety of beverages within business. The international foodservice industry provides millions of meals a day in a wide variety of types of operation.

■ *Food* can include a wide range of styles and cuisine types. These can be classified by country, for example, traditional British or Italian; by type of cuisine, for example, oriental; or a particular speciality such as fish, vegetarian or health food.

■ *Beverages* include all alcoholic and non-alcoholic drinks. Alcoholic beverages include wines and all other types of alcoholic drink such as cocktails, beers and cider, spirits and liqueurs. Non-alcoholic beverages include bar beverages such as mineral waters, juices, squashes and aerated waters, as well as tea, coffee, chocolate, milk and milk drinks and also proprietary drinks such as Bovril.

The various elements that make up a food and beverage operation can be summarised into the eight stages of the foodservice cycle, as illustrated shown in Figure 1.1. Foodservice operations are therefore concerned with:

1 The consumer needs and market potential in the various sectors of the foodservice industry.

2 The formulation of policy and business objectives that will guide the choice of operational methods that will be used.

3 The interpretation of demand in order to make decisions on the range and type of food and beverages to be provided, as well as other services, and the service levels and prices to be charged.

4 The planning and design to create the convergence of facilities required for the food and beverage operations and making decision s about the plant and equipment required.

5 The organisation of provisioning for food and beverages and other purchasing requirements to meet the needs of the food production, beverage provision and the service methods being used.

6 Operational knowledge of technical methods and processes and ability in the production and service processes and methods available to the foodservice operator, understanding the varying resource requirements (including staffing) for their operation, as well as decision-making on the appropriateness of the various processes and methods to meet operational requirements.

7 Control of costs of materials and other costs, such as labour and overheads, associated with the operation of food production, beverage provision and other services, and the control of revenue.

8 The monitoring of customer satisfaction to continually check on the extent to which the operation is meeting customer needs and achieving customer satisfaction.

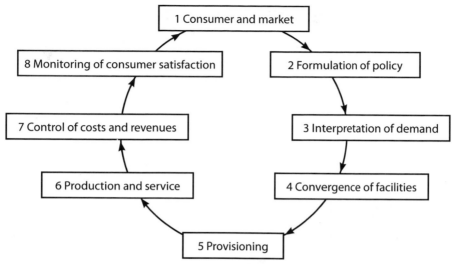

Figure 1.1: The foodservice cycle

Source: Cracknell, H.L. and Kaufmann, R.J., 2002, Practical Professional Catering Management, 2nd edn, Thomson Learning Vocational

The foodservice cycle is not just a statement of what food and beverage operations are concerned with. It is also a dynamic model in the sense that difficulties in one area of the cycle will cause difficulties in the elements of the cycle that follow. Thus, for instance, difficulties with purchasing will have effects on production and service, and control. Similarly, difficulties experienced under one element of the cycle will have their causes in preceding elements.

The structure of the book

The foodservice cycle, and the systematic approach it supports, has also been used to form the basis for the structure of this book. This is indicated by the presentation of the structure of the book in Figure 1.2, which has been developed from an application of the foodservice cycle.

Although presented in a form which is predominately linear, the actual management of food and beverage operations is organic. The structure of the book, given in Figure 1.2, therefore also attempts to indicate the nature of the interrelationship that exists between the various components. Thus all the issues that are raised in Chapter 1 have an impact on all the other issues that are considered in the rest of the book. Consequently any consideration of the customer and product development (Chapters 2 and 3); operational planning (Chapter 4); the methods used in food production (Chapter 5); beverage provision (Chapter 6): those used in food and beverage service (Chapter 7), and the management of events (Chapter 8) must be carried out taking account of, for instance, the systems approach, the nature of demand being met, the business environment and the legal environment. Equally any review of the performance of the operation, as discussed in Chapter 9, must also take account of all the preceding aspects. Additionally any strategic decisions, as discussed on Chapter 10, are as dependent on the outcome of appraising the performance of the operation as they are on appraising the trends in the business environment.

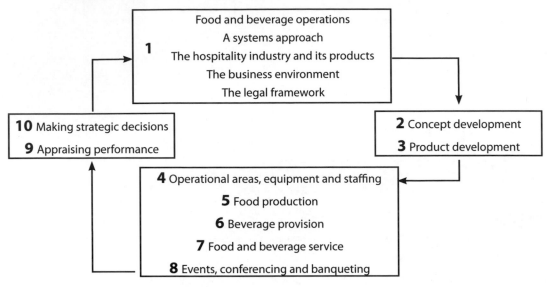

Figure 1.2: The structure of the book

Food and beverage management then, is the management of all the eight stages of the foodservice cycle. It is also systematic and organic; quantitative and qualitative; academic and pragmatic, and also both serious and fun. This is its fascination.

1.2   A systems approach

The underlying thinking behind much of this text relies on the application of a systems approach to the management of food and beverage operations. There are, however, two dimensions to a systems approach:

■ The first dimension of the systems approach is concerned with being systematic in the design, planning and control of a food and beverage operation.

■ The second dimension of the systems approach is concerned with the management of the operating systems within a food and beverage operation.

This systems approach varies from the traditional approaches to foodservice management. The differences are summarised and contrasted by the comparisons that are presented in Table 1.1.

The benefits of adopting the systems, or operations management, approaches have also been reinforced and further supported by various writers (see, for example, Johnston and Clarke, 2008; Jones *et al.*, 2003). Johnston and Clarke (2008) also discuss the nature of service operations management and identify the potential conflict between the demands of the short-term management of the day-to-day operations against the longer-term needs of developing an operations strategy. In addition they identify the constant need for operations managers to improve processes and to motivate people in order to carry out the operations more effectively, so as to achieve greater quality of service and /or productivity.

Table 1.1: Comparison of traditional and system approaches

Traditional approach	Systems approach
Based on assumptions of linearity in the marketplace	Sensitive to changes in business conditions
Depends on the experience of key people	Depends on staff experience and good data
Information not readily available	Information available as needed
Intuitive	Quantitative
Reactive in nature	Proactive in nature
Service driven	Cost and service driven
Vulnerable to turnover of key people	Less vulnerable to turnover of key people
Weak in accountability	Strong in accountability

Source: Developed from Records and Glennie (1991)

The application of systems thinking has also led to a different view being taken of the operating systems that exist within a food and beverage operation. Traditionally a food and beverage operation, and therefore food and beverage management, was seen as being concerned with the management of an operation as a whole. In systems terms this could easily have been seen as the management of three basic systems: a system for food production, a system for beverage provision and a system for food and beverage service. In this traditional view, food and beverage service was primarily seen as a delivery system. This in itself had obvious problems: the customer was largely seen as a passive recipient of the service rather than, as now more widely recognised, a participant in the service process. Fortunately the application of operations management approaches, and the systems thinking associated with it, leads to a different view of the management of food and beverage operations. One of the key outcomes of this was recognising that food and beverage service actually consists of two separate systems, albeit operating at the same time. These are the service sequence and the customer process, as identified below, and explored in more detail in Chapter 7.

Up until the late 1980s there was much discussion about differences between the production of goods and the provision of services. Most of the operations literature at the time was concerned with exploring the supposed differences between production operations management and service operations management. However Morris and Johnston (1987) initially settled much of this argument by taking a more holistic view. They put forward the argument that operations management, and therefore the management of any operation, is concerned with the management of three elements:

- The management of materials
- The management of information
- The management of people (customers).

By linking this thinking in the general operations management field, together with reconsidering the management of food and beverage operations, Cousins (1988) originally identified that there were three distinct systems operating within a single food and beverage operation. This identification had included beverage provision as part of food production, but this is now separated out into a system by itself. The four systems operating within a foodservice operation are then:

1 The system for food production
2 The system for beverage provision
3 The system for delivery or the service sequence
4 The system for customer management or the customer process.

These four systems are tangible systems whose properties are known and can be defined. Figure 1.3 presents a generic diagram for a foodservice operation, which summarises the four systems, their component parts and the relationship between them.

The four systems identified in Figure 1.3 interlink to form the whole operation. In turn each of the four systems can be further broken down into their component parts, or separate sub-systems, for example, 'purchasing'.

For a foodservice operation, food production and beverage provision may be seen as 'hard' systems, which are expected to behave predictably. The customer process however may be seen as a 'soft' system because it involves emotional reactions, personal values and attitudes and shifting expectations, which are personal rather than technical in construction. However the service sequence contains characteristics of both 'hard' and 'soft' systems. It is 'hard' in the technical and procedural aspects of service and 'soft' because there are aspects of it that are to do with interactions between staff and customers and between staff and staff in other departments.

Food and beverage management therefore is concerned with the management of an operation, which is constructed from four identifiable operating systems that are interlinked; and each of these four systems is made up from a variety of sub-systems. Thinking in this way can be useful. Others (see, for example, Johns and Jones, 2000; Jones *et al.*, 2003) support this view. For food and beverage managers understanding the characteristics of systems, and the ways in which they behave, can help in the control of resources (systems inputs), the efficient and effective operation (systems processes), and assure the achievement of the required objectives (systems outputs).

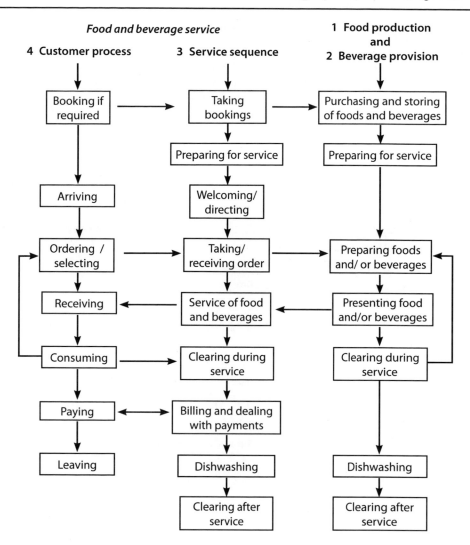

Figure 1.3: Outline of the relationship between the different operating systems within a foodservice operation

Source: Lillicrap and Cousins, 2010

1.3   The hospitality industry and its products

The hospitality industry is usually identified by its output of products that satisfy the demand for food, drink and accommodation away from home. The industry is often split into the accommodation and foodservice industry.

Over the years there has been much discussion, in a similar way to the discussion in the operations management field, about possible differences between products as being divided into goods and services. The approach of this book is to follow the lead of many in talking only about products.

All products, that are produced and sold, have production and delivery elements, although these may be separated by distance, time or both, as in the production of cars, which is separated from the selling of cars in showrooms. All products then have some form of tangible (or physical) element and all products have some intangible (or non-physical) element. In the hospitality industry these two are operating side by side, as part of the product.

Kotler *et al.* (2010) propose that there are particular dimensions of the hospitality industry's product that should be taken into account as they make the service conceptual in nature and difficult to manage. These are:

- **Intangibility** – referring to the nature of the service element of the product. The accommodation and food and beverages can be described and defined but the service element is potentially variable both in the process and in the way it is carried out.

- **Perishability** – the inability to sell tomorrow the rooms or restaurant seats which were not occupied today.

- **Inseparability** – Services cannot be separated from their providers.

- **Variability** – the potential for highly variable procedural execution and level of conviviality.

In addition Knowles (1996) had identified other dimensions that affect the provision of the food and beverage product such as:

- **Simultaneous production and consumption** – the product (from the customer's perspective) is not created until the customer requests it.

- **Ease of duplication** – the core (food, drink and accommodation) of the product is the most easily duplicated. The procedural aspects of service are less so, and the convivial aspects (the way the procedures are carried out by staff) the least easy to duplicate.

- **Demand variation** – demand for the hospitality product varies dramatically throughout the day, week, month, or the year and over a period of years. Sustaining consistency of the product within these fluctuations is a major challenge for the hospitality operator.

- **Difficulty of comparison** – the intangible elements of the service product make direct comparison of the service product difficult. Customers tend to use three comparators when purchasing. These are:
    1 **Search qualities** – attributes that can be identified before purchase.
    2 **Experienced qualities** – attributes that can be identified only after consumption.
    3 **Credence qualities** – attributes that customers may find impossible to evaluate because of a lack of experience, knowledge or evaluative skills.

Hospitality-related purchase decisions tend to derive from experience and credence decisions. Consequently customers tend to rely more on personal sources of information than they might for other products. This may explain the phenomenal demand for published reviews and guidebooks.

■ The sectors of the foodservice industry

There are many types of eating out premises but differing premises do not necessarily indicate the nature of the demand being met. For instance, a cafeteria may be found in industrial catering, motorway service stations, hospitals and retail operations. For marketing purposes, sectors are better identified based upon the nature of customer demand being met and not on the type of operation. The list of the sectors given in Table 1.2 (both in UK and international terminology) is based upon identifying the purpose of the sector, i.e. the nature of demand being met by the foodservice operations. This method of classification of sectors by purpose provides for either the small company to identify its immediate competitors, or for the larger company – which may be operating in a number of markets – to specifically identify immediate competitors within a specific sector. It also provides for the identification of other sectors where competition might exist for the specific sector under consideration, i.e. alternatives (hotels, popular catering, fast food) may attract the same customers at different times or as alternatives.

In order consider the sectors in more detail, each sector may be further analysed by reference to a set of variables that exist in the different sectors as indicated in Table 1.3. These variables represent elements that vary in particular sectors and thus provide a basis for examining the operation of different types of foodservice operation within specific sectors. They enable a comprehensive picture of industrial sectors to be compiled, and also provide the basis for the comparison of the different sectors.

There are many different industry sectors such as hotels, independent and chain restaurants, popular catering, pubs and wine bars, fast food, leisure attractions and banqueting where the hospitality provision and therefore the food and beverage provision is part of the main business. There are also sectors where food and beverages are provided as part of another business. These include transport catering, welfare, clubs, education, industrial feeding and the armed forces.

Some sectors are providing food and beverages for profit, whereas others are working within the constraints of a given budget, often called cost provision (for example, welfare and industrial). In addition, some sectors provide services to the general public whereas others provide them for restricted groups of people (this is further discussed on page 11 below). A summary of the sectors of the foodservice industry is given in Table 1.4, with the sectors categorised according to whether they are profit orientated or cost provision and also according to whether the market is general or restricted.

Table 1.2: Sectors of the foodservice industry (including UK and international terminology comparison)

Industry sector: UK terminology	Purpose of the foodservice operation	Industry sector: international terminology
Hotels and other tourist accommodation	Provision of food and drink together with accommodation services	**Hotel, motel and other tourist accommodation:** often referred to as the *Lodging industry*
Restaurants including conventional and specialist operations	Provision of food and drink generally at high price with high levels of service	**Separate eating and drinking places** Categories usually defined by reference to three criteria: Level of service, e.g. quick service to full service or fine dining Extent of menu, e.g. limited to full Price range, e.g. low to high
Popular catering including cafes, pizza, grills, specialist coffee shops, roadside restaurants and steak houses	Provision of food and drink generally at low/medium price with limited levels of service	
Fast food including McDonalds and Burger King	Provision of food and drink in highly specialised environment characterised by high investment, high labour costs and vast customer throughput	
Takeaway including ethnic, spuds, KFC, snacks, fish and chips, sandwich bars, kiosks	Provision of food and drink quickly	
Retail stores	Provision of food and drink as adjunct to retail provision	**Retail market**
Banqueting/conferencing/ exhibitions	Provision of large-scale food and drink alongside services such as conferencing	**Leisure and special event market**
Leisure attractions such as theme parks, galleries, theatres, airline terminals	Provision of food and drink to people engaged in another pursuit	
Motorway service stations	Provision of food and drink together with petrol and other retail services often in isolated locations	**Highway (interstate)**
Industrial catering either in-house operations or through catering contractors	Provision of food and drink to people at work	**Business and industry markets**
Welfare catering	Provision of food and drink to people in colleges, universities, the forces and to people through established social need	**Social caterer student, healthcare, institutional** and **military**
Licensed trade including public houses, wine bars, licensed clubs and members' clubs	Provision of food and drink in an environment dominated by licensing requirements	**Separate drinking places** but also some units included in separate eating and drinking places above

Transport catering including railways, airlines and marine	Provision of food and drink to people on the move	Transportation market
Outdoor catering (or off premises catering or event catering)	Provision of food and drink away from home base and suppliers usually associated with a major event	Catering market

Source: developed from Lillicrap and Cousins, 2010

Table 1.3: Variables in foodservice sectors

Historical background	Interpretation of demand/catering concept
Reasons for customer demand	Technological development
Size of sector:	Influences
In terms of outlets	State of sector development
In terms of turnover	Primary/secondary activity
Policies:	Types of outlets
Financial	Profit orientation/cost provision
Marketing	Public/private ownership
Catering	

Table 1.4: Summary of sectors in the foodservice industry

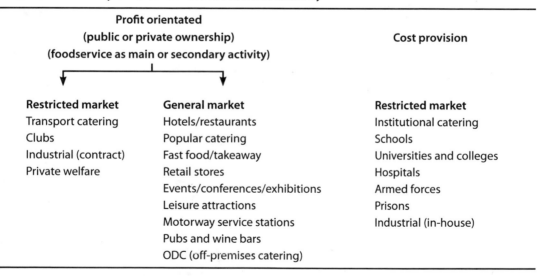

Profit orientated (public or private ownership) (foodservice as main or secondary activity)		**Cost provision**
Restricted market	**General market**	**Restricted market**
Transport catering	Hotels/restaurants	Institutional catering
Clubs	Popular catering	Schools
Industrial (contract)	Fast food/takeaway	Universities and colleges
Private welfare	Retail stores	Hospitals
	Events/conferences/exhibitions	Armed forces
	Leisure attractions	Prisons
	Motorway service stations	Industrial (in-house)
	Pubs and wine bars	
	ODC (off-premises catering)	

■ The nature of demand

There are many different kinds of food and beverage (or foodservice) operations that are designed to meet a wide range of types of demand. It is important, though, to recognise that it is the needs people have at the time, rather than the type of people they are, that these different operations are designed for. Customer make choices about food and beverage operations primarily on the needs they have at the time and not on the basis of the type of people they consider themselves to be. For example, the same person may be a business customer during the week, but a member of a family at the weekend; he or she may want a quick lunch on one occasion, a snack while travelling on another or a meal for the family at another time. Additionally the same person may be booking a wedding or organising some other special occasion. Clearly there are numerous reasons for eating out, other examples being: to do something different, to try different foods, or for sheer convenience because of already being away from the home, out shopping, at the cinema, a conference or an exhibition.

The reasons for eating out vary and with this, the types of operation that may be appropriate at the time. Differing establishments offer different service, in both the extent of the menu and the price as well as varying service levels. Also the choice offered may be restricted or wide. Basically there are three types of markets in which operations may be meeting demand. These are:

- **Captive markets** – where the customer has no choice, e.g. hospital patients or people in prison.
- **Non-captive markets** – those people who have a free choice of establishments.
- **Semi-captive markets** – where there is some restriction, e.g. people travelling by air who have a choice of airline but once the choice is made, are restricted to the food and drink on offer. This category also applies, for instance, to railways, some inclusive-term holidays and people travelling on motorways.

Identifying what business a foodservice operation is in then is not simply about what sector it is in or what type of operation: it is also about identifying the range of types of demand that are being met by the operation. This will then help with identifying the direct or indirect competition that might exist.

■ The nature of the foodservice product

To every product (and the foodservice product is no exception) there are two dimensions: *features* and *benefits*. Features are the physical characteristics of the product but marketers tend to stress benefits because of the realisation that products are bought for the satisfaction they provide.

The foodservice industry's products may be defined as the set of satisfactions or dissatisfactions which customer receives from a foodservice experience. The satisfaction may be physiological, economic, social or psychological or convenience as follows:

- **Physiological** needs: e.g. to satisfy hunger and thirst, or to satisfy the need for special foods.
- **Economic** needs: e.g. staying within a certain budget, wanting good value, a convenient location or fast service.
- **Social** needs: e.g. being out with friends, business colleagues or attending special functions such as weddings.

- **Psychological** needs: e.g. responding to advertising, wanting to try something new, fulfilling life-style needs or satisfying or fulfilling the need for self-esteem.
- **Convenience** needs: for example it may not be possible to return home or the desire may be there for someone else to prepare, serve and wash up.

Potential dissatisfaction falls into two categories:

- **Controllable** by the establishment: e.g. scruffy, unhelpful staff, cramped conditions.
- **Uncontrollable**: e.g. behaviour of other customers, the weather, transport problems.

Customers may be wanting to satisfy all or some of these needs identified above and it is important to recognise that it is the reason behind wanting or having to eat out, rather than the food and drink by themselves, that will play an important part in determining the resulting satisfaction or dissatisfaction with the experience. It is quite possible that the motivation to eat out is not to satisfy basic physiological needs at all.

Product augmentation

Sometimes the product delivered to the customer is different from that received by the customer. In other words, the reason for the customer buying the product may determine the satisfaction rather than specifically the product itself (e.g. out with friends). Distinctions are often drawn between the core, tangible and augmented concepts of the product: for example:

- The **core** of the product is the food and drink provision itself.
- The **tangible** elements of the product are the methods of delivery (silver service restaurant or vending machine) or portions of a certain size.
- **Augmentation** of the product takes into account the complete package.

Differing sectors of the foodservice industry are essentially meeting similar customer demands, i.e. offering the same core product. However, this can be modified and enhanced in cost-effective ways to make the product more attractive. Competition within specific sectors largely takes place at the augmented level. In the foodservice industry this augmentation might include:

- Speed of service
- Ordering/booking convenience
- Reliability
- Provision of special foods
- Cooking to order
- Home deliveries
- Availability of non-menu items
- Entertainment

- Privacy/discretion
- Acceptance of credit cards, or
- Availability of account facilities.

These various elements are often drawn together with the core and tangible elements under the heading *the 'meal experience'* (Lillicrap and Cousins, 2010).

■ The meal experience

If people have decided to eat out then it follows that there has been a conscious choice to do this in preference to some other course of action. In other words, the foodservice operator has attracted the customer to buy his/her product as against some other product, for example theatre, cinema or simply staying at home. The reasons for eating out may be summarised under seven headings:

- **Convenience**, for example being unable to return home as in the case of shoppers or people at work or involved in some leisure activity.
- **Variety**, for example trying new experiences or as a break from home cooking.
- **Labour**, for example getting someone else to prepare, serve food and wash up or simply the physical impossibilities of staging special events at home.
- **Status**, for example business lunches or people eating out because others of their socio-economic group do so.
- **Culture/tradition**, for example special events or simply because it is a way of getting to know people.
- **Impulse**, for example simply spur-of-the-moment buying.
- **No choice**, for example those in welfare, hospitals or other forms of semi or captive markets.

People are, however, a collection of different types, as any demographic breakdown would show. While it is true that some types of foodservice operation might attract certain types of customers this is by no means true all the time; for example, McDonald's is marketed to the whole population and attracts customers depending on their needs at the time.

The decision to eat out may also be split into two parts: first, the decision to do so for the reasons given above and then the decision as to what type of experience is to be undertaken. It is generally agreed that there are a number of factors influencing this latter decision. These factors extend the core, tangible and augmented distinctions drawn earlier. The factors that affect the meal experience may be summarised as follows:

- **Food and drink on offer** – the range of foods, choice, availability, flexibility for special orders and the quality of the food and drink.
- **Level of service** – depending on the needs people have at the time, the level of service sought should be appropriate to these needs. For example, a romantic

night out may call for a quiet table in a top-end restaurant, whereas a group of young friends might be seeking more informal service. This factor also takes into account services such as booking and account facilities, acceptance of credit cards and also the reliability of the operation's product.

- **Level of cleanliness and hygiene** – this relates to the premises, equipment and staff. Over the last few years this factor has increased in importance in the customers' minds. The recent media focus on food production and the risks involved in buying food have heightened awareness of health and hygiene aspects.

- **Perceived value for money and price** – customers have perceptions of the amount they are prepared to spend and relate these to differing types of establishments and operations. However, many people will spend more if the value gained is perceived as greater than that obtained by spending slightly less. (Also see the notes on price, cost, worth and value in Chapter 2 page 32.)

- **Atmosphere of the establishment** – this is difficult to quantify, as it is an intangible concept. However, it is composed of a number of factors such as: design, decor, lighting, heating, furnishings, acoustics and noise levels, the other customers, the staff and the attitude of the staff.

Identifying the meal experience factors is important because it considers the product from the point of view of the customer. All too often foodservice operators can get caught up in the provision of food and drink, spend several thousands on design, decor, equipment, etc. but ignore the actual experience the customer undertakes. Untrained service members of the staff are a good example of this problem. Operations can tend to concentrate on the core product and forget the total package. A better understanding of the customer's viewpoint or the nature of customer demand leads to a better product being developed to meet it. (The meal experience factors are explored in more detail in Chapter 3, pages 45 to 51.)

1.4   The business environment

Any foodservice business operates within the hospitality industry environment and this in turn operates within the wider business or macro-environment. Both the macro-environment and the industry (micro) environment are interrelated. Although the split between the two is not totally clean, it can be convenient to consider them as separate parts of the business environment before looking at the links between them. Clearly changes in the macro-environment can have an impact on the hospitality industry itself and then on the current and future competitors of any operation. These impacts can also be reciprocated.

■   The macro-environment – the PESTLE framework

The macro-environment is the broader environment outside the immediate environment of a particular foodservice business and the hospitality industry.

PEST, STEP, PETS, PESTEL and STEEPL are all variations of the acronym that might be used to refer to the relevant factors when carrying out an analysis of the macro-environment. The influences they stand for are:

P   Political

E   Economic

S   Socio/cultural

T   Technological

L   Legal

E   Ecological.

The value of whichever version of the acronym is chosen is that it offers a simple mechanism for grouping related factors, although this might hide the interrelationships between them.

Applying the PESTLE framework leads to the identification of possible influences, such as:

■ Political influences might include issues such as the availability of grants and subsidies, and the intervention of the Competition Commission.

■ Economic influences might include exchange rates (as they affect tourism), inflation and taxation.

■ Social issues might concern changing market needs, demographic changes and changing patterns of employment.

■ Technological issues might concern the operating systems of a business, channels of distribution (how a business communicates with its customers) and data and information gathering.

■ Legal issues might mean changes in legislation, e.g. hygiene and food safety, opening hours, employment contracts and responsibilities, trade descriptions, licensing, etc.

■ Ecological might mean the increasing requirements for energy conservation or the acceptability (or otherwise) of genetically modified foods.

It may be very difficult to detect the impact of many of the PESTLE factors directly on the foodservice industry. There is also a danger of sterility in using a formal approach to PESTLE analysis. At worst, it can become a ritual listing of all possible influences. This has three possible dangers:

■ Data overload.

■ Failure to try to assess the potential impact of an environmental change however unlikely it may initially seem.

■ Failure to recognise the combined impact of a number of influences.

So, looking outwards means also having to look inwards at the organisation to answer question such as:

- Why are we, or how can we be, successful?
- Is it because there is a growing market out there?
- Is it going to keep growing?
- Will customers still buy our products?
- Is it because our products are affordable?
- If so, what are the major influences on our costs?
- What changes of policy or price are we vulnerable to?
- How can the product life cycle be extended?

Interactions between PESTLE elements

It can be an instructive and creative exercise to look out for interactions between the PESTLE elements. This is well illustrated by the advancement of the environmental factor: the ecological movement. Technology has produced damaging effects on the environment. These have led to social concerns, which have manifested themselves in political action and legislation. This has in turn spurred companies on to seek out technological developments to address the issue and also to gain competitive advantage. Thus foodservice operations have to respond to, for instance, consumer mistrust of genetically modified foods with some firms making specific marketing claims based on not using such foods.

Additionally, one of the most important issues of the moment is sustainability. Sustainability refers to the ability to continue over time. This is not just about the environment (often also referred to as green issues). Foodservice operations need to be economically sustainable. Investment needs to continue in order to meet growing customer demands and increased national and international competition. Dealing with sustainability has now become a complicated combination of economic, social and environmental factors that present any business with having to make difficult decisions on trade-offs in order to be able to prosper in the longer term.

Identifying changes in the PESTLE elements

Also, in these turbulent times, it is important to keep a close watch on influences that may be unlikely to occur, but if they did, could have a major impact on the organisation. Many organisations are, or should be, aware of the main external influences that affect them at present. These could include factors that are fairly easy to identify and to monitor, such as the weather, government legislation, changes in the local business environment, changes in fashion, and developments in technology in directly related areas. Examples of these could be:

- The closure of a local manufacturing plant, which is a major source of local employment, directly affecting both business and leisure based demand for hotel and catering services and leading to a decline in the area generally.

- The opening of a major tourist attraction which creates an opportunity for local foodservice operations but may also encourage new businesses into the area and therefore increased competition.
- The introduction of parking restrictions around a restaurant which might seriously reduce direct access and therefore business.

Other areas are less easy to grasp. These can include:

- Developments that are so new or unknown that most people have not realised they may be important and virtually nobody has any knowledge of the impact they might have, or
- Developments that seem extremely unlikely but may have a massive impact on a foodservice business if they do occur.

There is no simple way of recognising and selecting developments. It can however be useful to try to identify reasons for the current success of an operation and the factors that might have affected them. It is also worth considering what developments might give a foodservice organisation the opportunity to build on its strengths.

The most difficult of all to pull together are those influences which, if taken separately, seem insignificant, but taken together can constitute a significant influence. It might not be recognisable by any one person or department because of the complex interlinking across many aspects of the organisation. Once again, this illustrates the need for cross-functional/cross-departmental creative forums to examine the interlinking of potential influences. This requires much more than a sterile listing of influences or naming of parts.

Most books on strategic management provide coverage of the macro-environment. Kotler *et al.* (2009) discuss it as one component of a marketing audit and Johnson *et al.* (2008) link together the macro-environment with industry analysis. However all cover the material summarised here in much more depth.

■ Industry micro environment – Porter's Five Forces

Porter (2004a, 2004b) proposes that competitiveness within an industry could be determined by reference to Five Forces. The famous Five Forces model is shown in Figure 1.4.

The central force is the rivalry amongst existing firms competing in the industry. But the strength of the model is that it includes four other competitive forces that influence the attractiveness and profitability of the industry. These are:

- The threat of new entrants and how easily they can break into the market.
- The bargaining power that can be exerted on the industry by its buyers.
- The bargaining power that can be exerted on the industry by its suppliers.
- The extent to which substitute products can take over from the existing industry.

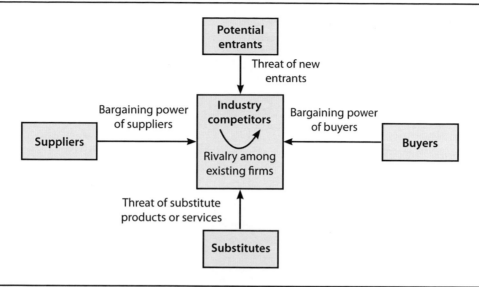

Figure 1.4: The Five Competitive Forces

Source: adapted from the original in Porter, 2004a

These five forces represent the industry environment and the extent and strength of these forces determine the attractiveness of the industry. Of crucial importance is recognising that both direct competitors and the nature and strength of the competitive forces change with time and sometimes very suddenly. These changes can be provoked by changes in the PESTLE factors.

Using the Five Forces model

The use of the Five Forces model provides for the systematic review of the organisation's competitive position at both corporate and business levels. What the module does is to help to focus attention not only on direct competitors but also on substitutes. For example better transport systems, which directly reduce the demand for overnight accommodation, are a clear, but not immediately obvious, example of a substitute for accommodation services.

Porter's full diagram of the Five Forces is shown in Figure 1.5. Here are added practical determinants of the relative power of each of the Five Forces. From this full version of Porter's full diagram it can be seen that many of the determinants are themselves determined either by PESTLE factors or, very importantly, by factors that the organisation can itself directly influence by changing its strategies at business or operational level.

The industry competitors are those organisations that a foodservice business identifies as being in direct competition and the rivalry among existing firms is the level of competition that exists between the existing operations.

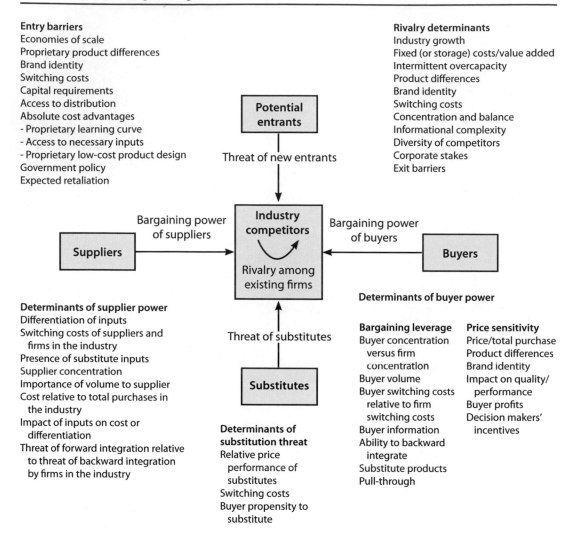

Figure 1.5: Porter's Five Forces Model

Source: developed from Porter, 2004a

> **Potential entrants** are the new organisations, which may threaten the business of existing organisations within the market. The barriers to entry into the market are the factors that might deter new operations. These include:
>
> ■ Capital cost of entry (for example plant and equipment)
>
> ■ Cost disadvantages such as licence requirements of adverse government policy
>
> ■ Entrenched customer loyalty to existing organisations
>
> ■ Economies of scale achieved by existing large businesses.

Buyers are the customers of the foodservice operation. Buyers can have varying degrees of power. A strong bargaining power of buyers will make it easier for buyers to attempt to force down prices whilst at the same time require better quality. Buyers will also tend to play off different foodservice operations against each other. The influence of buyers is greater if, for instance, they are large in terms of volume of business or spend or if the market is highly competitive.

Suppliers provide the materials and other stocks for the business. The bargaining power of suppliers tends to be powerful where, for instance:

■ They are integrated – operate as a cartel

■ They are suppliers of small organisations with essential materials

■ Their groups of products are integrated, e.g. brewer who is also a wine merchant

■ They integrate forward, e.g. a wine supplier which also operates wine bars.

Substitutes are those alternative products, which the buyers might choose instead of the foodservice operations product. This is complex. For a foodservice operation the nature of demand being met will be a key determinant of the substitution threat. Foodservice operations that are linked to another activity, such as retail or leisure, will be highly dependent on the customer carrying out the first activity. There are many alternative or substitute activities to retail or leisure pursuits that the customer might choose. This will then affect demand for the foodservice product. Even where this is not the case, substitutes for foodservice operations are also other types of foodservice operation that might not be seen initially as in direct competition; a customer choosing a McDonald's rather than choosing a fine dining restaurant for instance.

Organisations need also to be always aware that existing or potential competitors will also be modifying their strategies to attempt to be more competitive. In turn, many of these possible changes to strategy, or change to the relative competitiveness of an industry, are caused by changes to PESTLE factors.

Gaining an understanding of the macro-industry environment and the competitiveness within an industry can inform a foodservice organisation about how their strategies can be managed in order to be successful. We return to further consideration of making strategic decisions for a foodservice organisation in Chapter 10.

1.5   The legal framework

Part of considering the business environment is also about considering the legal framework in which the foodservice organisation has to operate. For foodservice operations there are aspects that are the subject of legal regulation. Summaries of the key responsibilities of the foodservice operator are given below. However these are highly summarised guidelines and many of the issues highlighted are affected by the particular circumstances at the time.

■ Health, safety and security

There is a common law duty to care for all lawful visitors. In addition establishments must not:

- Sell (or keep for sale) food and beverages that are unfit for people to eat
- Cause food or beverages to be dangerous to health
- Sell food or beverages that are not what the customer is entitled to expect, in terms of content or quality, or
- Describe or present food in a way that is false or misleading.

It is important for a foodservice operator to be able to demonstrate that steps have been taken to ensure good food hygiene (this is called *due diligence*).

An operator's responsibilities include ensuring that:

- Service standards comply with health, safety, environmental and food hygiene regulations
- There are adequate arrangements in place to ensure the safety, security and well-being of staff and customers
- Periodic risk assessments are carried out and recorded
- Emergency exits are clearly marked and regular fire drills are carried out
- Staff have been trained in fire procedures and how to use fire-fighting equipment
- Staff are aware of evacuation procedures in the event of fires or security risks such as bomb threats
- Health and safety notices are displayed in working areas
- Staff and customers are trained, as appropriate, on correct usage of equipment and facilities
- Food handlers have all been trained in safe and hygienic working practices
- Security policies and procedures are know and followed by all management and staff.

Further consideration of health and safety is given in Chapter 4, section 4.2. Health, safety and security issues related to staffing are identified in section 4.8.

■ The licensing framework

The sale of alcoholic liquor is subject to liquor licensing requirements, which have four key objectives:

1 The prevention of crime and disorder
2 Public safety
3 The prevention of public nuisance
4 The protection of children from harm.

There are usually requirements for:

- The display of a summary of the licence, including the days and times of opening, name of the registered holder, licence number and valid date
- Drinks price lists to be displayed
- Restrictions on under-aged persons being served or employed to serve alcohol
- Requirements for an authorised person to be on site at all times.

Restrictions and penalties for infringement are applied, not only to the licensee or their staff, but also to the customer. In all cases of doubt as to legal issues and concerns, a licensing solicitor should be approached.

Other types of licences may include, for example, licences for music (live or pre-recorded), dancing, gambling, theatrical performance and television display. In all cases the supervisor and the staff should be aware of the provisions and limitations of the licences to ensure compliance. (For more detailed information on the local licensing arrangements refer to the various national and local government websites.)

Selling goods by weights and measures

All sales of goods by weight or measure should be in accordance with the legislative requirements. This usually requires the following:

- Display of the prices and the measures used for all spirits, wines, ales and any other alcohol served.
- Ensuring the food and beverage items for sale are of the quantity and quality demanded by the customer and can include, for example, spirits that have been inadvertently (or deliberately) watered down. This can occur through the use of speed pourers, which effectively leave bottles open for long periods of time, leading to evaporation of the alcohol. Equally, if the pourers are washed and then replaced in the bottles when they are wet, the water can become introduced to the spirit and cause a reduction in the percentage of alcohol by volume (abv).

Contracts

A contract is made when one party agrees to the terms of an offer made by another party. In food and beverage service there are essentially two types of customer: those who pre-book and those who do not (often called chance or casual customers). All foodservice operations should be clear on how they will deal with these different types of customers including:

- Circumstances where the restaurant may seek compensation from the customer if they do not turn up or pay for their meals or services.
- Taking care when making contracts with minors (persons under 18).

■ Selling goods by description

It is good practice for the foodservice operation to ensure:

- All food, beverages and services provided are fit for purpose and of satisfactory quality in relation to price and description.
- Food, beverages and other services are accurately described in terms of size, quality, composition, production, quantity and standard.
- All statements of price, whether in an advertisement, brochure, leaflet or on the Web, or those given by letter or orally in person or over the telephone are clear and accurate.
- Food, beverages and other services correspond to their description in brochures/promotional material.
- Times, dates, locations and nature of service promised are adhered to
- Customer billing is fair, transparent and reflects the prices quoted either orally or in writing.

Care must therefore be taken when:

- Wording menus and wine lists
- Describing menu and beverage items to customers
- Stating if prices include local and/or government taxes
- Describing conditions such as cover charges, service charges or extras
- Describing the service provision.

■ Avoiding discrimination

The foodservice operator should be aware of, and work to ensure, that the operation and the staff do not discrimination on grounds of ethnic origin, race, creed, sex or disability. There are potentially three ways in which discrimination can take place.

Direct discrimination: for example, refusing service to customers of particular ethnic origin, race, creed, gender, sexual orientation or disability.

- *Indirect discrimination*: for example, denying consumer services by imposing unjustifiable conditions or requirements that have ethnic origin, race, creed, gender, sexual orientation or disability implications.
- *Discrimination through victimisation*: for example, by (a) refusal of provision, that is refusal of admission on the basis of ethnic origin, race, creed, gender, sexual orientation or disability; or (b) omission of provision, that is providing services to ethnic customers that are markedly inferior to those available to the public in general or which may only be available at a price premium.

It is the manager's responsibility to ensure that no such discrimination occurs.

■ Providing services

Generally a food and beverage operator is under no specific requirement to serve anyone. However, it is important that the managers and staff are aware of:

- Circumstances where there may be a mandatory requirement to provide servicesValid reasons for refusal.

■ Customer property and customer debt

Good practice usually means that the operator needs to ensure:

- Proper care is taken of customer's property so as to minimise potential loss or damage. Notices warning customers of 'no responsibility' may help in defence but do not guarantee exemption from liability for the food and beverage operator.

- Clear guidance is given on the procedures to follow if the customer is unable or unwilling to pay.

■ Data protection

Customers generally have a right to expect that data about them is kept secure and is only used for the published business purposes. The operator is generally required to ensure that:

- Information on customers is kept up to date, fairly, lawfully and securely.

- Customer information is not passed on to third parties without prior consent from the customerStaff are aware of the importance of the protection of customer information and the procedures to follow to ensure it is held securely.

For further information on these, and a broader range of other legal aspects, see for instance, Barth (2008) and also the various local and national government websites.

2 Concept development

Aim

This chapter aims to explore the nature of demand for food and beverage products through the application of a systematic approach to the development of the consumer–product relationship.

Objectives

This chapter is intended to support you in:

- Adopting a systematic approach to the development of a consumer product relationship

- Further identifying and appraising key issues associated with the nature of demand for food and beverage products

- Explaining the importance of market segmentation

- Developing the process of idea evaluation and understanding its relationship with concept development

- Setting organisational goals and objectives.

2.1　Systematic approach to developing a consumer–product relationship

In Chapter 1 we introduced issues regarding the nature of products, sectors of the industry, the nature of demand and the nature of the foodservice product. This chapter extends this material and proposes that a systematic approach needs to be adopted, in order to be effective in identifying the key issues, which shape the nature of demand for food and beverage products and create the consumer–product relationship.

Literature concerning consumers and markets is readily available, much of which applies specifically to food and beverage operations. The literature explores the nature of demand for products from different viewpoints. These viewpoints include marketing, psychology, anthropology, economics, sociology, geography and social psychology.

■　Considering the consumer

Consumers of food and beverage products are increasingly sophisticated, complex and dynamic. Psychology, sociology, social psychology, geography and anthropology all identify the behaviour of individuals and groups in an attempt to understand the human condition, and relate to the consumer through the examination of human needs, wants, demands, goals and values. Economics focuses on the examination of the human condition as it relates to the commercial and business world through the examination of the allocation of scarce resources and the link between supply and demand. Marketing focuses on the human condition as it relates to products, i.e. the study of the consumer. Kotler *et al.* (2010) explain that marketing is managing markets to attract profitable customer's relationships through identifying their needs and designing good product offerings. The consumer is the actual link. Without the consumer there is no link between the human needs and food and beverage products. A product is simply a consumer's satisfied need.

People who do not consume are not consumers. However obvious or trite this statement might appear it does eliminate the possible confusion between a consumer and a non-consumer. For example, families who eat four times a year in a motorway service area are consumers of the motorway service area food and beverage product, even if they rarely consume this product. They are potential consumers of many existing and future food and beverage products but at present are consumers of only one product from a vast range available, but are not consumers of the rest. At the same time they are consumers of many other products but are consumers of only one food and beverage product. They may have an unsatisfied food and beverage need, but a product is unavailable to them as yet which may satisfy this need.

When consumers are discussed they are often addressed as large groups comprising millions of people, who they are when all added together. But when consumers are examined in detail they are certainly not homogeneous; they consume, or choose not to consume, millions of products in a very dynamic and rapidly changing way. They are individuals who group together to form a market for a particular product. This market grouping may range from 300 people, as in a small rural exclusive restaurant, up to and beyond 300 million people for world-branded products like McDonald's. It is also true that the same consumers will group together at different time depending on the needs they have at the time. The question for food and beverage managers is: Who do we want our consumers to be?

Managers may say that their consumers are the same as the consumers they want them to be, i.e. 'We have achieved our objective of creating a consumer that fits our product.' However, even if such a desirable state exists, the nature of the consumer is continually changing and as such management need to understand their consumers and how changes are taking place, which affect consumers' choices. It is a clear argument for the establishment of a customer-oriented business. The first key issue in the framework is therefore centred on consumers.

■ Considering the product

The key issues concerning the nature of demand for food and beverage products are identified using a well validated, if somewhat oversimplified list of questions:

- Who are the consumers of the food and beverage product?
- What food and beverage product do they want?
- Why do they want a food and beverage product?
- When do they want a food and beverage product?
- Where do they want a food and beverage product?
- How do they obtain a food and beverage product?

These questions can be explored individually, but only one is key: What products do consumers want? Who, why, where, when and how are all part of the product and are inherent in answering the question as to the nature of the products consumers actually want. The second key issue in the framework is therefore centred on the product.

■ Being systematic in developing the consumer–product relationship

The two key issues, the consumer and the product, can each be examined by expanded them to identify their component parts. This expansion is illustrated in Figure 2.1. The component parts of the two frameworks represent the tasks required in order to develop a product–consumer relationship.

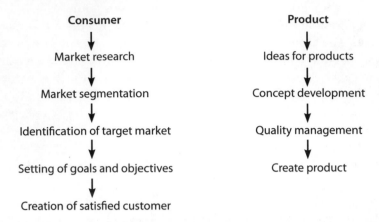

Figure 2.1: Consumer and product frameworks

The various component parts of the consumer and the product, as illustrated in Figure 2.1, may be merged together to form a single development framework, as exampled in Figure 2.2. This single framework then provides the basis for a systematic approach to the development of a consumer–product relationship. Although this framework can give the impression that it is a list of tasks, which are performed chronologically, in practice many of these tasks will be performed simultaneously. Additionally this is not a one-off process. It is a dynamic and organic process in which any food and beverage operation is continuously engaged. The initial stages of the process, through to setting goals and objectives, are covered in this within this chapter. The product development stages and the later stages are covered in Chapter 3.

Figure 2.2: Integrated consumer–product relationship development framework

2.2   Market research

Researching into the food and beverage market can be performed at various levels. Large food and beverage businesses may invest considerable resources in acquiring market information. Marketing departments will use consumer panels, questionnaires, interviews, mystery customers, sales analyses, market information from specialist publications, specifically commissioned market information and other generally available data. Small food and beverage businesses do not usually have a marketing department and in these instances the unit manager or owner-operator will perform the market research function. The growing use of personal computers assists small businesses to conduct secondary research into the business environment. This leads to the identification of current trends and also the competitors who are facilitating them.

■ The nature of needs

From Chapter 1 we saw that food and beverage needs arise as a consequence of the desire to satisfy a range of needs. Kotler *et al.* (2010) point out that these needs are inherent in human biology and the human condition and as such are not created by society or by marketers. This is reinforced by O'Gorman (2010) who demonstrates that hospitality is fundamental to human existence.

Food and beverage needs are basic needs for satisfaction but these needs do not arise independently. They are associated with other needs such as those for shelter, safety, belonging and esteem. Food and beverage wants are desires for satisfiers of this complex set of needs. A hamburger can be a want for food and a want for belonging and esteem. Younger children may want to go to McDonald's to satisfy their need for belonging to their peer group, to satisfy their need for esteem within their peer group and to satisfy their need for food and drink. Wanting to satisfy their belonging and esteem needs may outweigh their food and drink needs. A food and beverage product may therefore satisfy needs not initially stimulated by hunger and thirst.

■ The nature of demand

We saw from Chapter 1 that it is important to recognise that it is the needs people have at the time, rather than the type of people they are, that different operations are designed for. As an example, the Pizza Hut product may be demanded and purchased by customers wanting to satisfy their needs at the time. However some of the same customers could also want a different type of experience depending on the needs they have at the time.

Food and beverage demands are wants for specific food and beverage products but the level of demand is also affected by the capability of the consumer to buy them and to meet the other costs, which may be involved. Food and beverage operators should try then to influence demand by making their product desirable, valuable, available and affordable. In essence this is following the four Ps of the marketing mix: product, price, promotion, place (location and availability), (see, for instance, Armstrong *et al.*, 2009). They add that in service marketing, the four Ps are often extended to include process, people and physical evidence.

Consumers then have a variety of goals when they decide to choose a food and beverage product. These goals can include esteem, belonging, status, attention, entertainment, privilege, relaxation, intimacy, romance, convenience, physiological and psychological comfort, and satisfying hunger and thirst. Again sometimes satisfying hunger and thirst are not always goals needing to be achieved. The collection of goals an individual has when choosing a food and beverage product may be referred to as the goal set. Each food and beverage product has the capacity to satisfy different goal sets. Accordingly, a consumer may perceive a takeaway as providing greater convenience and as being less expensive than an up-market à la carte restaurant, but the restaurant may be perceived as providing greater attention (level of service) and a higher level of esteem and status. The consumer will make a choice as to which is the most satisfying product for their particular goal set at the time. If a consumer's goal set is prioritised as food, convenience and variety, different food and beverage products may satisfy them in different ways. A consumer with this goal set may satisfy these goals with a fish and chip shop product, whereas another consumer may satisfy the same goal set with a public house meal product. This has important implications, as the direct competitors for a foodservice operation are not only those operations that are similar, but also those that the consumer may choose simply as an alternative choice. This can be for instance where the consumer is making a choice primarily motivated by the desire to save money or reduce travel time.

Individual consumers then will have different priorities depending on their needs at the time. An individual may prioritise convenience when purchasing coffee and croissants on the way to work in the morning, and prioritise low price at lunchtime when purchasing a meal in the workplace restaurant and high levels of service and entertainment when purchasing a celebration meal in the evening. These priorities will also change during an individual's life cycle as his/her needs, wants and demands also change in relation to their circumstances. Individuals may desire a nightclub product in their youth, a fast food restaurant when they have young children and a reduced price product for a pensioner in their old age. Additionally, consumers may give differing importance to the same product or parts of a product. One individual may value silver service because it is perceived as increasing the status of the occasion, while others may not value silver service because it makes them feel uncomfortable in an unusual situation.

◼ Price, cost, value and worth

Although values are attached to various products because of the perception of the needs they can satisfy, the ability to realise those goals is dependent on the ability to pay. But payment is not just about having the required money. Choices are also made by considering the relationship between price, cost, worth and value:

- Price is the amount of money required to purchase the product.

- Cost includes, as well as price, the cost of not going somewhere else, the cost of transport and time, the cost of potential embarrassment, the cost of having to look and behave in a required manner and the cost in terms of effort at work to earn the money to pay the required price.

- Worth is a perception of the desirability of a particular product over another in order to satisfy a set of established goals.

- Value is not only the personal estimate of a product's capacity to satisfy a set of goals it is also a perception of the balance between worth and cost.

Good value is where the worth is perceived as greater than the costs, and poor value is where the costs are perceived as greater than the worth.

2.3   Market segmentation

Researching the market will facilitate the identification of consumers' needs, wants, demands, goals and values as they relate to food and beverage products. Having identified these it is possible to group them using a mix of criteria. These groupings are termed market segments.

There are many different ways to segment a market. Food and beverage operators will try different segmentation variables in the attempt to identify the needs, wants and demands of possible market groupings. These variables are most usually grouped using the following four sets of criteria:

1 Geographic segmentation
2 Demographic segmentation
3 Psychographic segmentation
4 Behavioural segmentation.

Geographic segmentation

This involves dividing the market into geographical areas such as nations, regions, cities, districts and neighbourhoods. Food and beverage products such as J D Wetherspoon and Harvester target regions of the UK's food and beverage market. Up-market restaurants may target a district, and a fish and chip shop may only target a neighbourhood. Starbucks coffee shops have a global approach targeting major cities worldwide.

A food and beverage product may operate in areas with different geographical needs, satisfying these different needs by making alterations to their product mix. Menu items vary between the restaurants of a chain operating in different European cities. Well-known fast food restaurants operate discriminatory pricing by applying a different price to the same product in relation to location, e.g. higher prices at airports than on high streets, and different prices in relation to different countries. The reason this is done is because the needs, wants and demands vary by geographical location, and the product/marketing mix will be altered in an attempt to exploit and/or accommodate the differences.

◼ Demographic segmentation

This will involve dividing the market into groups using such variables as age, gender, stage in the family life cycle, income, occupation, education, religion, race and nationality. A public house may segment their markets into, for instance, single, 25–35-year-old men with average incomes, whose education finished at 16, and who are employed in manual skilled and semi skilled professions. Another public house however may segment its market in a similar way but substitute married couples with two small children for the 25–35-year-old single males. The first public house could be located in a city centre, and the second in a seaside holiday resort. The needs, wants and demands of these two segments are very different and this will have implications for the nature of the food and beverage product being required and offered.

◼ Psychographic segmentation

This is a stage further on from demographic grouping and identifies the social class, life style and personality characteristics of a consumer. Social class exists in all areas of our society with various individuals forming into sets whose patterns of behaviour and attitude vary widely. Food and beverage consumers may be segmented as to their social class with products designed specifically to satisfy their demands.

Different social groupings exhibit preferences for particular food and beverage products. Some social groupings will prefer seclusion and formality when consuming a food and beverage product while another group may prefer informal and crowded atmospheres. Life-style segmentation can be seen in the development of food and beverage products such as TGI Friday and Wagamama, appealing to consumers who see themselves as young, fashionable, informal and adventurous. Personality segmentation is used to develop beverage products such as beers, appealing to consumers who see themselves as sharp and quick-witted (lager), or discerning traditionalists (real ale).

◼ Behavioural segmentation

This divides the market into groups depending on the way in which customers use the product. The food and beverage product may be used as a place to meet others, or as a place of anonymity. The behaviour exhibited will relate to consumer needs which the product must try and satisfy, i.e. lots of open areas in the former, and booths in the latter.

Behavioural segmentation also includes identifying the position of consumers in the hierarchy of usage, from having never used the product through regular users to ex-users. Consumers who have never used the product before may need to be made psychologically comfortable by a genuinely friendly welcome and an informative introduction to the food and beverage product. Some steakhouse chains ask customers if it is their first visit to the brand as standard practice, with different procedures for either of the two, yes and no, responses.

First-time buyers

Attracting first-time buyers necessitates the identification of how first-time buyers behave. How often the product is consumed is another behavioural variable. A consumer may use a bar every day, a takeaway once a week, a pizza restaurant once a month or go to a dinner dance twice a year. Identifying the usage rate enables the identification of the needs, wants and demands of that segment, and will contribute to product design. Consumers may perceive a dinner dance as a special occasion and they must therefore be made to feel special with personalised attention from senior staff. A bar may be perceived as a place to rest and unwind after work and may therefore be designed to be peaceful and comfortable.

Loyalty

Loyalty is another behavioural variable that applies to food and beverage products. This is the ratio between the consumption of a range of products. If a customer only eats in one restaurant he/she is 100 per cent loyal to that restaurant. If a customer eats in a mix of six restaurants, he/she may be 50 per cent loyal to one, and 10 per cent loyal to the rest. The consumer's needs, wants and demands may be different at different loyalty levels.

■ Identifying changes in variables is a continuous process

Using segmentation variables allow for a more objective view of food and beverage consumers, and adopting this approach assists in the identification of consumers with similar needs, wants and demands. However new groups are continually forming and older ones becoming no longer relevant, therefore the need to make the identification is also continual.

Apart from the traditional methods to segmentation as discussed above there are other approaches that achieve the same goal just in a different way. One method is detailed in Figure 2.3. This looks at the combination of the consumer's time availability and the budget (cash) and then identifies the possible dining experience that might be sought.

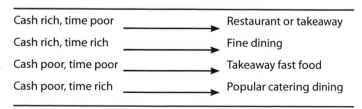

Figure 2.3: Cash/time model

Another approach used by large companies is that of typologies, which may include groups of consumers who are categorised and named and targeted as follows:

- Empty nest career ladies
- Comfortable retired couples
- Stretched single mums
- Career focused females/males, or
- Competitive male urbanites.

The ACORN classification is a UK based system that uses geo-demographic segmentation to organise neighbourhoods into different consumer types and categories. Examples include: wealthy executives; affluent greys; flourishing families; aspiring singles; prudent pensioners and burdened singles. (For more on the ACORN classification go to http://www.caci.co.uk/acorn-classification.aspx).

The identified groupings or market segments must be the focus of the food and beverage operators' business. Choosing which segments the product will be targeted at will then depend on the financial, technological, material and human resources available. Once a target segment has been decided this will then drive how the company will create its product, price, promotion and distribution to fit the consumers. Food and beverage management is then concerned with the manipulation of these various resources to achieve customer satisfaction, organisational efficiency and effectiveness, and ultimately profitability.

2.4   Idea evaluation

How market segments are chosen, shaped, reached, targeted and satisfied by the operation, begins by generating ideas. Ideas can be generated using a variety of techniques and sources.

Ideas can come from examining how existing food and beverage products are meeting the demands of various segments. Researching how well one's own and the competition's products satisfy customers' demands may stimulate ideas and identify key factors for success. Other methods of generating ideas include management and staff brainstorming sessions, and asking customers, with the focus for these approaches always being clearly on establishing customers' needs, wants and demands.

The generation of many ideas, which will then need to be considered, enables a more objective appraisal to be made. It is a sad situation that many new food and beverage operations fail because only one idea has been generated and alternatives have not been considered. Idea generation should be sought from all the stakeholders of the operation in an open and supportive atmosphere. If one idea is criticised, other ideas may not be forthcoming for fear of ridicule. Food and beverage operators can also benefit by formalising the idea generation process and by giving their employees information about segmentation variables. This would lead to a continuous flow of good new ideas to meet customer needs.

A flow of product ideas focused on consumers' needs, wants and demands should be screened. Screening out ideas and progressing the remainder into the next stage of concept development can be achieved by setting up processes through which the idea must successfully pass. Screening processes will be drawn up by the stakeholder(s) and applied accordingly. An example idea-screening process is as follows:

- Does the idea meet consumers' needs?
- Is the group of consumers with these needs large enough to make the idea worthwhile?
- Does the food and beverage operator or potential operator have the necessary resources available to deliver the idea?
- Will the idea generate customer satisfaction?
- Will the idea generate a benefit to the operation, economically, managerially and socially?
- Is the idea different form the competition?

This idea-screening process asks questions which may be very difficult, and sometimes impossible, to answer, but trying to answer them will give indications of what will be needed to make the idea worth investing in further. This approach to idea screening should reduce the amount of ideas considerably, but is by no means a foolproof system. Good ideas may still be discarded and poor ones adopted no matter how sophisticated the screening processes are.

These approaches to market research, market segmentation and idea generation and screening apply to all situations where new products are being developed. A restaurant concept, such as Nando's, will have gone through this development process, as will a change in the opening times, service methods and decor of an existing food and beverage product. All ideas need to be screened according to the stakeholders' objectives and resources. Screening processes should be individually tailored to suit the objectives of the business. It is also necessary to review the screening process periodically as business objectives may change. If a successful food and beverage operation decides to expand and open other operations, the idea-screening process may need to be changed to accommodate product branding, continuity and consistency issues.

2.5   Completing the concept development

It is helpful to consider the generated ideas, which pass a screening process, in terms of how they might be conceptualised as products or parts of products. For example an idea to introduce a self-service buffet operation could be conceptualised as:

- An informal continental-style all-day restaurant
- A family meal occasion to satisfy all appetites, or
- An inexpensive, value for money, eat as much as you like concept.

Turning the ideas into concepts allows for the identification and consideration of the potential market as well as the potential competition if the concept was converted into a product.

Evaluating the competition, using for example, a relative strengths and weaknesses analysis, will help position the new product. The position of the product is related to key consumer needs variables. These variables will be directly related to a particular market segment and should be clearly focused on customers' needs. Product positioning draws a map of the food and beverage market and places the various products in relation to each other. For example, if speed of service and convenience are identified as key consumer needs for a particular target market, the perceptions of various products might be related against each other as shown in Figure 2.4.

Figure 2.4: Perceptions of various products for a particular target market

Other variables, which may also be used to position a concept/product, include price, flexibility, availability, reliability, amount of choice, quantity, consumers' quality perceptions and the likely amount of product usage. It is also possible to set up a three-dimensional model using three customer needs variables.

Once the idea has been converted into a concept it should be tested in the

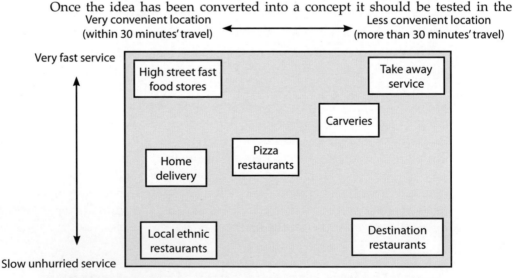

identified market segment by asking consumers and potential consumer's questions about the concept. These questions might include:

- How they view the concept in relation to the competition?
- If they would purchase the product and how frequently, time of day, what price might they be prepared to pay?

- What they see as the benefits of the product?
- What improvements to the product could be made?

Asking these sorts of question can help to position the new concept more accurately.

Testing new product concepts is essential. Even if performed badly it is probably better than not testing at all. Large operations will test their new concepts thoroughly using consumer panels and sometimes actually create the real product in selected areas to test consumer reaction. Smaller operations with fewer resources to test the concept can still be thorough by talking, and most importantly, listening, to existing customers and likely competitors' customers. Well-structured interviews relating to a product's benefits and image will produce valuable data to inform the development of the new concept. Well-tested food and beverage concepts have a reduced risk of failure.

2.6   Setting goals and objectives

As well as generating ideas for concept development, the organisation also needs to consider its potential goals and objectives. Developing an understanding of the business environment leads to greater confidence in determining appropriate goals and objectives for a foodservice organisation. This is important as the setting of goals and objectives will play a crucial role in the determination of the direction of a particular foodservice organisation and its likely success.

Goals, or aims, are the broad intentions of an organisation. Objectives are the measurable outcomes, which will indicate the progress being made by an organisation towards meeting its specific goals. Having goals and objectives is important: as the old adage says: if you have no idea of where you are going then you won't know if you are ever going to get there.

The orientation of organisational objectives can be classified under three broad headings as:

- Economic
- Managerial
- Social responsibility.

Economic objectives

Economic objectives assume that the sole purpose of an organisation is to maximise profit for its owners. This approach tends to be predominant where the foodservice operation is owner-managed and provides a single product, or a limited range of products, under near perfect market conditions. It is also likely to operate most successfully under the assumption of a unitary perspective; that is, where everyone within the organisation shares the same objectives.

There are however some problems when objectives are based purely on the economic theory of the firm. It can be difficult to define exactly what is meant by profit maximisation. Does it mean profit, for instance, in absolute terms or profit expressed as return on capital employed, return on equity or profit margin (that is profit as a percentage of sales) or some other measure of profit? The other dimension which needs to be determined is the time-scale over which this to be achieved; short-term profits, one, two, three years, or a much longer period?

Creating economic objectives also relies on the assumption that the achievement of profitability can actually be measured in a meaningful and consistent way. It also assumes that customers make their purchasing choices solely on economic grounds.

Moreover, it is easy to argue that such an approach ignores the reality of organisational life in today's complex organisations. Clearly, many organisations have non-economic goals, especially but not exclusively those in the public and charitable sectors. There are also likely to be circumstances under which the interests and objectives of the organisation's owners and its managers may be in conflict.

■ Managerial objectives

The maximisation of profit for the owners of a foodservice organisation may not always be perceived to be a desirable objective for the managers. For example, food and beverage managers may seek to:

- Maximise revenue through a high market share, thereby increasing their own prestige in their industry
- Increase the assets of the organisation (for example, by acquisition), thereby increasing their own power and personal reward
- Empire-build inside the organisation, again increasing their own status, salary and associated perks
- Increase the technical sophistication and complexity of the organisation (for example, in products and processes) thereby achieving growth, increasing managerial independence and providing fresh challenges.

The existence of these types of managerial objectives can be very prevalent, especially in the private sector.

On the other hand it can also be argued that the best interests of a firm are actually served by its managers. They may be more interested, for instance, in the long-term success of the organisation than its owners, whose interest may be transitory as they can sell the business or their shares in it.

The complexities of organisational life mean that managers are often faced with conflicting objectives. These may arise from their personal objectives, those of the owners, customers, suppliers, different groups of employees, the government, and possibly other interested stakeholders. Under such conditions they may seek a compromise that satisfies every party to some extent. Such behaviour is termed 'satisficing'.

■ Social responsibility objectives

Such objectives stress the ethical aspects of a foodservice organisation's objectives. These can include objectives related to:

- Safety of products
- Working conditions for staff
- Honesty, for example, not offering or accepting bribes or other inducements
- Equal opportunities
- Ethical business practices
- Sustainability of the business, and
- Concern over pollution and other environmental concerns.

For many organisations a code of business and social ethics is seen as good for business. It is also important, as increasingly businesses will only seek to trade with other businesses that have clear social responsibility policies. Additionally for many public, charitable and voluntary sector organisations, the entire raison d'être is allied to particular social and/or ethical objectives. However the issues raised under the preceding section on managerial objectives often also apply in the cost provision sectors.

It is also sometimes worth speculating as to whether social and ethical concerns among a profit seeking organisation's managers and owners derive from genuinely held beliefs, or whether they merely exist to satisfy the concerns of external stakeholders such as pressure groups, governments or society at large.

■ Summarising the need to set objectives

Generally, objectives for an enterprise tend to be a mixture of economic, management and social responsibility factors. In all cases, though:

- The goals of a foodservice organisation are bound to affect the strategic options that it will consider appropriate and the particular objectives that will be set.
- Organisational objectives have an implicit impact on planning when strategic choices are being considered.
- Setting objectives for a foodservice organisation provides a basis for making choices about the policies and plans to be adopted in order to achieve the goals of the organisation.
- Having agreed objective which are also made explicit means that there is something to measure the performance of the organisation against.
- The agreed objectives may also be the criteria which are used when making future strategic choices and determining the resulting policies and plans.

3 Product development

This chapter aims to detail the process of developing the food and beverage product to meet the needs of its target consumer.

Objectives

This chapter is intended to support you in:

- Identify key stages of product development
- Developing detailed knowledge of the meal experience factors
- Identifying and applying various approaches to the development of a consumer–product relationship
- Gaining an insight into service quality and quality management issues
- Setting standards for food and beverage operations
- Developing an integrated approach to service quality management
- Balancing customers service requirements with resource productivity
- Developing the consumer–product relationship as a dynamic process.

3.1   The food and beverage product

In order to progress from the concept development phase, the next requirement in developing a consumer–product relationship is to consider the nature of a food and beverage product. Within this phase questions need to be addressed, and decisions made, in order to turn a consumer focus (the abstract concept that consumers purchase) in to an operational focus.

Customers may view a food and beverage product as a quick snack, a night out, a celebration, an indulgent extravagance or an absolute necessity. These concepts are what customers purchase, but the food and beverage product is what operators construct and provide.

Marketers tend to identify the product as: a central consumer concept known as the core concept; a surrounding layer of tangible features, and an outer layer of augmentation (see Chapter 1, section 1.3). Placing this framework on a food and beverage product might show that the core product is, for example, a wedding celebration, the tangible product is a full wedding banquet, and the augmented product includes the opportunity to pay in instalments. It is helpful to apply this product framework to the development of concepts. This is also where frameworks such as the meal experience can be useful. The meal experience, which was introduced in Chapter 1, comprises five factors: the food and beverage itself, the level of service, the cleanliness and hygiene, the price and the atmosphere.

As there are five factors of the meal experience to consider, the inevitable question arises as to which one should be addressed first. Most food and beverage operators immediately explore the food and beverages, with the construction of a menu and beverage list being given the highest priority. However, it might be more appropriate to explore the price first, or the style and level of service that will be provided, the level of cleanliness and hygiene or the atmosphere and ambience to be created. The intended core, tangible and augmented concepts of the product, considered in the form of benefits to the consumer, will guide an operator when ranking the meal experience factors in order of priority to the consumer. Table 3.1 gives examples of how differing core concepts might change the order of importance, to the customer, of the meal experience factors.

When setting out to design a tangible product it is therefore appropriate to consider the core concept in order to establish the weighting of the meal experience factors and the priority given to them by the customer so that the operation can develop the product from this perspective.

The other dimension, which this approach can also demonstrate, is that limitations in the operation in one part of the meal experience provision will create stronger expectations in the customers' minds from the other parts. For instance a limited menu operation will find that customers are more concerned with value for money and speed of service than they would be in an operation where the menu offered greater choice. In all cases then, although the meal experience factors can be identified in all operations, the intended product will determine the emphasis or limitations placed on them. This in turn will affect the potential customer's expectations of them and this in turn should determine the priorities for operational development of the product.

Table 3.1: Possible meal experience factor ranking for different meal experiences

Core concept	Possible factor ranking
Night out	1. Atmosphere 2. Food and drink 3. Service 4. Price 5. Cleanliness and hygiene
Gourmet event	1. Food and drink 2. Service 3. Atmosphere 4. Cleanliness and hygiene 5. Price
Cheap meal	1. Price 2. Food and drink 3. Cleanliness and hygiene 4. Service 5. Atmosphere
State banquet	1. Service 2. Atmosphere 3. Food and drink 4. Cleanliness and hygiene 5. Price

Exploring the meal experience further

In order to continue to explore product development more fully it can be useful to consider each of the five meal experience factors separately. The factors are:

- Food and drink
- Level of service
- Cleanliness and hygiene
- Price and value for money
- Atmosphere.

Food and drink

The food and drink itself, usually in the form of a menu and beverage lists, must clearly focus on the needs and demands of the consumer. Operators need to focus on what food and beverages the different market segments want. The permutations of range, tastes, textures and presentations of food and beverages are almost endless. However, the menu and beverage offerings are a list from which customers construct a package to suit their own needs, and therefore the range of food and beverages offered should be considered in this light. There may be vegetarians, dieters, customers who are hungry (and ones who are not), ones who like seafood and those who do not, ones who like steaks and not much else; all are potentially part of any intended market segment. However, if there are a very wide variety of demands in the intended market segment, it may be appropriate to consider further market segmentation. Trying to satisfy everyone can lead to satisfying no one.

The type of food and beverages that are offered is often used to identify operations. Food can include a wide range of styles and cuisine types. These can be by country, e.g. traditional British, Italian or Thai, by type of cuisine, e.g. oriental, or aiming for a particular speciality such as fish, vegetarian or health food. These operations can all be identified by their cuisine. Other operations can be identified principally by the beverage provisions, e.g. pubs, wine bars and clubs. The food and beverage offering therefore will play a considerable part in influencing the customers' perceptions and expectations of the product and consideration of the market's needs, wants and demands in terms of the food and beverages is important. Ideas can be generated and tested on consumer panels to identify these demands more specifically rather than relying on instinct and a propensity to deliver what the operator knows how to deliver as opposed to what the customer wants.

Level of service

Service is a part of the product and may be considered the human (usually) interface between the product and the consumer. The exception is vending operations where the machine is the interface. Food and beverage operators usually identify service as different service methods, such as silver service, buffet service, cafeteria service and so on, from which can be selected the most appropriate service method to meet the demands of their customers: Quick service when the customer is in a hurry, slower service for an intimate dinner, and stylish service for customers who want to be entertained are examples of service methods meeting demand. However, service also involves a personal interaction between customers and service personnel. This interaction can deliver benefits to the customer, such as feeling valued, and should therefore be designed into the product rather than just hoping these benefits will be delivered. So in food and beverage service there are two factors. One factor is 'efficiency', which includes how timely, consistent and organised the service is (procedural), and the second is 'conviviality', which includes the way the service is carried out and the friendliness and attitude of the staff. These two factors can be used to construct a framework into which service styles can be placed. Figure 3.1 indicates what consumers might think and say about particular the service depending on the combination of the service dimensions: efficiency and convivial.

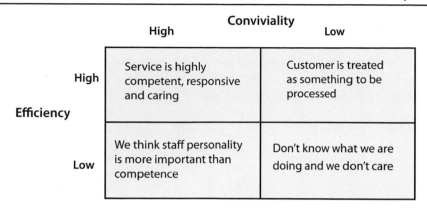

Figure 3.1: Service dimensions framework

Source: developed from Martin, 1986

The two dimensions of efficiency and conviviality are interdependent and if the procedural element of the service is poorly designed and delivered, resulting in overworked and poorly motivated staff, it is more likely that conviviality will also deteriorate. A food and beverage operator must ensure that both elements are addressed and considered and design them into the product. Training and feedback concerning service performance should also be built into the product to ensure the standards required by consumers are delivered.

The level of service can also be affected by the standards being achieved. However the level of service should not be confused with standards of service. Low levels of service, such as in a fast food operation are often achieved with very high standards, which are consistent over time. On the other hand an operation offering a high level of service, such as silver service, can be poorly regulated and standards can be low and variable.

The level of service provided can also be augmented and this can have a considerable influence on the success of a foodservice operation. Being able to reserve a table, pay by various credit cards, vary portion size, access health information and availability of highchairs, for example, will be factors that will influence consumer choice. They may be factors which particular market segments value highly and should be researched, and if thought worthwhile, introduced.

Cleanliness and hygiene

Cleanliness and hygiene issues are relevant to the premises, equipment and staff. Over the last few years the significance of this factor has increased substantially. The media focus on food hygiene and the risks involved in buying food have heightened awareness of health and hygiene aspects. Customers are now far more aware of, and prepared to complain about, issues of cleanliness and hygiene. Overall operations should be concerned about assuring the proper levels of cleanliness and hygiene all the times as a normal part of the working practices, rather than doing it to avoid being caught out.

As well as ensuring that food and beverage product is prepared in hygienic conditions and that customers are provided with a clean environment in which to consume the product, there is also the need to reinforce the perception of the foodservice operation as being clean and hygienic. Tidy premises, smart uniforms and the use protective gloves, for instance, can all have a positive effect on this perception. Negative impressions can be created by, for instance, scruffy staff, fiddling with hair, eating or holding equipment badly (e.g. holding cups and glassware by the rim rather than the handle or the base), poor standards of personal hygiene amongst staff, poorly presented food items or food not being served at the right temperatures.

Price and value for money

Price is that element of the meal experience that relates to value, and is also directly related to profitability. However, price is also very flexible and can be changed relatively easily, thereby changing value perceptions and possibly changing profitability. (Chapter 9, on operations appraisal, covers profitability in more detail.)

In Chapter 2 we also saw that good value is where the worth is perceived as greater than the cost, and therefore a successful operator must add value for the consumer into the product. Prices should also be set in relation to the quality and value perception that operators want consumers to have. A high-priced product might be perceived as either good value or a rip-off, and a low-priced product as poor quality or good value, indicating that it is more than just the absolute price which determines value, but rather price and other costs relative to worth.

When developing, changing or supporting a product concept it is good practice to establish a price range within which the consumer will be prepared to pay. Another price range can be established within which the operator is prepared to offer the product. The overlap is the range available to the operator. Setting prices within ranges, which the consumers will pay, should be accomplished with reference to the particular market segment and the core concept. Market research can determine a range within which families travelling on motorways are prepared to stop and pay for food and drink, and will also be able to determine a price range for a particular menu item. This can be achieved through setting up consumer panels and asking them about price and product. The information to be gained from researching customers' attitudes and behaviour towards price will reveal that lowest price is far from always the main consideration, as Table 3.1 indicated.

Pricing methods used by operators vary in their appropriateness and sophistication. The various pricing methods include the following:

- **Cost plus**: This is the most common method. The ingredient cost is established – not always very accurately – and the required profit (referred to as gross profit) is added. The result is a selling price that gives the operator the required profit for that dish (although it should be noted that this required profit would only be realised when that dish is actually sold). This method is attractive because of its simplicity but it ignores price sensitivity and demand (price is a determinant of demand) and that value for money must be factored into the pricing decision. It also makes the assumption that the required profit can be established by making it a set percentage of the selling price (often between 65 and 75 per cent), fails to account for different restaurant types and different menu categories and does not take into account that each dish/beverage is only part of a collection of items purchased to produce the meal experience. Where this method is applied, differentiated percentages are used so that low-cost starter items earn proportionately more gross profit than higher-cost main course items.

- **Prime costing methods**: These attempt to factor-in the labour cost of a dish, and actual cost pricing attempts to include fixed and variable costs as well as labour. These additional costs are also established as a percentage of the final selling price (e.g. labour at 25% and variable costs at 10%). These methods are flawed in the same way as cost plus: labour is a factor related to the time needed to prepare a dish, not to the value of the ingredients used to prepare it; no account is taken of volume of business or item popularity in assessing the labour content of a dish, therefore not taking into account economies and diseconomies of scale; and allocating fixed and variable costs to each menu item should at least be related to the volume of each dish sold rather than a fixed percentage figure to be used for each menu item.

- **Backward pricing**: This attempts to match costs to a price previously established for a desired potential market. This market-driven approach – which is not really backwards – is a good starting point in new product development but it is still difficult to establish the necessary gross profit, ingredient and labour costs, and care must be taken to avoid the problems of using percentages. However identifying what the customer is prepared to pay for a particular product and investigating whether the operation can provide the product, profitability, at that price may avoid an operation being created that was never going to be profitable anyway.

- **Rate of return pricing**: This method tries to establish price based on a forecast of sales and costs and may be used to produce a break-even matrix for the operation. This approach may help give a guide to the price range but will not in itself establish individual selling prices.

- **Profit-per-customer pricing**: This establishes the total profit required and allocates this to a forecast demand resulting in an average profit per customer. This 'profit' is then added to the material and/or other costs to produce a selling price for each dish. Again this may be used to produce a break-even matrix, but caution should be exercised because profit is a factor of demand, which is a factor of price, which is a factor of demand, and so on. However, as with backwards pricing above, relating the required profitability of an operation to a given level of demand and within a price range that the customer is likely to pay can be used in determining if the operation can in fact ever be successful.

- **Elasticity pricing**: This asks how sensitive a market is to price changes. In order to determine menu prices the operator will try to determine the effect a price change may have on demand. It should be remembered that it is possible to increase demand and profitability through price decreases. However, it is very difficult to predict market responses to price changes, but considering elasticity may inform the pricing decisions.

- **Competition pricing**: This is copying the competitors' price. However, there is no guarantee that the cost structure of any competitor offering a similar product will be similar, so a particular market price may produce higher or lower profits. Copying the competition may also take the form of special offers, premium promotions, special meals, free wine and the provision of children's toys, all or which are short-term tactics, which can potentially lead to increasing costs and fierce price based competition. (Sales promotion is discussed in more detail in Chapter 7.)

Other pricing methods include: marginal analysis; break-even analysis; cost margin analysis; individual menu item profit and loss, and frequency distribution pricing (see, for example, Bowie and Buttle, 2004; Kotler *et al.*, 2010). Whichever methods are used, an operator should always have a clear pricing policy or objective in mind. Some of these pricing objectives might include:

- **Sales volume maximisation**, where the pricing objective is to achieve the highest sales possible.

- **Market share gain**, where the objective is to increase your number of customers relative to the total possible market and the competition.

- **Profit maximisation**, where the pricing objective is to achieve the highest profit possible.

- **Market penetration**, where the pricing objective is to move from a position of a zero or low market share to a significant market share.

Once a clear pricing objective is established, the pricing methods most suitable to that particular objective can be drawn from the various methods available, often being a combination of a range of pricing methods. (The nature of and the relationships between revenue, costs and profits are explored in more detail in Section 9.1, Operational appraisal.

Atmosphere

Atmosphere development leads to the creation of emotions. It is created through the combination of a number of factors such as: design, decor, lighting, heating, furnishings, acoustics and noise levels, the other customers, the staff and the attitude of the staff. There are happy atmospheres, gloomy, stressful, joyful, cheerful, angry, bustling, sedate, calming, invigorating, indulgent, peaceful, comfortable, uncomfortable, boring and inviting atmospheres. All of these different types of atmospheres can be created, and examples abound. The bright, young, clean atmosphere of McDonalds; the lively, musical atmosphere of a Hard Rock Cafe, the farmhouse atmosphere of Harvester, the luxurious atmosphere in the Queens

Grill on the Queen Mary 2, the cosy and informal atmosphere of a local French bistro, are all created. With so much control available, food and beverage operators clearly have opportunities to match the atmosphere with the concept.

Atmosphere is sensed through sight, sound, touch, taste and smell. Food and beverage operators' use:

- The sense of **sight** through the presentation of food and beverage products, furniture and textures, equipment, lighting, colours, employees, shapes, spaces and their own customers.

- The sense of **sound** can be controlled through acoustics, the use of materials and shapes, which alter sound, and the use of music, televisions, and operational sounds including speech.

- The sense of **touch** will be incorporated though, for instance, the quality of the air and the fabrics and equipment with which customers come into contact, the texture of the foods and the touching of other people.

- The sense of **taste** has great volumes of documentation dedicated to it through recipe and wine books and the variations are almost infinite.

- The sense of **smell** is used by many food and beverage operators to attract customers through coffee, bread, roast meat, etc. and any other aromas which may be associated with the core consumer concept.

Atmosphere is also created through the attitude of the staff. A pleasing environment soon becomes an unbearable one if members of staff are unhelpful, lacking in competence, unresponsive and rude. Conversely a potentially poor environment can be enhanced through genuine interest in customer needs, competence and good interpersonal skills.

Other customers have an impact on atmosphere. There is a range of customer related factors that operations need to consider which can affect the atmosphere. The proximity of other customers through the spacing of table in a restaurant for instance will affect the feeling of privacy or otherwise. Additionally operations need to make decisions, for example, about policies for:

- Customer dress requirements
- Mobile phone usage
- Maximum group size
- Accepting children
- Alcohol over-consumption
- Minimum levels of acceptable customer behaviour
- Mix of customers (e.g. a bar showing a football match).

Having policies for these factors means that they also have to be reinforced. Procedures for dealing with this need to be developed so that the consistency in the application of the policies is maintained, and the potential for customer relations problems minimised. (Also see the discussion in Chapter 7, section 7.4, on customer relations.)

There are always structural and cost constraints to atmosphere creation, but operators should invest in atmosphere to their best ability. If the right atmosphere is not created, in the hope that business success will finance further atmosphere development, success might not come at all. It might be better to consider targeting a different market for which atmosphere creation is less expensive, and then moving on to the original target market when the atmosphere-creation funds are available.

Some consumers want hot, sweaty, noisy, dark, vibrant and exciting atmospheres, while others will prefer quiet, comfortable, light, relaxing atmospheres. Specialist designers are available to construct an atmosphere for a food and beverage operation, and some large businesses employ their own design teams. These designs can be used to test the concept further by showing them to consumer panels and recording the reaction. At whatever level a food and beverage operation is resourced, investing in a part of the product, which so heavily influences the customers' perception of the product, should be a priority.

3.2   Quality in the management of food and beverage operations

The term 'quality' is currently used in a variety of ways to mean a variety of things. To support the approach of this book, the term 'quality' relies primarily on the approach of the British Standard Quality Award BS EN ISO 9001, on an assessment: 'in the fitness for purpose and safe in use sense: is the service provided or product designed and constructed to satisfy the customer's needs'.

■ British Standard EN ISO 9001

BS EN ISO 9001 identifies the systems, procedures and criteria that ensure that a product or service meets a customer's requirements. The key elements in quality management for most organisations in the hospitality industry include:

- Management responsibility: policy, objectives, and identification of key personnel.
- Quality system procedures: all functions must be covered.
- Auditing the system: it must be audited internally.
- Quality in marketing: honest promotional activities.
- Material control and traceability: supplies must be traceable.
- Nonconformity: ensuring that faulty products/service do not reach the customer.
- Corrective action: identifying reasons for faults, the measures taken to correct them and records to be kept.
- After-sales service: procedures for monitoring quality of after-sales service.

- Documentation and records: records of checks and inspections, action taken, audit reports.
- Personnel and training: identification of needs, provision and verification of training.
- Product safety and liability: procedures for handling, storing and processing materials, e.g. foods.

BS EN ISO 9001 can be important to foodservice operations for two reasons. First, when purchasing goods and services BS EN ISO 9001 indicates that a supplier operates a quality system of a high standard. Secondly, foodservice operators, such as contract caterers, may find that they will not be considered as potential tenderers if they have not achieved BS EN ISO 9001. Additionally, BS EN ISO 9001 may even provide useful evidence that due diligence had been exercised, for example, in the event of a foodservice operation being prosecuted under food safety legislation.

In an increasingly competitive marketplace, and with increasing uniformity between operations, the level of service provided and its quality become ever more important. It is the front-line members of staff that offer this service: hence their training and development are crucial to the successful running of an operation. Total quality management offers a framework by which members of staff are given the scope to treat customers as individuals, and thereby offer superior service.

However, the costs involved can be high and therefore, the introduction of BS EN ISO 9001 needs to be carefully assessed before implementation takes place. On the other hand, the reviews from many of the organisations moving towards BS EN ISO 9001 have suggested that it is cost-effective. The complete documents on BS EN ISO 9001:2008 are available from the British Standards Institution (BSI), at http://www.bsigroup.com.

European Foundation for Quality Management Excellence Model

The various approaches to quality management all support the systems approaches, and are intended to achieve total quality management within an organisation. This is summarised by the European Foundation for Quality Management Excellence Model (2010) shown graphically in Figure. 3.2.

The EFQM Excellence Model is a non-prescriptive framework, which recognises that there are many approaches to achieving sustainable excellence in all aspects of performance. The model is based on nine criteria. Essentially the model tells us that results for people (employees), customers and society are achieved through leadership driving policy and strategy, people management, partnership and resources and processes, leading ultimately to key performance (business) results.

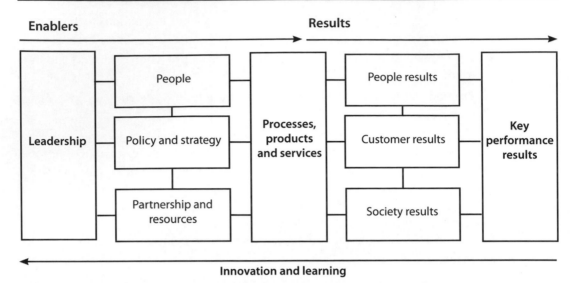

Enablers   **Results**

Figure 3.2: European Foundation for Quality Management Excellence Model

Source: adapted from EFQM, 2010

Each of the nine elements shown in the model is a criterion that can be used to appraise an organisation's progress towards total quality management. The four results criteria are concerned with what the organisation has achieved and is achieving. The five criteria for enablers are concerned with how results are being achieved. The arrows shown in Figure 3.2 are intended to emphasise the dynamic nature of the model. They indicate that innovation and learning help to improve enablers and that this in turn leads to improved results. The overall objective of a comprehensive self-appraisal and self-improvement programme is to regularly review each of these nine criteria and, thereafter, to adopt relevant improvement strategies. (Further information on quality matters can be obtained from **European Foundation for Quality Management** at http://www.efqm.org.)

■   Technical and service standards

Within foodservice operations service standards may be seen under two headings:

- **Technical standards** refer to the items on offer, the portion size or measure, the cooking method, the degree of cooking, the method of presentation, the cover, accompaniments, the cleanliness of items, etc.

- **Service standards** refer to two aspects: first, the procedures for service and second, the way in which the procedures are carried out. Procedures include meeting and greeting, order taking, seeking customer comment, dealing with complaints, payment and customers with additional needs. The method in which the service is carried out includes paying attention to the attitude of staff attentiveness, tone of voice, body language, etc.

Accepting that any standard must be achievable and measurable then this is quite possible with technical standards and with some aspects of service standards. However, it becomes increasingly difficult to set actual standards for the way that the service should be carried out.

Below are a number of possible aims for the service to achieve but is it arguable whether all of these are in fact standards or simply intentions:

- The supervisor should be visible in the room.
- The supervisor will visit all tables at least once during the customers' meal.
- Service employees should have positive attitudes.
- Servers should be noticeably comfortable in their respective roles.
- Co-operation between staff should be noticeable.
- Customers should be addressed by name.
- All customers should be addressed by name at least once during the meal.
- Customers' needs will be met.
- Ninety per cent of customer requests will be met.
- Menu items can be substituted or combined.

The other difficulty is that these intentions may not suit all customers all the time and therefore the service staff in endeavouring to meet these intentions may not be providing good service when considered from the customer perspective.

An alternative to this approach is first to recognise that the product is the totality of what the customer receives. The customer makes no real distinction between the physical product and the intangible aspects of service. It is probable in this context that the manager should also view the product as a whole, setting standards only where it is actually possible.

■ Customer service and resource productivity

On the one hand, a foodservice operation is designed to provide customer service and on the other the achievement of profit is largely determined by the efficiency of the use of resources. Customer service can be defined as being a combination of five characteristics. These are:

- **Service level**: the intensity of or limitations in, the individual personal attention given to customers.
- **Availability of service**: e.g. the opening times, variations in the menus and drinks lists on offer.
- **Level of standards**: e.g. food quality, decor, equipment cost, staffing professionalism.
- **Reliability of the service**: the extent to which the product is intended to be consistent in practice.
- **Flexibility of the service:** the provision of alternatives, variations in the standard product on offer.

The resources used in foodservice operations are:

- **Materials**: commodities and equipment
- **Labour**: staffing
- **Facilities**: basically the premises and the volume of business which the premises are able to support.

The customer service characteristics and the resources can be summarised as a model, shown in Figure 3.3. The management of the operation must therefore take account of the effect that the level of business has on the ability of the operation to maintain the service while at the same time ensuring a high productivity in all the resources being used. (This application of this model is discussed in more detail in Chapter 7 page 71.)

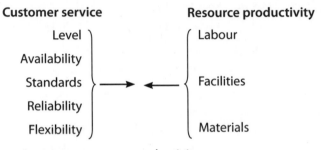

Figure 3.3: Customer service versus resource productivity

■ An integrated approach to quality management and service standards

Total Quality Management has had a controversial existence. Burill and Ledolter (1999) for example, identified that the concept had on the one hand been praised by those who have successfully interwoven the TQM concepts into their organisational culture and, on the other hand it has been panned by those organisations that have had problems with it.

There can be a tendency for quality management to be applied as a highly structured approach, which becomes internalised in the organisation, and as such is often supported by a weighty bureaucracy. Orientation to quality customer service is seen as a strategic dominant competitive tool, but, any strategy taking on board service quality must also consider the human element both within and external to the organisation. The customer can be too easily lost sight of in the highly regulated system of operating a business. In many ways the aim of management has been to reduce the aggregate cost of quality and so the cost of failure is likely to be reduced. Also businesses have often spent more money on prevention strategies, whereas the more prudent strategy is one of getting the job done correctly the first time.

One further dimension is that most of the quality assessment processes do not include some external measure of the customers' satisfaction with a particular operation. They are primarily concerned with evidence of systematic processes, which are employed within an operation, which can demonstrate that there is a link between customer demand and the services and products on offer.

More recently however, for the hospitality industry in the UK, under the aegis of the Institute of Hospitality, an accreditation programme has been developed which is based on quality management assessment systems that do take into account a measure of the reality of customer service. This is the Hospitality Assured programme. You can find more information on this from the website at http://www.hospitalityassured.com.

3

Identifying the question of balance

The question then is how can highly structured and systematised approaches to quality really allow personnel to contribute from the heart – the very essence of genuine good service? Product quality (in terms of technical standards) and service quality (in terms of service standards) are by their very nature different. Technical standards can be identified, measured and compared. Service though is highly varied. This is its distinguishing feature, and the essence of it is individuality.

However, it is possible to create an expectation that helps the customer to both perceive consistency and to recognise the variable factors that make that service what it is. There is a need then to develop a culture which views quality as a natural part of what everyone is doing. Establishing standards, having operational manuals and regular auditing are appropriate as part of the process but it can only really ever work if everyone in the organisation is focussed on real quality as viewed by the customer. There needs to be cohesion in moving toward ensuring emotional added value for the customer (doing the things your customers appreciate – but genuinely).

Overall, the extent to which customers appreciate a foodservice enterprise and its people is a function of the emotional value that has been added to the relationship, the product and the core-design. When no emotional value exists in this relationship, there is in essence, no relationship. How can a foodservice organisation blame customers from moving on to another business, when that other business recognises the importance of, and can support, rich, rewarding, physical and emotional relationships with its clientele? The level to which customers can appreciate a foodservice business and its people clearly has a critical impact on the success of the business. Consequently the benefits of true service quality probably come from giving service staff more freedom to do what they feel is in the best interests of their customers within a loose strategic framework.

Towards an integrated approach

Taking account of the various thoughts about on quality management, the place of standards within it and also ensuring that there is scope for developing a relationship between the organisation and the customer, then it is possible to bring these various ideas together and to develop an integrated approach to service quality management. It is also very necessary as the food and beverage manager is having to manage the relationship between the four food and beverage systems: food production, the beverage provision and between the service sequence (or service delivery system) and the customer process (for the relationship between these four systems see Chapter 1, Figure 1.3).

The first stage of the integrated approach to service quality management is to draw up a customer service specification, using the five meal experience factors (identified on page 48) and the five customer service factors identified in Figure 3.3. The importance here is to define technical and procedural standards where they can be defined (and achieved, measured and compared) and then also to describe what the customer experience should be like from their perspective. The next step is first to check that this customer service specification can be achieved and supported over time by the physical capabilities of the operation. Following this it is important to check that the customer service specification can actually be delivered through the service system (including being supported by the service staff). This can be seen as an integrated service quality management model. It is a six-stage process and can be summarised as shown in Figure 3.4.

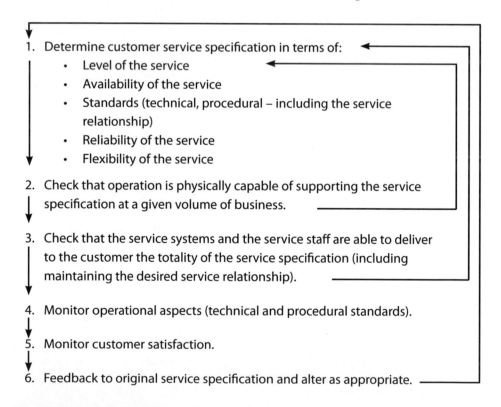

1. Determine customer service specification in terms of:
   • Level of the service
   • Availability of the service
   • Standards (technical, procedural – including the service relationship)
   • Reliability of the service
   • Flexibility of the service

2. Check that operation is physically capable of supporting the service specification at a given volume of business.

3. Check that the service systems and the service staff are able to deliver to the customer the totality of the service specification (including maintaining the desired service relationship).

4. Monitor operational aspects (technical and procedural standards).

5. Monitor customer satisfaction.

6. Feedback to original service specification and alter as appropriate.

Figure 3.4: Integrated Service Quality Management Model

This integrated approach to quality management ties in with the systems approach to operations and also follows from the philosophy of the various approaches to quality management.

3.3   Creating the consumer–product relationship

Once products to satisfy particular market segments have been designed it is necessary to undertake the steps to complete the product–consumer relationship. This final element in the process may be viewed as a four-stage sequence.

1   Determining promotional channels

2   Estimating profitability

3   Planning product launch

4   Offering product and appraising performance.

■   Determining promotional channels

Determining promotional channels is important because it will identify how consumers will be reached and attracted to the product. Food and beverage operators should identify and monitor consumers in order to be informed as to which promotional channels are best for their product. When choosing promotional channels the target market segment variables are considered in relation to the product message and the medium through which it may be delivered. The message to be delivered should relate to the consumer's needs, wants and demands, and be delivered through a medium used by the target consumers, reflecting their life styles and self-images. Table 3.2 shows possible messages and media for different food and beverage products.

Table 3.2: Possible message and media for food and beverage products

Product	Possible message	Media
Branded pizza restaurant	Meet friends and have fun	Television, local radio and press, mailshots
New Year's Eve dinner dance	Celebrate in style and spoil yourself	Local radio and press, in-house literature, direct suggestive selling to existing customer base
Local bistro	A touch of Continental style	Word of mouth
Public house	Traditional British hospitality	Word of mouth, local press, food guides

Choosing the message and the medium is a critical element in promoting the product. Large businesses will spend millions of pounds promoting their product through national television, radio, press and billboards. Small operations may only spend hundreds of pounds but the criterion is the same, namely is it effective? Regular reviewing of promotional activity and spending and how it relates to increased sales and profits, will enable effective evaluation of the process to take place. Consumers' responses to promotional activities should be researched.

Websites are a common way to communicate one's product to a wide audience. Nowadays the organisation's website is one of the first stops for consumers when deciding on a product. Therefore operators need to ensure that their websites are easy to use, presentable, communicative, current and a true reflection on what is offered. Furthermore, the website is now a platform to receive reservations directly through built-in online booking systems, provide virtual menus and to stay in contact with customers through blogs and comments. Third-party booking sites (restaurant marketing portals) for example Toptable.com are a current way to source bookings and to promote and monitor customer experiences. (For an example of a restaurant marketing portal visit http://www.toptable.com)

In addition, when considering marketing activity an emerging trend is the use of web 2.0 applications within hospitality organisations. Web 2.0 applications are tools that are user-generated content websites; these may include trip advisor, Facebook, Twitter, etc. These tools include applications that may include blogs, social networks, metaverse, podcast, wiki, tags and RSS.

Currently the utilisation of these applications is being used more at the luxury end of hotels than budget and small independent operators. Table 3.3 details some examples of different applications being used and their uses within hospitality and food and beverage operations.

Table 3.3: Examples of Web 2.0 applications and their potential uses within the hospitality industry

Examples	Potential uses
Tripadvisor, Toptable websites	Consumers regularly post comments and ratings of their experiences of hotels and restaurants on specialised websites. These opinions are for the most part neutral and unbiased and can have a powerful impact on consumer decision and overall image. In an age of new media tools, consumers are more inclined to trust the recommendation of friends, relatives, or even strangers who have had a similar experience rather than generic marketing messages (see for example William, 2002 or Sink, 2006).
Facebook and Twitter	Operators can now use such social network sites as part of their customer relations management (CRM) system in order to have a better understanding of their customers and as a way to keep in contact. It is also a vast platform for advertising. Qualman (2011) notes that if Facebook were a country it would be the fourth largest in the world.
You Tube	Media such as You Tube is becoming very powerful because it is convenient for customers to upload videos with recommendation and critiques of visits to restaurants and other hospitality organisations. Organisations can also upload videos of their own to promote and showcase their operations.
Hotel websites	Some hotels are now encouraging complete interactivity with their customers allowing them to upload comments and videos of their experiences.
Podcasts	Chains, such as Jumeirah, now provides podcasts on its website informing potential customers of their facilities and what is taking place within their hotels.
Industry blogs	Operators should monitor and participate in industry blogs. There are various tools and resources available to inform operators when comments have been made about their business and brands.
Applications (Apps)	Many large restaurant chains now use applications for iPhones and iPads to inform customers of product updates, events and promotions.
Voucher sites	Some restaurants now use commercial voucher sites to inform consumers of discounted promotions.

Some of the benefits that social media presents include:

- A way to distribute, promote, monitor and keep in touch with customers and potential customers.
- A more cost-effective media for many operators.
- More of a level playing field for independent operators against larger competitors.

Some challenges include:

- No strategic plans or rules can govern what happens in other words it is an untamed beast.
- Operators constantly have to be there to interact and engage and as a result it is extremely time consuming.
- For some consumers very little information is considered to be private, therefore anything is posted and they expect operators to do the same.
- Once information is posted via these applications it is permanent as it is often repeated on other sites.
- Operators are unsure how to use these applications to their advantage, as they are very customer driven.

Estimating profitability

Estimating profitability is a case of budgeting costs and sales. How these budgets might be set is addressed in Chapter 9 but when launching new products and changing existing ones the art of predicting outcomes is extremely indefinite. Methods used can however be very sophisticated. Some operators will measure the size of their selected target and segmented market, apply usage or uptake measures between competing products and multiply the resultant number of customers for their product by an estimated average spend per head. This may be performed for each hour, day and month to produce the sales budget. Applying 'profitability on sales percentage' approach will determine the budgeted profit. However, the measures used cannot be guaranteed correct, and therefore a best and worst scenario should be considered. This may take the form of a break-even chart to show an operator what the profitability levels are for various levels of demand or numbers of customers.

Having said this, outcomes are usually different from those expected. Estimating profitability will at least give some indication as to what might happen, and progress after launch can be evaluated against the estimates.

Planning the product launch

Planning the product launch is an operational as well as a promotional issue. Operationally, the new food and beverage product will need testing. This will involve staff scheduling and training, specifying and sourcing the necessary ingredients and equipment and if possible testing full-scale production. If a full-scale test production run is not possible, perhaps due to cost restraints, a reduced-scale test should be performed. There will always be elements of the product that will not work entirely as planned, and finding out about these before the product launch enables these elements to be rectified. Not being able to deliver the product as promoted will result in consumers' expectations not being met, and this could negatively affect the market segment's uptake of the product. It is also worth remembering that customers seem to remember bad experiences more than good ones.

The launch of a new product gives rise to promotional opportunities. Special sessions can be organised by offering the product free, or at reduced prices, to selected groups on a one-off basis, thus gaining good public relations exposure. This would also be a good operational test of the product without the repercussions of not meeting customers' expectations. Special offers can also be introduced to initially attract customers to the product, such as two items for the price of one, or free bottles of wine with a meal. However, special consideration must be given to the market segment's perception of the promotion, as free offers or reduced prices may not project the required image.

The timing of the product launch is also an important consideration. There are two issues regarding timing; one is getting the time right, and the other is having enough time available to get the product right. Getting the time right involves choosing a launch date that provides the best advantage to the operator. This will mean investigating the possibility of other events, which are going on at the same time and which may detract from or enhance the product launch. If demand is expected to fluctuate, and demand for food and beverage products does fluctuate between time of day, week, month and year, the planned launch time should be set to take this into account. It may be appropriate to launch the product before a busy period, in order to be able to build up to full capacity. Operations which do not give themselves enough time to develop and launch their product can find themselves offering products which are not successful, and the time available to develop a product may often be seen as insufficient. However if the product is not ready to be introduced in time, it is probably worth considering delaying the launch rather than offering a sub-standard product.

■ Offering the product and appraising performance

Offering the product and appraising performance are about putting the plan into action and monitoring the result. Chapter 9 details approaches to operations performance appraisal and to product performance appraisal.

3.4   The consumer–product relationship as a dynamic process

Issues surrounding the consumer-product relationship have been explored in Chapter 2 and in this chapter. Although presented and discussed primarily as a sequence (see Figure 2.2), the process of developing a consumer–product relationship is a dynamic and organic one, which is also continuous. As consumers' needs, wants and demands change, and as the competition increases and technology offers new opportunities, managing the process of creating a consumer–product relationship is also about managing change.

Various frameworks have been suggested to help to develop and evaluate the consumer–product relationship. These frameworks may be viewed as tools to be applied as required, but they are also tools that will need to be applied continuously. Food and beverage operations will often engage in different stages of developing a consumer–product relationship at the same time. Market research should be an ongoing commitment; generating ideas and concepts should be built into the management of an operation; and searches for new and developing market segments is a major management responsibility. With so many variables changing all the time, including the operator's own personal and business objectives, it can be seen how promoting the status quo and relying on consumers to remain fixed over time is a dangerous assumption. As product life cycles continue to shrink the importance of managing these changes in order to defend against threats and respond to opportunities, is increased.

Managing change effectively and profitably in a food and beverage environment is as complex and as difficult as in any other type of business. In order to really embrace change there must be a management vision of where they want to be. The focus of this vision will be satisfying the consumers of the food and beverage product. Management's first commitment is to communicate this vision with their staff, for without members of staff who are convinced of the need to change, and of the need to do things differently, the vision will not happen. Managing relationships within food and beverage operations, between groups of personnel, will play an ever-increasing role for management in the successful development of, or changing the consumer–product relationships.

4 Operational areas, equipment and staffing

Aim

This chapter aims to outline key considerations in the planning, design, equipping and staffing of foodservice operations.

Objectives

The chapter is intended to support you in:

- Developing a systematic approach to the planning, designing, equipping and staffing of foodservice operations

- Identifying the factors to be taken into account when making operational choices

- Ensuring compliance with health and safety requirements.

4.1 General considerations

The food and beverage manager responsible for a large operation, as well as dealing with staff reporting directly, reviewing financial performance, monitoring quality standards, overcoming obstacles and fine tuning the operation, also has to consider innovation. Creating new operations, or renovating existing ones, means being involved in developing new concepts or rethinking old ones. This can include activities such as creating new design, developing new menus, beverage lists and rethinking approaches to production and service, which then includes looking for new plant, equipment such as crockery, glassware, flatware and cutlery, through to uniforms, and so on.

Trends in the international market have an impact on foodservice businesses so it is necessary to stay in touch with forming trends. The dangers for foodservice businesses are that they can flounder because too much has been spent on interior design that could not be afforded or the business has suffered because the concept is not harmonised with effective staffing and menu and beverage list design.

There is a tangible relationship between the nature of the market, the type of demand being met and the budget available. In a competitive market unless the operation is unique, it has to be more attractive. Customers need a reason for coming to a particular operation rather than another offering similar products.

4.2 A systematic approach

The systematic approach to designing, planning, equipping and staffing of a foodservice operation includes giving consideration to a wide variety of factors. These can be grouped under six broad headings:

- The market needs
- Operational needs
- Space allocation and requirements
- Finance availability
- Sustainability
- Hygiene, health, safety and security.

■ The market needs

The needs of the market, or rather the need of the establishment to provide products to meet the determined market needs, may be ascertained by working through the first three stages of the foodservice cycle (see Chapter 1, page 2). These are:

1 Consideration of the potential market and the needs of the consumer.

2   The determination of policies and the business objectives, including the determination of the scope of the market needs that the operation is intended to serve.

3   The interpretation of demand, which identifies the type, range and scale of the food and beverage services to be provided.

Giving consideration to and making decisions within the first three stages of the foodservice cycle, (much of which has already been discussed in Chapters 1 to 3), a framework will have been established within which systematic consideration can be given to the planning and design of the facilities for the food and beverage operation and determining the plant, equipment, and staffing required.

Operational needs

Included in the consideration of the planning and design of facilities and the staffing of the operation, is the determination of the various operational methods that will or are to be used. This includes:

- Receiving and storage methods
- Production systems and methods
- Service system and methods
- Dining arrangements
- Clearing methods
- Dishwashing methods
- Control methods
- Disposal of waste and waste products.

The movement of food and beverages through a foodservice operation should follow a logical sequence starting with receiving and storage functions and continuing through to the disposal of waste products and waste. This can be illustrated as shown in Figure 4.1.

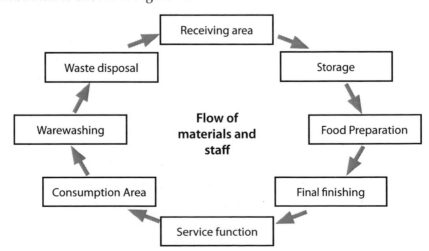

Figure 4.1: The flow of materials and staff (Source: developed from CESA, 2009)

Operation aspects also include consideration of, and establishing, food and beverage control systems. This involves many different areas and individuals within a foodservice facility. Specific areas that should be looked at, and control procedures that should be established include:

- Cash control
- Sales analysis
- Control of the customers' bills and receipts
- Food production forecasting
- Control over the various storage areas, including refrigeration
- Purchasing and receiving control
- Portion control, and
- Quality control.

Planning for these control mechanisms before the project has been completed, or even before it is under construction, is highly recommended. Operators significantly increase their chances for success when all of these areas have been critically examined and sufficient controls have been established.

The consideration of operational aspects also needs to take into account the customer usage of food and beverage service areas. This will include issues such as access to the premises and facilities such as toilets. It should also include the needs of the disabled and of children.

■ Finance availability

The main financial objectives of the operations will have been considered under stage two of the foodservice cycle (determination of policy). Under this stage the finance available will have been determined. Consideration will also have to be given to:

- The cost of the space to be used
- The purchasing policies, e.g. buying equipment, leasing equipment, lease/ rental, new or used
- The expected life of the operation in terms of the product life cycle and therefore the expected life of the equipment.

■ Space allocation and requirements

Taking into account the various considerations outlined above, Table 4.1 gives a rough guide to the space allocation required for different types of foodservice operations.

Table 4.1: Space allocations for foodservice operations

Meals	Square metres per meal served/hour		
	Up to 200	200–500	500+
Cafeteria	0.45–0.70	0.35–0.45	0.25–0.35
Hotels	0.35–1.60	0.35–0.70	0.35–0.45
Restaurants	0.35–0.90	0.35–0.45	0.30–0.35

Fast food outlets

The average size of most fast food outlets is currently around 1000–1500 m²

Restaurant and other dining areas

(NB Space allocation includes sideboards, aisles, etc.)

Style	Space per cover (m²)
Traditional restaurant	1
Banqueting	0.9
High-class restaurants	2

(NB For safety reasons all aisles should be 1 metre wide)

Food production areas	Space per cover (m²)
Up to l00 covers	0.5
100–1000	0.3–0.4
1000 or more	0.25

Source: developed from Croner's Catering, 1999

■ ## Sustainability

When designing or refurbishing premises, and when selecting equipment, careful evaluation of potential energy and water saving should be a part of each business's cost-saving, sustainability and corporate social responsibility (CSR) strategy. This should also consider the longer-term use of the premises and the equipment. Apart from improved environmental credentials and a positive perception of the business there is potential for increased energy savings. In addition any sustainability programme is aimed at encouraging reduction, reuse and recycling, sometimes known as R³ and depicted as in Figure 4.2.

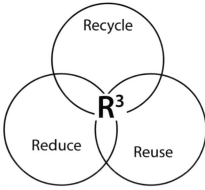

Figure 4.2: R³ – Reduce, Reuse, Recycle (Source: developed from CESA, 2009)

■ Hygiene, health, safety and security

The design of foodservice facilities must at all stages reflect the need for safe and hygienic working practices. The early involvement of the local environmental health officer (EHO) will reduce the risk of costly later amendments bearing in mind the legal powers of the EHO to close catering premises considered unfit for food production. Similarly the local fire officer should be consulted prior to any significant alterations or changes of use. Security must also be taken into account in the design process to allow for the protection of the premises, stock, equipment, cash, data and of course people (staff and customers).

4.3　Health and safety

The dual responsibility of employers and employees at work is to ensure that the premises and equipment are safe and that they are kept safe so as to prevent accidents. Employers need to assess any hazards or risks and implement procedures to deal with any accidents. All employees should receive training in accident prevention. Safety signs must be used to inform and instruct people using the premises so as to prevent accidents, or what they must do in the event of an accident.

■ Developing a positive health, safety and hygiene culture

It is an important function of management to develop a culture of safety. Good management involves stimulating staff interest and motivating them to set goals to achieve the highest standards of hygiene and safety within the organisation.

Figure 4.3: Developing a health and safety culture

A positive safety culture establishes health and safety systems; effectively achieving the culture requires time and effort from management. Management must be caring, committed and well organised. It must identify named individuals who are competent to guide company policy and knowledgeable staff who are able to contribute to the business through health and safety committees. A summary of an approach to the development of a health and safety culture for a foodservice operation is given in Figure 4.3.

■ Developing health and safety policies

Management are required to develop workable policies, which address real workplace issues that are of practical use and are tailored to the operation and processes. Health and safety policies should lead to the identification of all potential hazards found within the business and attempt to deal with them, reducing the risk of injury *in so far as is reasonably practicable*. There is, therefore, an inseparable link between policy and risk assessment, the first stage of development of a comprehensive health and safety policy.

The policy sets down a commitment by the company, organisation or operation to encourage food hygiene practices within the organisation. These must be seen as laying down clear guidelines and objectives for management and staff. Some of these policies have been modelled closely on health and safety lines giving a detailed set of broad objectives with guidance in relation to particular processes. Emphasis must be on clear accurate guidance to ensure that members of the staff comply and that all who work for the organisation accept the policy. Some establishments ask staff to sign a form to indicate that they understand the policy and that they mean to comply with its objectives to maintain high standards of hygiene. Failure to comply, once signed, may lead to disciplinary action. The success of the policy must be judged on the commitment of the workforce, therefore before formulating any document it is advisable to consult with staff. It is important that any policy is simple to understand and is practical to operate.

■ Control of substances hazardous to health (COSHH)

Substances dangerous to health are labelled very toxic, toxic harmful, irritant or corrosive. While only a small number of such chemicals are used in foodservice operations for cleaning, persons using such substances must be made aware of their correct use, proper dilution where appropriate and to wear protective goggles, gloves and face masks. It is essential that members of staff are trained to take precautions and not to take risks.

■ Risk assessment

Prevention of accidents and preventing food poisoning in foodservice establishments are essential, therefore it is necessary to assess any possible hazard or risk and decide what action is to be taken. The purpose of regularly assessing the possibility of risks and hazards is to prevent accidents. First it is necessary to monitor the situation to have regular and random checks to observe that the standards set are being complied with. It is essential that an investigation is made if any incidents or accidents occur. The investigation must aim to track down any defects in the system and proceed to remedy these at once. The outcome of the assessment is that potential hazards or risks can be classified under four levels:

1   Minimal risk – safe conditions with safety measures in place.

2   Some risk – acceptable risk; however, attention must be given to ensure safety measures operate.

3   Significant risk – where safety measures are not fully in operation, also includes foods most likely to cause food poisoning. Requires immediate attention.

4   Dangerous risk – requires the cessation of the process and/or discontinuing of the use of the equipment in the system and the complete checking and clearance before continuation.

■ Health and safety committees

Health and safety involves everyone in the foodservice operation from goods inwards to final product to service. In order to focus attention on the subject and to maintain a continued interest throughout the workforce it is advisable to set up a committee. Such a committee comprises those who have immediate responsibility for maintaining hygiene standards, quality control, production, service, training, etc. Staff representatives from various areas should be involved. Members should be changed from time to time to avoid complacency and to maintain interest.

■ Temperature control

Generally there are two important temperatures: 8°C and 63°C. Foods, which may be subject to microbiological multiplication, must be held at no higher than 8°C or no lower than 63°C. There are a few exceptions, which include foods in display. These foods can be displayed for up to four hours. Low risk and preserved foods can be stored at ambient temperature. It is possible to re-use food that has been displayed at ambient temperatures providing it has not exceeded four hours at that temperature, and is then subsequently served directly from a refrigerator. Food, which is served hot, should be held at over 63°C. Under Scottish regulations reheated food must attain a temperature of 82°C providing this does not adversely affect the quality of the food.

■ Hazard analysis and critical control point (HACCP)

HACCP is a process that examines each stage in the process, which may appear vulnerable in terms of introducing a hazard into the food. Particular attention is then given to this stage in the process. HACCP critically examines each stage of food production through to the final product and the consumer.

Once potential hazards in the processes have been identified, whether it is within the preparation, processing, storage or service, then particular attention must be given to either eliminating or minimising the hazard. One of the advantages of HACCP is that a multi-disciplinary team is involved because it covers the wide range of activities associated with the food product. Staff must be trained in HACCP and for the process to be successful they too must have commitment.

HACCP can be adapted by all sectors of the foodservice industry. The process is not just confined to large operators. On introducing the HACCP process into food production the following elements have to be implemented:

- A detailed flow chart needs to be drawn up showing the path of the food (including beverages) throughout the production process.

- All production details need to be identified so that any special characteristics are noted that could become a cause for concern.

- Each stage in the production must be carefully examined to see if there is the possibility that a hazard could occur. The risks are then recorded as high, medium or low. Monitoring controls are then implemented. In all cases records must be kept.

- Taking food samples and bacterial swabs also help to complement the HACCP programme.

Examples of critical control points (CCPs) include:

- Inspection (including temperature checks) of goods on delivery and before use

- Separate storage and handling of ingredients and the finished product

- Correct temperature ranges for refrigerated and frozen goods

- Cleaning procedures for equipment and utensils

- Cross-contamination with other menu items in process

- Personal hygiene and health standards

- Proficiency in use and cleaning of equipment.

Maintaining HACCP requires:

- Monitoring the information (e.g. temperature record charts) and take effective action when appropriate;

- Altering the HACCP system as necessary if any feature of ingredients, processes or environment changes;

- Carrying out periodic checks to ensure the accuracy of any necessary instruments;

- Periodic laboratory testing of the microbiological condition of raw materials, equipment environment and product should be made wherever possible

- Ensuring adequate personnel monitoring, training and retraining.

■ Safer food, better business

As HACCP is a system principally designed for manufacturing it is seen by many foodservice operators as being too complex. Therefore, a simpler system was developed which takes a slightly different approach in that it takes a generic view of all operations in a kitchen, for example, temperature monitoring. Safer Food Better Business is based on the HACCP approach but looks at the many steps or individual sub-processes involved in getting all the supplies from the supplier, processing them and then getting them to the customer. At each point where a risk is identified a control measure needs to be designed, implemented and monitored. These may include:

- ■ Examining sub-processes such as:

  □ Specification   □ Cooking

  □ Buying   □ Holding: hot or cold

  □ Receiving   □ Re-heating

  □ Storage   □ Serving

  □ Preparation   □ Waste disposal

                           □ Cleaning

- ■ Identifying potential risks from:

  □ Contamination

  □ Temperature

  □ Cross-contamination.

- ■ Taking measures such as:

  □ Supplier checks

  □ Checks for condition

  □ Temperature checks

  □ Colour coding knives and boards.

The Safer Food Better Business system is based on the principles of HACCP but in an easy to understand format. It is divided into two parts. The first part is about safe methods, e.g. avoiding cross-contamination, personal hygiene, cleaning, chilling and cooking. The second part covers opening and closing checks, proving methods are safe, recording safe methods, training records, supervision, stock control and the selection of suppliers and contractors. The system also includes pre-printed pages and charts to enter the relevant information such as temperatures of individual dishes.

■ Food hygiene audits

Food hygiene audits are intended to record deficiencies and areas for improvement and to monitor performance at certain points. These may be linked to any quality assurance (including ISO9001) criteria. The audit usually requires a suitably qualified person to carry out an in-depth inspection of the premises, plant and practices. The report is presented to management and includes observations and makes recommendations.

Many foodservice establishments change their techniques and procedures of operation without being aware of hazards that are introduced. It is all too easy for people who are familiar with the operation to fail to see what to outsiders are obvious problem areas emerging. Buildings may also be suffering from wear and tear and lack of repair. Equipment may also need overhauling. Often a hygiene audit is the only way of looking critically at the environment and thus picking up the problem areas or practices.

The frequency of these audits may vary, depending on the type of premises. High-volume production will justify more frequent audits. Establishments processing high-risk fresh commodities will also require more frequent audits. All in-depth inspections require properly recorded documentation, which provide the basis for reports to go to the people who are able to take action. Otherwise their value is diminished. Reports should prioritise, to assist management in their decision-making, especially when financial implications have to be assessed and considered.

4.4   Food production areas and equipment

Factors that influence kitchen planning and design are:
- The size and extent of the menu and the market that it serves
- Services: gas, electricity and water
- Labour, level of skills of people
- Amount of capital expenditure, costs
- Use of prepared convenience foods
- Types of equipment available
- Hygiene and food safety
- Design and décor
- Multi-usage requirements.

The size and space of the food production area should enable the staff to be able to work safely, efficiently, speedily and in comfort. The aim when planning a kitchen is for food to be prepared and served without waste of both time and effort. Therefore, layout design must consider working methods that improve productivity and utilize equipment to reduce labour.

The main considerations are:
- Ensuring an efficient workflow
- Providing adequate work space

- Creating suitable work sections
- Ensuring access to ancillary areas
- Determining number, type and size of equipment
- Ensuring ease of cleaning and disinfecting.

Food production areas must be also designed so that they can be easily managed. The management must have easy access to the areas under their control and have good visibility in the areas that have to be supervised.

■　Workflow

Food preparation rooms should be planned to allow a 'workflow' whereby food is processed through the premises from the point of delivery to the point of sale or service with the minimum of obstruction. The various processes should be separated as far as possible and food intended for sales should not cross paths with waste food or refuse. Staff time is valuable and a design that reduces wasteful journeys is both efficient and cost-effective.

Newly-built premises should comply fully with the requirements of the appropriate hygiene and safety legislation. Plans should be discussed with the enforcement officers, as it is much easier and cheaper to provide satisfactory finishes and facilities at the design stage rather than having to replace later.

The use of satisfactory building materials and a well-planned layout is also essential to achieve high standards of hygiene. Within the food production design there must also be adequate facilities for cleaning and disinfection of utensils and equipment.

For planning purposes stationary equipment must be sited to allow for the cleaning of wall and floor surfaces. Alternatively, the machines should be fixed firmly to the floor without a gap. However, the design must avoid narrow areas or angles in contact with the floor.

■　Work space

The size of the premises must be adequate to allow efficient operation and the site must be large enough to accommodate possible future expansion. Approximately 4.2 m2 (45 sq ft) is required per person; too little space can cause staff to work in close proximity to stoves, steamers, cuffing blades, mixers, etc. which creates the potential for accidents. Aisle space of approximately 1.37 m (4½ ft) is desirable as aisles must be adequate to enable staff to move safely. The working area must also be suitably lit and ventilated with extractor fans to remove heat, fumes and smells.

Premises should take full advantage of natural lighting through large, well-placed windows. In addition efficient, artificial lighting is always required in food production areas. Adequate lighting is also essential in passageways, storerooms, stairs and in areas outside the building where staff need to go, such as refuse areas and delivery bays. Wall and ceiling finishes should be chosen to enhance available light by using light-reflecting colours.

Modern buildings are often equipped with air conditioning, which provides a balanced system of purified air in each part of the building, and a separated ducted extraction of stale air. As ventilation is a specialist subject always consult a ventilation engineer.

■ Working sections

The size and style of the menu and the ability of the staff will determine the number of sections and layout that are necessary. A straight-line layout would be suitable for a snack bar while an island layout would be more suitable for an hotel restaurant.

The kitchen and food premises must also have adequate facilities for hand washing and drying in all areas of the kitchen where food processing, preparation and handling are carried out.

■ Access to ancillary areas

A good receiving area needs to be designed for bringing in supplies easily, with nearby storage facilities suitably sited for distribution of foods to preparation and production areas.

Refuse containers must be situated outside the building preferably in a covered but not totally enclosed area. Refuse can be divided into two types:

■ Dry waste – paper, cardboard boxes
■ Wet waste – food and kitchen debris.

The best type of container for wet waste is a metal or plastic bin with a tight-fitting lid that keeps out vermin and insects.

Areas must also be planned so that kitchen equipment can be cleaned and all used equipment from the dining area can be cleared, cleaned and stored, Stillroom facilities may also be required.

■ Type, amount and size of equipment

The type, amount and size of equipment will depend on the type of menu being provided. Not only should the equipment be suitably situated but also the working height is very important to enable the equipment to be used without causing excess fatigue. Kitchen equipment manufacturers and gas and electricity suppliers can provide details of equipment relating to output and size.

The various preparation processes require different types for consideration depending on what food is involved. A vegetable preparation area means that water from the sinks and dirt from the vegetables are going to accumulate and therefore adequate facilities for drainage should be provided. Pastry preparation alternatively entails mainly dry processes.

Whatever the processes, there are certain basic rules that can be applied which not only make for easier working conditions but which help to ensure that the food hygiene regulations are complied with.

Kitchens can be divided into sections, based on the production process:

Dry areas	Stores, storage
Wet areas	Fish preparation, vegetable preparation, butchery, cold preparation
Hot wet areas	Boiling, poaching, steaming
Equipment	Atmospheric steamers, pressure steamers, combination oven, bratt pans, steam-jacketed boilers
Hot dry areas	Frying, roasting, grilling
Equipment	Cool zone fryers, pressure fryers, bratt pans, roasting ovens, charcoal grills, salamanders, induction cookers, halogen cookers, microwave, cook and hold ovens
Dirty areas	Refuse, pot wash areas, plate wash
Equipment	Compactors, refuse storage units, pot wash machines, dishwashers, glass washers

Prepared foods will require different types of equipment and labour requirements compared with part-prepared food or raw state ingredients.

Prepared food examples:
- ☐ Sous-vide products
- ☐ Cook–chill
- ☐ Cook–freeze
- ☐ Prepared sweets.

Part prepared:
- ☐ Peeled and cut vegetables
- ☐ Convenience sauces and soups
- ☐ Portioned fish/meat.

Raw state:
- ☐ Unprepared vegetables
- ☐ Meat which requires butchering
- ☐ Fish requiring filleting and portioning.

Consideration must be given to the management policy on buying raw materials, and ensure plans incorporate facilities that allow raw materials are to be handled efficiently and safely.

The final selection of equipment will be made after detailed consideration of:

- ■ The functions that will be carried out within the cooking area of the kitchen
- ■ The amount of equipment, which will depend upon the complexity of the menus offered
- ■ The quantity of meals served.

The policy of management in use of materials from the traditional kitchen organisation using only fresh vegetables and totally unprepared items, to the use of prepared foods, chilled items, frozen foods, where the kitchen consists of a regeneration unit only.

Given, however, that a certain amount of equipment is required, the planner has the choice of a number of possible layouts, within the constraints of the building shape and size and the location of services. The most common are the island groupings, wall siting and the use of an L- or U-shaped layout and variations upon these basic themes.

◼ Ease of cleaning and disinfecting

Equipment must be so designed, constructed finished and arranged so that it can be easily cleaned and disinfected, safely, thoroughly and rapidly, without the need for skilled fitters or specialised tools.

Equipment such as gravity feed slicers, mixers, processors, etc. which do require dismantling for cleaning must be easy to take apart and reassemble. All edges must be smooth and rounded. Rough and sharp edges constitute a serious hazard to cleaners. If equipment is difficult to dismantle because of poor design and may result in a danger to operatives, it will mean that those responsible for cleaning will be reluctant to dean it. This results in a lowering of hygiene standards and possible health risks.

The buyer of the equipment should also observe that all joints and welds are smooth, and that nuts, bolts and screw heads are absent from food contact surfaces. All hinges should be capable of being taken apart for cleaning. No crevices in fitting panels, open joints and rough seams should be present in the equipment, if any of these are, they have a tendency to become filled with accumulations of food, grease and dirt which in turn will support bacterial growth and may then provide a food source for pest infestation.

(For a more detailed consideration of kitchen design see Foskett *et al.*, 2011, Chapter 5.)

4.5 Food and beverage service areas and equipment

Food and beverage service areas fall into two categories, those for customers and staff usage and those for staff usage only. Staff and customer usage areas include consumption areas such as dining areas and service areas such as in cafeterias, bars and the associated services. Staff areas include stillroom, wash-up, storage and cellar areas. The general considerations for staff usage areas are:

- ◼ Appropriate siting and with logical layout of equipment
- ◼ Ease of delivery access

- Ease of service
- Ensuring hygiene, health and safety requirements are met
- Ease of cleaning
- Sufficient storage space for service equipment and food items
- Security.

The general considerations for areas used by both customers and staff include first the general considerations for staff-only areas as above and in addition also take into account the meal experience factor of atmosphere (see Chapter 3, page 50). This includes consideration of:

- Decor and lighting
- Heating and ventilation
- Noise, and
- The size and shape of the areas.

Decor and lighting

The general considerations on decor are:

- Appropriateness to the type and style of the operation
- Sufficient flexibility especially where the space has multi-usage, e.g. function rooms
- Functional reliability
- Ease of maintenance
- Industrial rather than domestic quality
- Ease of cleaning and general housekeeping needs.

Lighting, itself an architectural feature, is a pivotal ingredient in foodservice operational design. Contemporary lighting and colour designs tend towards a versatile system of lighting by which a food and beverage service area may have brighter lighting at lunchtime and a more diffused form of lighting in the evening. Lighting can create image, generate atmosphere and seamlessly communicate a marketing and merchandising message. In tandem it can determine quality, price, and speed of turnover. The principal rule in lighting provision is that it be neither too bright nor too dark. Brilliant lighting does not create comfortable or intimate surroundings. Dim lighting limits sensory evaluation and may inhibit safe working practices. It can also be an advantage to be able to change the colour of the lights for special functions and today's technology enhances these possibilities.

Heating and ventilation

There are two dimensions to heating and lighting:

- The maintenance of a reasonable temperature
- The ventilation of the areas.

The temperature of food and beverage service areas will change depending on the volume of customers and how long they stay in an area. For every ten people this is equivalent to a 1 kw fire being turned on. Temperature control will therefore need to take this into account especially where customers are in dining areas for a long period such as in function operations. Temperature also has an actual and a perceived reality. Customers will have preferred locations depending on their perceptions of the heating; asking to sit by windows, for example, as this is considered a cooler part of the room, or not by doors because of suspected draughts, or not near buffets because of the heat or cold. In all these examples the actual temperature may be the same as other areas of the room.

In areas where food and beverages are served there are inevitable smells, which come from these areas. It is a truism that a single food smell is generally liked, for example fresh coffee or freshly baked bread, but that a combination of food smells is usually unpleasant. Some restaurant environments however, utilise the smell of food and beverage effectively to promote customer comfort and promote sales as part of merchandising. In general though, food smells are best avoided and the ventilation systems should be able to take account of this requirement.

Ambient noise

Because of equipment movement and customer and staff conversation, food and beverage service areas can be noisy. The customer expectation is that generally the higher the service level and price, then the lower the noise level that will be tolerated. This is also affected by the time of day; for instance breakfast can be more acceptably noisy than dinner. Care needs to be taken in the design and selection of materials and equipment in order to contain noise at appropriate and acceptable levels. Sound absorbing materials in walls, floors and ceilings can assist greatly. Acoustical materials for ceilings and walls are generally the largest target areas for noise control. The floor space is another major surface area which when carpeted actively controls noise. Window treatments and tabletop linen also absorb noise pollution.

Another issue is that of noise transmission from one area to another as in an adjacent bar, lounge and kitchen. Sound transmission should really be considered and alleviated at the planning phase; afterwards it is a matter of control and the effective use of acoustical materials. Background music systems can also cause problems. It is an area of great controversy with very clear views being expressed as to why background music systems can aid or hinder operations. In general it depends on the particular style of operations and the image that the operation is trying to project. If background systems are to be used then it is worth investing in high-quality equipment. Having cheap and badly regulated equipment is both distressful and fatiguing for customers.

■   The size and shape of the areas

Not only do the size and shape of the room affect the customers' enjoyment of the meal but also in table service areas the location of the tables becomes important. Some issues to consider are:

- The location of tables in a food service area especially taking into account the needs of the single diner and couples
- Facing positions (e.g. not towards service areas, walls, doors, or too close to service stations)
- Access for those with disabilities
- Ease of workflow
- Evenness of temperature and ventilation (including avoiding air-conditioning, heating and extraction hot spots)
- Access to exits and toilets
- Avoiding being directly in the path of live or piped music systems.

■   Food and beverage service equipment

The general points to be considered when purchasing equipment for a food and beverage service area are:

- Flexibility of use
- Type of service being offered
- Type of customer and the nature of demand being met
- Design, shape, colour, and durability
- Ease of maintenance and replacement
- Stackability
- Costs and funds available
- Storage
- Rate of breakage, e.g. for crockery
- Psychological effect on customers, and
- Delivery time.

Furniture

Furniture must be chosen according to the needs of the establishment and the variation in human body dimensions. The type of operation being run determines the specific needs as far as the dining arrangements are concerned. A summary of possible dining arrangements is given in Table 4.2.

Table 4.2: Examples of dining arrangements

Type	Description
Loose random	Free-standing furniture positioned in no discernible pattern within a given area
Loose module	Free-standing furniture positioned within a given area to a predetermined pattern with or without the use of dividers to create smaller areas within a module
Booth	Fixed seating, usually high-backed, used to create secluded seating
High density	Furniture with minimum dimensions and usually fixed in positioned within a given area to create maximum seating capacity, e.g. for cafeterias
Module	Seating incorporates table and chairs constructed as one and may be fixed
In-situ	Customers served in areas not designed for service, e.g. in aircraft and hospital beds
Bar and lounge areas	Customers served in areas not conventionally designed for eating

In determining the specification for furniture for foodservice operation the following factors might be taken into account:

- Comfort
- Cost
- Design
- Durability
- Function
- Movability
- Multi-functionality
- Safety
- Structure and materials
- Storage capacity (if required).

Very often by using different materials, designs and finishes and by careful arrangement the atmosphere and appearance of the food and beverage service area can be changed to suit different occasions. Restaurant and bar furniture needs careful consideration. It needs to reinforce the aesthetics, style and ambience of the business. The ergonomics have to be carefully considered. Furniture needs to be sturdy yet easily moved, versatile, durable, low maintenance and with a superior finish. Where possible prior to purchase, performance evaluation should be carried out. This should definitely be requested where consultants are employed.

With seating requirements generally there is a relationship between comfort and the time the customer will tend to spend in the seat. Thus less comfortable but adequately functional seating tends to be used in fast service operations and in higher-level service areas more comfortable seating is provided. It is also true because of differences in physiology, women tend to sit up straighter for longer than men. Therefore chairs with arms are more useful in operations meeting the needs of a male-dominated clientele.

Consideration also needs to be given to the needs of children, people with disabilities and the manoeuvrability and stacking capability of seating especially for function operations.

Trays

Trays are used throughout foodservice operations. Their use ranges from carrying equipment and food to service on a tray, as in hospital, airline and room service operations. Additional considerations in the purchase of trays include:

- Lightness and strength – trays should be able to be carried when fully loaded and not become misshapen when weight is placed upon them
- Stackability
- Heat resistance
- Ease of cleaning
- Resistance to slippage of items place on them
- Resistant to damage from spilt items or damp.

Tables

Tables generally come in four shapes: round, oval, square and rectangular. An establishment may have a mixture of shapes to give variety, or tables of all one shape according to the shape of the room and the style of service being offered. These tables will seat two or four people and two tables may be pushed together to seat larger parties, luncheons, dinners, weddings, etc. By using extensions a variety of shapes may be obtained allowing full use of the room and getting the maximum number of covers in the minimum space.

Chairs

Chairs come in an enormous range of designs, materials and colours to suit all situations and occasions. Because of the wide range of styles, the chairs vary in height and width, but as a guide, a chair seat is 46 cm (18 in) from the ground, the height from the ground to the top of the back is 1 m (39 in) and the depth from the front edge of the seat to the back of the chair is 46 cm (18 in).

Additional purchasing considerations are the size, height, shape and the variety of seating required – banquette, armchairs, straight-backed, action–backed and padded chairs, giving the customer a choice, and also including high chairs for toddlers and kiddy boosters or cushions for children. Care also needs to be taken in matching chairs and seating generally with table heights, especially where chairs and tables in both metric and imperial measurements are being used.

Sideboards/workstations

The style and design of a sideboard or workstations vary from establishment to establishment. The majority of commercially available sideboards are insufficient in strength of construction, storage capability and worktop provision. It is now more usual for operations to design and build their own sideboards or workstations, often incorporating them as part of the design of the dining area.

Linen

There are many qualities of linen in present-day use, from the finest Irish linen and cotton to synthetic materials such as nylon and viscose. The type of linen use would depend on the class of establishment, type of clientele and cost involved and the style of menu and service to be offered.

Operations need to make arrangement to ensure the availability of linen to meet operational requirements. Decisions need to be made on whether the operation should:

■ Have an in-house laundry and its own linen

■ Purchase own linen and use an off-site commercial laundry, or

■ Have a linen rental or contract with an external commercial laundry.

Essentially it comes down to the requirements and size of the business or organisation and the capacity in terms of available space to site a laundry and available capital for initial steep outlay. If the business is part of a group, another option may well be to utilise a centralised laundry service for the group.

Crockery

When purchasing crockery the key factors to consider are:

■ Every item should have a complete cover of glaze to ensure a reasonable length of life.

■ Items should have a rolled edge, which will give added reinforcement at the edge and reduce the possibility of chipping.

■ The pattern should be under rather than on top of the glaze. However, this demands additional glaze and firing. Patterns on top of the glaze will wear and discolour very quickly. Therefore, although crockery with the pattern under the glaze is more expensive its life will be longer.

There are now many more manufacturers in the marketplace than ever before. Foodservice operations can now choose not simply in terms of durability, but with bespoke design, size, colour, weight and shape as just part of an overall package. There is a wide range of traditional items available and their exact sizes vary according to the manufacturer and the design produced. There is also increasing use of more modern service ware such as that made from glass or plastics and also in a variety of shapes other than rounds. When purchasing service ware key considerations are:

- The extent to which there is to be common usage of items thus reducing the level of stock, e.g. using one size of plate for fish and sweet courses or using one bowl for items such as soup, fruit and cereal.
- The extent to which different service areas and different service times might have different crockery. For example different banqueting crockery from coffee shop crockery or larger cups for breakfast.
- The extent to which the various crockery items should match. It has become quite common to have differing designs of crockery according to different types of dishes and also to mix complementary patterns.

Tableware

The term tableware traditionally covers:

- Flatware; all forms of spoon and fork
- Cutlery; knives and other cutting implements, and
- Hollow-ware; any item made from silver, apart from flatware and cutlery, e.g. teapots, milk jugs, sugar basins, oval flats.

Although traditionally referred to separately as *flatware* and *cutlery*, the term most commonly used now is *cutlery*, which refers to both.

The majority of foodservice areas use either plated silverware or stainless steel. Plain cutlery and flatware are more popular than patterned for the simple reason that they are cheaper and easier to keep clean. General considerations for choosing a selection of tableware items also include the extent to which items will have more than one purpose. For example using jugs for hot water, hot milk or cold milk or using standard ranges of cutlery such as sweet/soup spoons, and general-purpose knives and forks rather than having, say, separate fish knives and forks.

Glassware

Glass also contributes to the appearance of the table and the overall attraction of the room. There are many standard patterns available to the foodservice operator. Most manufacturers now supply hotel glassware in standard sizes for convenience of ordering, availability and quick delivery.

Except in certain speciality restaurants or high-class establishments, where either coloured glassware or cut glassware may be used, hotel glassware is usually plain.

A good wine glass should be plain and clear so the colour and brilliance of a wine can be clearly seen; it should have a stem for holding the wine glass so that the heat of one's hand does not affect the wine on tasting; there should be a slight incurving lip to help hold the aroma and it should be large enough to hold the particular wine being tasted.

Disposables

The main varieties of disposable available are often used in the following areas:

- Storage and cooking purposes
- Service of food and beverages, e.g. plates, knives, forks, cups
- Decor – napkins, tablecloths, slipcloths, banquet roll, place-mats
- Hygiene – wipes
- Clothing, e.g. aprons, chefs' hats, gloves
- Packaging – for marketing and presentation purposes.

A considerable advance in the range of disposable available has been the intro-duction of disposables whose approximation to crockery and tableware is very close. For instance, they may have a high quality, overall finish and a smooth hard white surface. The plates themselves are strong and rigid with no tendency to bend or buckle, and a plasticising ingredient ensures that they are grease and moisture proof, even against hot fat and gravy. Oval luncheon plate, snack trays and compartment plates are all available to the caterer.

Advantages of disposables include:

- Equipment and labour: disposables reduce the need for washing-up equip-ment, staff and materials.
- Hygiene: usage improves the standard of hygiene in an establishment.
- Capital: usage reduces the amount of capital investment.
- Cost: disposables are cheaper than hiring conventional equipment.

Disadvantages of disposables include:

- Acceptability: customer acceptability may be poor.
- Cost: disposables can be more expensive than some conventional equipment.
- Storage: back-up quantities are required.
- Supply: there is heavy reliance on supply and delivery time.

■ Bar areas

There are certain essentials necessary in the planning of bars. These are outlined as follows:

- **Area**: The bar staff must be given sufficient area of space in which to work and move about. There should be a minimum of 1 m from the back of the bar counter to the storage shelves and display cabinets at the rear of the bar.
- **Layout**: Careful consideration must be given, in the initial planning, to the layout. Everything should be easily to hand so that the bar staff do not have to move about more than necessary.

- **Plumbing and power**: It is essential to have hot and cold running water for glass washing. Power is necessary to provide the effective working of cooling trays, refrigerators and ice-making machines.

- **Storage**: Adequate storage should be provided, in the form or shelves, cupboard and racks, for all the stock and equipment required.

- **Safety and hygiene**: Great care must be observed so that the materials used in the make-up of the bar are hygienic and safe. Flooring must be non-slip. The bar top should be of a material suited to the general decor that is hardwearing, easily wiped down and has no sharp edges. The bar top is usually of average working height – of at least 1 m (3 ft) and a width of 0.6 m (20 in).

■ Automatic vending

In the broadest sense, automatic vending may be defined as 'time saving selling by automation' for convenience. Vended goods have 24-hour availability and the units can be sited wherever required. It is a form of automatic retailing using one of the following:

- Coin
- Token
- Banknote
- Moneycard, or
- Credit/debit card.

The types of service available may be broken down into two main groups: namely services and facilities such as car parking, toilets, baggage store, or consumables such as hot and cold meal/snacks and beverages. Within foodservice, automatic vending refers to the supply of a wide range of beverages, both hot and cold, through coin/token-operated machines. Vending machines used for foodservice operations include:

- **Merchandiser**: Customers can view the products for sale, for example, confectionery machines. Can also be used for refrigerated drinks (bottles and cans) and prepackaged meals and snacks as well as for hot meals and snacks through internal heating.

- **Hot beverage vendor**: This mixes the powdered ingredients with hot water to produce the product.

- **In-cup system**: Ingredients are already in individual cups to which hot water is added.

- **Cold beverage vendor**: Post-mix syrup mixed with water (carbonated or non-carbonated).

- **Micro-vend system**: Provides a range of hot or cold foods from which the customer may make a selection and heat in an accompanying microwave oven.

The numbers and types of machines required depends on their location, the type and number of people they are providing a service for, the cost factor and the variety of food and beverage items required.

The machines required might be installed either individually or in small groups, to supplement the conventional catering establishment or to cover a small-scale demand that does not warrant the expense of employing the extra labour and plant. The opposite to this would be the installation of a complete vending service where demand is highly volatile, space is limited and the use of staffed operations would be uneconomical.

Automatic vending machines are not self-cleaning, self-maintaining or self-filling. Therefore, regular service maintenance is required and should be guaranteed if the vending service is to run smoothly and without the problems of mechanical breakdown. The type of vending machine and the service demand upon it will help to determine the regularity of the service requirements. All vending machines come with instructions about cleaning, maintenance and stocking, which do need to be followed for the machines to perform at optimum efficiency levels.

4

4.6   Staff management considerations

How management deals with key staffing issues can significantly affect the success of any operation. Areas that to be addressed include:

- Determining the amount of required labour
- The establishment of employee work schedules
- The determination of operating hours
- Staffing patterns
- The various benefits that will be offered to employees
- The varying skill and knowledge levels that will exist among the employees
- The level of supervision that will be required
- Issues that are centred on the remuneration package.

Addressing these issues will help to determine the organisational structure of the operation and the kind of management team needed to operate the facility in an effective and efficient manner.

Many successful restaurants are owned and operated by one individual whose personality becomes a part of the customers' dining experience. On the other hand, the management of the food and beverage department of a large hotel, or the foodservice in a large hospital or university, may be under the control of more than one person and is usually part of a more complex organisational team. In these cases, the policies and procedures of the foodservice facility should be laid out in an operations manual, to assure consistent implementation of management policies.

Staff have a critical influence on the success of a foodservice business. Within a foodservice operation there are a range of roles. These include staffing for:

- Food production
- Food service
- Beverage service
- Marketing
- Sales promotion
- Merchandising
- Financial and physical resource management
- People management.

The true strength of a foodservice operation is the opportunity for human interface and the quality of its people to maximise that opportunity. Although this might appear trite, achieving this requires a systematic and analytical approach. When selecting customer contact personnel it is crucial to have people who are likely to be liked by customers and whose personal attributes include a positive attitude and a customer-oriented approach. Foodservice businesses solely investing in greater efficiencies and mechanistic interactions can sacrifice the invigorative energies required to sustain positive and rewarding relationships between staff and customers.

■ Optimising human resources

The key selection attributes of enlightened food and beverage personnel are clear. What is needed is an intrinsic ability to help people; it is an inner genuineness, and ability respond to and attempt to satisfy the needs of others. Willingness to learn is also important, as is a sense of urgency.

People are a major resource and maximising the potential of this resource requires the management of staffing to be at the forefront of the organisation and not within the traditional personnel (or human resources) department. It should be as upfront in the requirements of management responsibilities as are the management responsibilities for the operations, finance and sales and marketing: it's a strategic partner with the organisation.

With more and more individuals entering the industry with improved educational qualifications, which is presenting its own challenges to achieve a positive outcome, people need to be challenged and motivated through opportunity. Compensation through rewards and recognition should support this approach. The quality of the human resources should be the businesses strength: the essence of the core competence.

The management of people is not and should not be primarily an administrative function. Managing people, developing teams and individuals, are all activities that are integral parts of the management of operations.

■ Health, safety and security

There are common-law duties on employers, which are to:

- Select reasonably competent staff (or provide training to bring new recruits up to a reasonable standard of competence)
- Provide adequate materials required for the job
- Provide a safe system of working.

Employees may claim damages from the employer for any injury sustained as a result of any breach of these requirements.

In turn, members of staff have responsibilities to contribute to maintaining the health and safety requirements of the foodservice operation. The implications for staff are that they should:

- Understand the food hygiene regulations and that it is their responsibility to act within the bounds of these regulations
- Notify management of any major illnesses
- Perform duties in any area concerned with the handling of food in a hygienic manner, paying attention to food and hygiene regulations
- Wear uniforms and protective clothing as required
- Make themselves familiar with all escape routes and fire exits in the building
- Ensure that fire exits remain clear at all times
- Participate in fire evacuation drills and practices
- Take reasonable care for the health and safety of themselves and of others, and ensure that health and safety regulations are followed
- Report to heads of department or duty managers any hazards which may cause injury or ill-health to customers and/or staff.

Employers and members of staff also take steps to ensure security. Depending upon the nature of the establishment, the security measures that are laid down may vary considerably. Procedures should be known and understood by all members of staff and management. This often includes:

- Using identity badges
- Being observant and reporting 'suspicious' persons and/or packages
- Not discussing work duties with customers or outside the workplace
- Allowing for the searching of bags, packages and the person
- Ensuring external fire doors are kept shut but not locked;
- Maintaining procedures for handling keys and restricted access
- Specific procedures for handling cash and other payment systems
- Ensuring that all areas have been vacated before locking up
- Having procedures for dealing with a suspicious item or package
- Having procedures for dealing with a bomb threat

■ Having well developed and rehearsed procedures for the evacuation of the premises.

■ Facilities for staff

Within the space allocation of the premises, provision must also be made for staff facilities. Good clean facilities for staff are essential, if they are to be encouraged to work cleanly and hygienically. If clean conditions are provided and kept clean for staff they will be encouraged to take ownership of the working practices necessary to provide an ideal hygienic working environment.

The staff facilities must be readily accessible to staff and while in smaller premises where only one or two are employed, a single lavatory may suffice, in larger premises involving numbers of employees, it will be necessary to have separate facilities for each sex, which should be situated at each floor level.

Adequate storage space must be provided for outdoor and other clothing and footwear not worn by the staff during working hours. These articles of clothing must not be stored in a food room and therefore, must be stored in separate lockers allocated to each member of staff. It is advisable that a separate room be designated as a cloakroom so that clothes can be stored conveniently. Adequate washing facilities should be provided in the cloakroom, to encourage staff to wash their hands frequently and to reinforce personal hygiene.

■ Staff organisation

Staff organisation in food and beverage operations is focused upon having sufficient trained and competent staff on duty to match the expected volume of customer demand.

The staffing required will be as much dependent on the nature of the various methods being adopted, e.g. food production method, service method, control method, as it is on determining the staffing levels to meet the expected volume of customer demand.

Customer demand, or throughput can be determined from sales records. There is clearly also a relationship between the volume of customers served and the length of time they stay on the premises. The time customers take in different types of operation varies. This can range from, for example, ten minutes in a cafeteria through to three hours in a fine dining restaurant.

Opening times are determined by the consideration of:

■ Local competition
■ Local attractions, e.g. theatre
■ Location of the premises, e.g. city centre/country/suburb
■ Catchment area
■ Transport systems

- Staffing availability
- Volume of business
- Local tradition.

Customer throughput

Customer throughput can be calculated for different types of operation. Examples of how this can be determined for different types of operation are as follows:

Table and assisted service operations

Since all customers are usually seated in both table and assisted service methods, throughput can be estimated for new operations as the level of throughput will be limited by the length of seating time and the opening hours of the operation. For existing operations, sales records will provide a guide to potential throughput. Staffing for each service period can then be estimated and allocated to specific duties. Staffing will also need to be estimated for preparation before and for clearing following service. Thus a restaurant open for two and a half hours at lunchtime may require staff for up to five hours.

To calculate the total staffing required:

1 Estimate the number of staff required for each range of duties per service period in one week.

2 Multiply the number of staff per service period by the number of hours to be worked in each period.

3 Divide total staff hours by full-time working week hours. This will give the full-time equivalent of number of staff required.

4 Mix full-time, part-time, casual, seasonal and temporary staff hours to cover all service periods.

5 Draw up staff rota which may need to be on two or three-week cycle to allow for days off, etc.

The number of staff to each service period can now be calculated and a rota drawn up. However the actual staffing levels for these types of operations are determined taking account of various ratios. This can be as covers per head, such as in determining the number of covers covered by a station in a restaurant, or revenue per head.

Cafeteria operations

There are five factors that influence potential throughput in cafeterias. These are:

- Service time: the time it takes each customer to pass along or by the counter and reach the till point
- Service period: the time the cafeteria is actually serving
- Till speed: the time it takes for customer to be billed and payment taken
- Eating/seating time
- Seating capacity.

The main criterion is seating capacity. The speed required in the queue is determined by the seating capacity and the average seating time. For example: a cafeteria with say, 186 seats and with a till speed of nine per minute, will take 20.66 minutes to fill the cafeteria. If the customers' seating time is 20 minutes, then the cafeteria will be filled just after the first customers are leaving. A faster till speed will mean that the last customer through the till will have nowhere to sit. Too slow a till speed will mean the cafeteria is not being fully utilised. For one till, four to six people per minute is a maximum.

Generally, if the seating time is greater than the service period then the actual number of seats will need to equal the total number of customers. If the seating time is less than the time it takes to serve all the customers then the number of seats may be less than the actual number of people to be served. However, the queue may need to be staggered to avoid excessive waiting before service.

The staffing levels will take account of the number of till points that need to be open as well as the level of food production, counter service, clearing and dishwashing required.

Single-point service operations

Customer throughput in single-point service operations may be taken from records of till transactions. Increases and decreases in the customer throughput are provided for by increasing or decreasing the number of till points that are open (or in the case of vending, additional machines). If seating areas are provided then similar calculations as for cafeterias can be carried out, assuming there is a known percentage of customers using the seating facility.

Again staffing levels will take account of the number of payment points that need to be open as well as the level of production, clearing and dishwashing required.

Specialised forms of service

For hospital and airline tray methods there is a capacity limitation. For other forms of specialised service methods there are records or estimates of potential take-up of services in specific locations, e.g. hotel rooms, lounges or home delivery.

Organising duties

All duties required within the foodservice operation can be broken down into a listing of tasks. These can then be rostered. The exact nature of a duty roster will vary with depending on the type of establishment according to the duties to be performed, the number of staff required, having time off, and whether a split/straight shift is worked.

The purpose of the duty roster is to ensure that all the necessary duties are covered in order that efficient production and service may be carried out. There is an old adage that 'everyone's responsibility is no one's responsibility'. It is crucial therefore for foodservice operations that all the required duties are covered and that all managers, supervisors and staff are responsible and accountable for specific tasks.

It is also important that a high level of discipline is observed during service periods. Loosing a grip on the flow of the food production and service through staff not knowing their responsibilities, or not carrying them out, or misguidedly trying to help others, can lead to chaos, which customers easily detect. Care also needs to be taken to ensure that plans are made for contingencies such as unexpected increases in business levels or shortages of staff.

Having properly detailed tasks and duty lists also provides the basis for staff training. Task and duty lists for each of the tasks and duties given are drawn up and these should identify standards to be achieved. These are often brought together in standards of performance manuals.

4

■ Staff training

It is essential that all managers, supervisor and members of staff fully understand their responsibilities, have been trained to carry out their duties and also know the standards of performance, which are expected of them. The basis for achieving this can be through having precise, agreed and written job descriptions. These are then backed up by agreed standards of performance manuals that are regularly reviewed and updated. And all of this is then reinforced through regular training and briefing sessions. The advantages of well-produced training programmes include:

- Clearer identified and specified responsibilities
- Compliance with required standards of performance
- Improved competence and confidence of staff
- More efficient, safe and hygienic working practices.

For further information on human resource management in the hospitality, tourism and leisure industries, see for example Nickson (2006) or Mullins (2007).

5 Food production

This chapter aims to demonstrate the importance of sound menu planning and emphasise its importance in the planning, implementation and management of food production systems.

Objectives

This chapter is intended to support you in:

- Identifying types of menus and the classic menu sequence
- Planning menus
- Identifying key influences on modern menus
- Managing food production as an operating system
- Managing volume within food production systems
- Developing and managing the purchasing function
- Developing and applying operational control procedures.

5.1   Types of menus

Menus may be divided into two main classes, traditionally called à la carte (from the card) and table d'hôte (table of the host). The key difference between these two is that the à la carte menu has dishes separately priced, whereas the table d'hôte menu has an inclusive price either for the whole meal or for a specified number of courses, for example, any two or any four courses. There are, however, usually choices within each course.

All menus, no matter how simple or complex, are based on the two basic menu classes of table d'hôte or à la carte. Some menus also offer combinations of these two classes, with a number of menu items being offered together at a set price and other menu items being priced separately.

Sometimes the term 'menu du jour' is sometimes used instead of the term 'table d'hôte menu'. Another menu term used is 'carte du jour' (literally 'card of the day'), or 'menu of the day', which can also be a fixed meal with one or more courses for a set price. A 'prix fixe' (fixed price) menu is similar. A 'tasting menu' ('menu degustation') is a set meal with a range of courses (often between six and ten). These tasting menus are offered in restaurants where the chef provides a sample of the range of dishes available on the main menu. These tasting menus can also be offered with a flight (selection) of wines (sometimes this can be a different wine for each course). For all menus the price of the meal might also include wine or other drinks.

■   Classic menu sequence

Over the last 100 or so years the sequence of the European menu has taken on a classical format or order of dishes. This format is used to layout menus as well as to indicate the order of the various courses. Although the actual number of courses on a menu, and dishes within each course, will depend on the size and class of the establishment, most follow the classic sequence. This sequence is given in Table 5.1.

Although beverages are listed in Table 5.1 to indicate the sequence for meals, beverages are not counted as a course as such and therefore should not be included when the number of courses for a meal is stated. Thus if a meal is stated as having four courses, this means that there are four food courses and that the beverages at the end are an addition to these. Additionally although the sequence outlined in Table 5.1 shows the cheese course after the main course and before the sweet course, the sweet course is still sometimes offered before the cheese course.

Table 5.1: Classic menu sequence

1 **Hors-d'oeuvres**	Traditionally consisted of a variety of compound salads but now includes such items as pâtés, mousses, fruit, charcuterie and smoked fish.
2 **Soups** *(potages)*	Includes all soups, both hot and cold.
3 **Egg dishes** *(oeufs)*	There are a great number of egg dishes beyond the usual omelettes, but these have not retained their popularity on modern menus.
4 **Pasta and rice** *(farineux)*	Includes all pasta and rice dishes. Can be referred to as farinaceous dishes.
5 **Fish** *(poisson)*	Consists of fish dishes, both hot and cold. Fish dishes such as smoked salmon or seafood cocktails are mainly considered to be hors-d'oeuvres dishes and therefore would be served earlier in a meal.
6 **Entrée**	Entrées are generally small, well garnished dishes which come from the kitchen ready for service. They are usually accompanied by a rich sauce or gravy. Potatoes and vegetables are not usually served with this course if it is to be followed by a main course. If this is the main meat course then it is usual for potatoes and vegetables to also be offered. Examples of this type of dish are tournedos, noisettes, sweetbreads, garnished cutlets or filled vol-au-vent cases.
7 **Sorbet**	Traditionally sorbets (sometimes now called *granites*) were served to give a pause within a meal, allowing the palate to be refreshed. They are lightly frozen water ices, often based on un-sweetened fruit juice, and may be served with a spirit, liqueur or even Champagne poured over.
8 **Relevé**	Refers to the main roasts or other larger joints of meat, which would be served together with potatoes and vegetables.
9 **Roast** *(rôti)*	Traditionally refers to roasted game or poultry dishes.
10 **Vegetables** *(légumes)*	Apart from vegetables served with the Relevé or Roast courses, certain vegetables (e.g. asparagus and artichokes) may be served as a separate course, although these types of dishes are now more commonly served as starters.
11 **Salad** *(salade)*	Often refers to a small plate of salad that is taken after a main course (or courses) and is quite often simply a green salad and dressing.
12 **Cold buffet** *(buffet froid)*	Includes a variety of cold meats and fish, cheese and egg items together with a range of salads and dressings.
13 **Cheese** *(fromage)*	Includes the range of cheeses and various accompaniments, including biscuits, breads, celery, grapes and apples. This course can also refer to cheese-based dishes such as soufflés.
14 **Sweets** *(entremets)*	Refers to both hot and cold puddings.
15 **Savoury** *(savoureux)*	Sometimes simple savouries, such as Welsh rarebit or other items on toast, or in pastry, or savoury soufflés, may be served at this stage.
16 **Fruit** *(dessert)*	Fresh fruit, nuts and sometimes includes candied fruits.
17 **Beverages**	Traditionally this referred to coffee but nowadays includes a much wider range of beverages being generally available, including tea, coffee (in both standard and de-caffeinated versions) and a range of other beverages such as tisanes, chocolate, milk drinks (hot or cold) and proprietary drinks such as Bovril or Horlicks. These are commonly available throughout the day, with a choice of milks, creams (including non-dairy creamers) and sugars (including non-sugar sweeteners).

5

The classic menu sequence outlined in Table 5.1 is based on a logical process of taste sensations. This classic sequence also provides the guide for the compilation of both à la carte and table d'hôte menus, as is evident in many examples of modern menus. However, a number of courses are often now grouped together. At its most simple this might comprise:

- Starters – courses 1 to 4
- Main courses – courses 5, 6 and 8 to 12
- Sides – potatoes and vegetables and salads
- Afters – courses 13 to 16
- Beverages.

This sequence is also used as a guide for the compilation and determination of the order of courses for event and special party menus.

The modern European classic menu sequence outlined above is derived from traditional European (mainly Franco-Russian, Swiss and English) cuisine and service influences. The menu structure and menu sequence can change considerably within the various world cuisines. Menu terms also vary, for instance in the USA a main course is commonly called an entrée and sweets are commonly called dessert. The term 'dessert' is also now becoming more commonly used to denote sweets generally.

Many modern cuisine terms are derived from the classic European cuisine. French terms are mostly used mainly because it was in France that cuisine terms were codified through, for instance, the development and publication of the *Le Répertoire de la Cuisine* (Saulnier, 1982, 17th edn). This is much the same as the use of Italian terms for music (musical terms being codified in Italy), French terms in ballet (dance terms being codified in France) and English being the international language for aviation traffic control.

■ Other menu types

With the advent of all-day dining menus, the traditional division of mealtimes is also changing. However as well as menus for main meals, such as luncheon or dinner, there are also requirements for other defined meals types, such as breakfast and afternoon tea menus.

- **Breakfast menus** – The current trend is for breakfasts to be offered in a variety of establishments. There are also a variety of terms indicating the various forms in which a breakfast may be offered, for example:
  - □ *Café complet* – continental breakfast with coffee as the beverage. The term 'thé complet' is also used, with tea provided as the beverage.
  - □ *Café simple or thé simple* – just the beverage (coffee or tea) with nothing to eat.
  - □ *Continental breakfast* – traditionally consisted of hot croissant, brioche or toast, butter and preserves and coffee as the beverage. The current trend for the continental breakfast menu is to offer a wider variety of choice,

including cereals, fruits, juices, yoghurts, ham, cheese, assorted bread items and a wider selection of beverages.

☐ **Full breakfast** – may consist of from two or more courses and usually includes a cooked main course. The term 'full breakfast' is also becoming more common. Modern full breakfast menus have changed to include a much more varied choice of items. Today customers expect to see such items as fresh fruit juices, fresh fruit, yoghurt, muesli, continental pastries, homemade preserves, margarines, decaffeinated coffee and mineral waters on the full breakfast menu. There is also a trend toward the provision of buffet breakfasts that contain a wide range of items and also offer a range of international menu item. Menus for buffet breakfasts are often offered and priced at three levels:

1 *Continental*: Including juices, bread items and beverages.

2 *Cold buffet*: Including those items of continental breakfast plus a selection of cold items from the buffet.

3 *Full breakfast*: Full selection from the buffet including hot cooked items.

■ **Afternoon tea menus** – Afternoon tea is served in many establishments and in a variety of forms. It may be classified into two main types: Full afternoon tea (often now simply called 'afternoon tea') and high tea. The key difference between these two is that a high tea includes items such items as grills, toasted snacks, hot and cold fish and meat dishes, salads, cold sweets and ice creams.

(Detailed information on a variety of gastronomy topics can be found in, for instance, *New Larousse Gastronomique* 2009.)

5.2   Menu planning

The menu is considered to be the prime selling tool of a foodservice operation and therefore it should be written to inform and sell. The menu, or bill of fare, is a means of communication, informing the customer of what the establishment has to offer. The compiling of the menu is one of the foodservice operator's most important jobs, whether it is for establishments in the profit sector, or for those working to a budget, such as hospitals, schools or other similar institutions. The menu is a central management document that directs and controls the foodservice operation. It establishes what is going to be purchased, the cost, what staff and other resources are required and the types of service needed. In addition the beverage offer, the decor, atmosphere, theme or logo and service system, etc. all revolve around the provision of the menu.

■ Food and restaurant styles

Over the past few years a number of terms have been adopted to signify differing types of food and establishment styles. Examples of these are given in Table 5.2.

Table 5.2: Examples of cuisine and restaurant styles

Cuisine/restaurant style	Description
Bistro	Often a smaller establishment, with check tablecloths, bentwood chairs, cluttered decor and friendly informal staff. Tends to offer honest, basic and robust cooking.
Brasserie	Generally a largish, styled room, with a long bar, normally serving one-plate items rather than formal meals (though some offer both). Often it is possible just to have a drink, coffee or just a snack. Service by waiters, often in traditional style of long aprons and black waistcoats.
Cafeteria	Primarily self-service with customer choosing selection from a counter or counters in varying designs and layouts. Originally developed for the industrial feeding market but now seen in a variety of sectors.
Classic/haute cuisine	Classical style of cooking evolved through many centuries. Greater depth of flavour. Style does not necessarily mean the most expensive ingredients – can include simply poached and boiled dishes such as chicken, tongue and offal. Classical presentation of food with full table service.
Coffee shop	Similar to brasserie-style operations, often themed. May be open all day and serve all meal types from breakfast through to supper.
Country house hotel	Varies from establishment to establishment but food is often modern British style with some influence from classic or even farmhouse style. Often the home of high-end destination restaurants.
Farmhouse cooking	Simply cooked with generous portions of basic, home-produced fare using good, local ingredients.
First class restaurant	Tend to be formal fine dining restaurants with classical preparation and presentation of food and offering a high level of table service. Often associated with classic/haute cuisine.
Fusion/eclectic cuisine	As the world is getting smaller through efficient transport and tourism, modern cuisine uses a variety of ingredients from all over the world. This has led to an inter-mix of cuisine cultures, for example a fusion of particularly western and eastern styles. Sometimes also described as eclectic cuisine.
Health food/vegetarian restaurant	Increasing specialisation of operations into vegetarianism and/or health foods (though vegetarian food is not necessarily healthy), to meet lifestyle needs as well as dietary requirements.

International destination restaurant	Often Michelin-starred fine dining restaurants, offering a distinctive personality, cuisine, ambiance, beverages and service. Usually table service at various levels but mostly personal and highly attentive. Generally considered as the home of gastronomy. Expensive but also value laden.
International restaurant	Indian, Oriental, Asian, Spanish, Greek, Italian, Creole and Cajun are just some of the many types of cuisine available, with establishments tending to reflect specific ethnic origins. Many of the standard dishes are now appearing within a range of other menu types.
New wave brasserie (gastrodome)	Slick modern interior design, coupled with similar approaches to contemporary cuisine and service. Busy and bustling and often large and multileveled.
New/modern British/French	Cuisine drawn from the classical style but with new style saucing and the better aspects of nouvelle presentation. Plated in the kitchen, allowing the chef the final responsibility for presentation
Popular catering and fast food outlets	Developed from table service teashops and cafés through to steakhouses, and now incorporating snack bars, kiosks, diners, takeaways and cafeterias, with modern-day burger, chicken and fish concepts, and with ethnic foods also being incorporated. Meeting the needs of all-day meal taking (grazing) and also the need for 'grab and go' service, especially for the leisure, industrial and travelling markets.
Public houses	Licensed environment primarily for drinking alcoholic beverages. May be simply a serving bar with standing room for customers or may have more plush surroundings incorporating the offer of a variety of foods. These can range from simple plated dishes through to establishments offering full restaurant service (sometimes called gastropubs).
Restaurant	Term used to cover a wide variety of operations. Price, level and type of service, decor, styles, cuisines and degree of choice varies enormously across the range of types of operation. Service ranges from full table service to assisted service such as in carvery-style operations.
Themed restaurant	Often international in orientation, for example, Icelandic hot rock with food prepared and cooked at the table, 'Beni-hana' oriental theme, again with food prepared and cooked at table. Also includes themes such as jungle, rainforest or music/opera, where waiting staff will perform as well as serve.
Wine bars	Often offering a mixture of bar and brasserie-style operation, commonly wine themed, serving a variety of foods.

5

■ # Developing a menu policy

When compiling the menu for an operation it is necessary to consider the creation of a menu policy that will govern the approach to the composition of the menu. This policy will determine the methods the operation will take to:

- Establishing the essential and social needs of the customer
- Accurately predicting what the customer is likely to buy and how much he or she is going to spend
- Ensuring a means of communication with customers
- Purchasing and preparing raw materials to preset standards in accordance with purchasing specifications and forecasted demand
- Portion and cost the product in order to keep within company profitability objectives
- Effectively control the complete operation from purchase to service on the plate.

■ # Approaches to menu construction

In addition to traditional defined meal types, different menus are required to meet different customer needs and in a variety of locations. These can include:

- **Special party or function menus:** These are set menus for banquets or functions of all kinds from finger, fork and bowl food buffets to full banquets.
- **National or speciality menus:** These can be both table d'hôte or à la carte menus specialising in the food (or religion) of the country or in a specialised food itself.
- **Hospital menus:** These usually take the form of a menu card given to the patient the day before service so that his or her preferences can be ticked. Both National Health Service and private hospitals cater for vegetarians and also for religious requirements. In many cases a dietician is involved in menu compilation to ensure nothing is given to the patients that would be detrimental to their health. Usually hospital meals are of two or three courses.
- **Menus for people at work:** These are menus that are served to people at their place of work in a range of cuisines and service styles. Such menus vary in standard and extent from one employer to another.
- **Menus for children:** These should emphasise healthy eating through a balanced diet. Those areas with children of various cultural and religious backgrounds should also have menus that reflect this cultural diversity.
- **Floor/room service menus** – floor or room service menu requirement varies from basic tea and coffee making facilities in the room, and possibly a minibar, to vending machines on floors, or the service of a variety of meals served in rooms.

- **Lounge service menus** – lounge service may include the service of continental breakfast, morning coffee, luncheon snacks, afternoon tea, dinner or late evening snacks as well as alcoholic beverages.

- **Airline tray service menus** – on many short-haul routes, only snack-type meals or sandwiches and beverages are offered. For some operators the provision of food and beverages is provided for an additional charge to the customer. On long-haul flights, airlines provide a more extensive service of food and beverages. The airline will provide dishes to meet its passengers' particular needs, for example, meals that meet a range of dietary requirements.

- **Rail service menus** – foodservice on trains is provided on the move and away from the home base and suppliers. The logistics of providing on-train foodservice are therefore similar in organisation to off-premises catering. Food and beverage operations on trains generally fall into one of five categories:
  1 Conventional restaurant (including having kitchen facilities on board)
  2 Kiosk (takeaway)
  3 Trolley service operations
  4 Tray service operations especially in First Class
  5 Limited type of room service for sleeper trains.

Cyclical menus

These are menus that are compiled to cover a given period of time, i.e. one month or three months. They consist of a number of set menus for a particular establishment, e.g. industrial restaurant, cafeteria, canteen, directors' dining room, hospital or college refectory. At the end of each period the menus can be used over again, thus limiting the need to keep compiling new ones. The length of the cycle is determined by management policy, by the time of the year and by different foods available. These menus need to be monitored carefully to take account of changes in customer requirements and any variations in weather conditions which are likely to affect demand for certain dishes. If cyclical menus are designed to remain in operation for long periods of time, then they must be carefully compiled in order that they do not have to be changed too drastically during operation if for instance stock availability changes.

Advantages of cyclical menus

- They save time by removing the daily or weekly task of compiling menus, although they may require slight alterations for the next period.
- When used in association with cook–freeze operations, it is possible to produce the entire number of portions of each item to last the whole cycle, having determined that the standardised recipes are correct.
- They give greater efficiency in time and labour.
- They can cut down on the number of commodities held in stock and can assist in planning storage requirements.

Disadvantages

- When used in establishments with a captive clientele, then the cycle has to be long enough so that customers do not get bored with the repetition of dishes.
- The foodservice operator cannot easily take advantage of 'good buys' offered by suppliers on a daily or weekly basis unless such items are required for the cyclical menu.

Preplanned and predesigned menus

These are often found in for instance banquet or function operations. Before selecting dishes the foodservice operator is able to consider what the customer likes and the effect of these dishes upon the meal as a whole.

Advantages

- Preplanned or predesigned menus enable the foodservice operator to ensure that good menu planning is practised.
- The menu construction can be well balanced in terms of texture, colour ingredients, temperature and structure.
- Menus which are planned and costed in advance allow banqueting managers to quote prices instantly to a customer.
- Menus can be planned taking into account the availability of kitchen and service equipment and the capability of the service staff, without placing unnecessary strain upon any of these.
- The quality of food is likely to be higher if kitchen staff are preparing dishes that they are familiar with and have prepared a number of times before.

Disadvantages

- Preplanned and predesigned menus may be too limited to appeal to a wide range of customers.
- They may reduce job satisfaction for staff who have to prepare and serve the same menu repetitively.
- They may limit the chef's creativity and originality.

■   Key influences on the menus

Modern-day menus are the result of a combination of a number of factors. Menu content, traditionally based on classic cuisine, is continually being influenced by changes in consumer requirements and taste. Because of these influences there is now a greater emphasis on offering alternatives such as low fat milks (for example, skimmed or semi-skimmed), non-dairy creamers for beverages, alternatives to sugar such as sweeteners, sorbets alongside ice creams and polyunsaturated fat and non-animal fats as alternatives to butter. These influences have also affected cooking ingredients and methods, with the development of lower fat dishes, lighter cuisine and attractive and decent alternatives for non-meat eaters, with greater use of animal protein substitutes such as Quorn™ and tofu. The key influences affecting customer demand include:

- The relationship between health and eating
- Dietary requirements
- Cultural and religious influences
- Vegetarianism
- Ethical influences
- Trends, fads and fashions.

Each of these is discussed below:

Health and eating

The key issue in the relationship between health and eating is having a healthy diet. This means eating a balanced diet rather than viewing individual foods as somehow less or more healthy. The use of the word 'food' here also refers to beverages.

Customers are increasingly looking for the availability of choices, and are requiring information on foods and beverages including more specific information on methods of cooking used, which will enable them to make choices to achieve a balanced diet. General consensus suggests that the regular diet should be made up of at least one third based on a range of bread, cereals, rice and potatoes; one third based on a variety of fruit and vegetables; and the remainder based on dairy foods, including low fat milk, low fat meats and fish and small amounts of fatty and sugary food.

Customers are also becoming increasingly interested in food hygiene and food safety generally. There are also particular reactions to developments in food technology such as irradiation and genetically modified organisms and how these technologies are being used. Some customers are seeking to avoid these foods and some operations are already using the avoidance of these foods as a marketing feature. Additionally the use of organic foods is being promoted in a similar way.

Dietary requirements

There are a variety of medical conditions, including allergies, which are more common than was previously understood. Customers may therefore require a certain diet for medical reasons (including the prevention of allergic reactions). Such customers will need to know about the ingredients used in a dish since eating certain things may make them very ill and may even be fatal. Although such customers will usually know what they can and cannot eat, it is important that when asked, a server is able to accurately describe the dishes so that the customer can make the appropriate choice. The server should *never* guess and if in doubt, should seek further information.

Cultural and religious influences

Various faiths have differing requirements with regard to the dishes/ingredients that may be consumed, and these requirements often also cover preparation methods, cooking procedures and the equipment used. In all cases professional specialist advice should be sought.

Vegetarianism

Vegetarianism may derive from cultural, religious, moral or physiological considerations. There are also various forms of vegetarianism, which will affect the food that are eaten by difference customers. As always the customer is always the best person to check with if there is any doubt.

Ethical influences

Customers have become increasingly aware of ethical issues, such as:

- Ensuring sustainability of foods consumed
- Fair trade
- The acceptability or otherwise of genetically modified foods or irradiated foods
- Reducing food packaging and food waste
- Reducing the effects that food production and food transportation have on the environment generally.

There is also a greater trend towards using more seasonal and locally sourced food and beverage items, when the quality, taste, freshness and nutritional value are all at their peak, and when supplies are more plentiful and cheaper. For foodservice businesses, the benefits can also include:

- Improved menu planning, as suppliers can give information in advance on what they are able to provide
- More reliable products and service, with greater flexibility to respond to customer needs
- Increased marketing opportunities through making a feature of using locally sourced food and beverage items and through special promotions related to local seasons and food and beverage specialities, and
- Support for training of staff from local suppliers.

Trends, fads and fashions

Like any other product, cuisine and menus are subject to trends, fads and fashions. A clear distinction can be drawn between culinary innovation and culinary fashion; with Nouvelle Cuisine being identified as belonging to the former, fusion cuisines identified as belonging to the latter, and molecular gastronomy, or at least the new restaurant concepts being referred to by that term, yet to be identified as either (Cousins *et al.*, 2010). Trends also include the established range of technical innovations such as: cook–chill; cook–freeze; *sous vide*, and induction hobs.

Fads and fashions also include things that appear, are widely adopted, and just as quickly disappear. Examples include: everything with a coulis; kiwi fruit; food being set on a bed of wet potato purée; being on a bed of a variety of other things; a rösti of potato or various other ingredients; shaved vegetables; everything with a *jus* (juice or gravy); over-use of balsamic vinegar in dressings and in sauces; roasted vegetables and foams.

(For more a detailed consideration of influences on menus see Lillicrap and Cousins, 2010, Chapter 4 and Foskett *et al.*, 2011, Chapter 4.)

■ Essential considerations in menu planning

Prior to compiling menus there are a number of essential considerations. In addition to the key influences on menus, already identified above, they include:

- *Location of an establishment:* This location should allow easy access to both customers and suppliers as and when required. A difficult journey can be off-putting no matter how good the quality of food on offer and can affect repeat business and profitability. If the establishment is in an area noted for regional speciality foods or dishes, the inclusion of a selection of these on the menu can give extra menu appeal.

- *Competition in the locality:* It is important to be aware of what is offered by competitors, including their prices and particularly their quality. Knowing this information enables an establishment to make decision about how to compete with local competition.

- *Suitability of a particular establishment to a particular area:* A self-service restaurant situated in an affluent residential district, or a very expensive seafood restaurant in a rundown inner-city area may not be very successful. Anticipating and analysing the nature of demand that the operation is planning to appeal to will contribute to ensuring that the menu will be developed to satisfy, for example,' office workers in the city, with a fast lunch service. Also opportunities may exist for outdoor catering.

- *Spending power of the customer:* A most important consideration is how much the potential customer is able and willing to pay. (Pricing methods were also considered in more detail in Chapter 3, page 48).

- *Customer requirements:* It is the customer not the foodservice operator who selects his or her menu, so the analysis of dish popularity is necessary and those dishes that are not popular should not stay on the menu. Customer demand must be considered and traditional dishes and modern trends in food fashions need to be taken into account.

- *Number of items and price range of menus:* It is essential to determine the range of dishes and whether table d'hôte or à la carte type of menus are to be offered. Decisions regarding the range of prices have to be made. A table d'hôte menu may be considered with an extra charge or supplement for more expensive dishes, or several table d'hôte menus of different prices may be more suitable.

- *Throughput:* If space is limited, or there are many customers (and control of the time the customer occupies the seat is needed) then the menu can be adjusted to increase turnover, e.g. more self-service items or quick preparation items, or separate service for beverages.
- *Space and equipment in the kitchen:* Both of these will influence the composition of the menu and production of dishes. The menu writer must be aware of any shortcomings or deficiencies in equipment and may be wary of offering dishes that are difficult to produce. Also, certain items of equipment should not be overloaded by the menu requirements, e.g. salamanders, steamers, fritures.
- *Amount, availability and capability of labour:* The availability and capability of both the preparation and service staff must be considered when planning a menu. Enough able and willing staff, both in the kitchen and the restaurant, are necessary to achieve customer satisfaction with any menu.
- *Supplies and storage:* Menu planning is dependent on availability of supplies, that is, frequency of deliveries of the required amounts. Storage space and seasonal availability of foods need to be taken into account when planning menus.
- *Cost factor:* When an establishment is run for profit the menu is a crucial consideration; but, even when working to a budget, the menu is no less crucial. Costing is the crux of the success of compiling any menu.
- *Nutritional information:* there are various initiatives to encourage people to be aware of the relationship between health and diet and also to address the problems associated with obesity. These initiatives include providing the nutritional content information on menus.

(For a more detailed consideration of menu planning see Foskett *et al.*, 2011, Chapter 7.)

■ Menu copy

Items or groups of items should bear names people recognise and understand. If a name does not give the right connotation, additional descriptive copy may be necessary. Mistakes in approaches to menu copy can include:

- Descriptive copy is left out when it is required.
- The wrong emphasis is given.
- Culinary terms are misused.
- Emphasis is lost because print size and style are not correctly used.
- The menu lacks creativity.

Carefully devised descriptions can help to promote the individual dish, the menu generally and in turn the establishment. However, descriptions should describe the item realistically and not mislead the customer as this has legal implications. Care should be taken therefore in the use of terms such as fresh, British or organic, etc. and also cooking terms such as fried, roasted, etc. The description should always be a true one. (In the case of organic it is only the food item that can be described as organic.)

Being able to write interesting descriptive copy is a skill; a good menu designer is able to illuminate menu terms or specific culinary terms and in doing so is able to draw attention to them. Simplicity in menu copy enhances the communication process and enables better understanding.

Some menus can be built around a general descriptive copy featuring the history of the establishment or around the local area in which the establishment is situated. Descriptive copy can alternatively be based on a speciality dish, which has significant cultural importance to the area or the establishment. In so doing the description may wish to feature the person responsible for creating and preparing the dish – especially if the chef is reasonably well known and has appeared on national or local television or radio. The chef may have also had his/her recipes featured in the local press. This too may be included in the menu to create further interest.

Menu copy should be set in a style of print that is easily readable and well spaced. Mixing typefaces is often done to achieve emphasis; if overdone the overall concept is likely to look a mess and therefore unattractive to the eye. Emphasis may also be achieved by using boxes on the menu. Also the menu paper and colour of the print can carefully be contrasted to make certain dishes stand out.

5.3   Food production systems

A food production system has to be organised to produce the right quantity of food at the correct standard, for the required number of people, on time, using the resources of staff, equipment and materials effectively and efficiently.

As costs of space, equipment, fuel, maintenance and labour continue to rise, more thought and time have to be given to the planning of a production system and to kitchen design. Research is often lacking in this area of the foodservice industry, although research from equipment manufacturers concentrating on new technology is increasing.

The requirements of the production system have to be clearly matched to the type of food that is to be prepared, cooked and served, to the required market, and at the correct price. All allocation of space and the purchase of the different types of equipment have to be justified, and the organisation of the kitchen personnel also has to be planned at the same time.

Many food production operations today are based on the process approach, as opposed to the 'partie' (product approach) system. The process approach concentrates on the specific techniques and processes of food production. The system places importance on the identification of these common techniques and processes across the full range of required dishes. In developing the production system, groupings are not then based on the types of dishes or foods, which is the basis of the 'partie' system, but on the clustering of similar production techniques and processes which apply a range of common skills and encourage flexible open-endedness.

Food production is an operating system and can be managed through the application of the systems approach. A whole range of different cuisines are able to fit more neatly into this approach, because the key elements focus on the process, the way the food is prepared, processed (cooked) stored and served. Using this approach, food production systems may be identified using the input/process/output model of systems and the basic process may be set tabulated as in Figure 5.1

Foods in	Storage	Preparation	Cooking	Holding	Regeneration	Presentation
Fresh	Ambient	Weigh/measure	Blanch	Chill	Regithermic	Bain-marie
Fresh cooked	Cool	Clear/open	Warm	Vacuum	Microwave	Service flats
Fresh prepared	Refrigerated	Chop/cut	Simmer	Freeze	Convection	Plates
Canned	Deep frozen	Combine/mix	Boil	Tray	Traditional	Trays
Frozen	Dry store	Blend	Steam	Hot cupboard		Vending
Chilled		Shape/coat	Grill	Cold cupboard		Buffet
Vacuum		Form	Sauté	Insulate		Trolley
Dehydrated			Brown	Ambient		Dishes
Smoked			Bake			Timbale
Salted			Roast			
Crystallised			Broil			
Acidified			Fry			
Pasteurised			Microwave			
Bottled						
UHT						

Foods in → ——————————Process—————————→ Foods out

Figure 5.1: Input process output model for food production

The identification of the seven stages of food production in Figure 5.1 shows the types of **foods in**, the **processes** and the **foods out** or presentation stages. Using this approach a generic model of food production can be developed and this is shown in Figure 5.2. Developing this approach further nine standard food production methods can be identified and these are summarised Table 5.3.

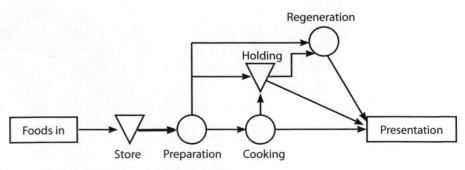

Figure 5.2: Generic model of the food production system

Table 5.3: Food production methods

Method	Description
Conventional	Term used to describe production utilising mainly fresh foods and traditional cooking methods
Convenience	Method of production utilising mainly convenience foods
Call order	Method where food is cooked to order either from customer (as in cafeterias) or from waiter. Production area is often open to customer area
Continuous flow	Method involving production line approach where different parts of the production process may be separated (e.g. fast food)
Centralised	Production not directly linked to service. Foods are 'held' and distributed to separate service areas
Cook-chill	Food production storage and regeneration method utilising principle of low temperature control to preserve qualities of processed foods
Cook-freeze	Production, storage and regeneration method utilising principle of freezing to control and preserve qualities of processed foods. Requires special processes to assist freezing
Sous vide	Method of production, storage and regeneration utilising principle of sealed vacuum to control and preserve the quality of processed foods
Assembly kitchen	A system based on accepting and incorporating the latest technological development in manufacturing and conservation of food products

■ Centralised production

Centralised production has recently been considered by a large number of businesses in the foodservice industry. Centralised production systems involve having a central food production kitchen where the bulk of foods are prepared, held and packaged and then transported to finishing kitchens where the final meals are produced ready for service. This can be in a single large-scale operation servicing various out-stations within the complex, or a separate food production facility proving food for a range of outlying operations, some distance away.

Considerations for adopting a centralised production system are mostly based on:

■ Labour cost – using staff more effectively and efficiently

■ Food costs – greater control over wastage and portion sizes linked to standardised recipes and standardised purchasing specifications

■ Equipment – more use of technology reducing commitment in individual units.

The centralised system also relies on a range of technology for holding food for transportation. These include cook-chill, cook freeze, sous vide and water bath cookery, which are discussed in more detail below.

Cook-chill system

Cook-chill is a foodservice system based on normal preparation and cooking of food followed by rapid chilling, storage in controlled low temperature conditions above freezing point, 0–3ºC and subsequently reheating immediately before consumption. The chilled food is regenerated in finishing kitchens, which require relatively low capital investment and minimum staff.

The cook-chill process

The purpose of chilling food is to prolong its storage life. Under normal temperatures, food deteriorates rapidly through the action of microorganisms and enzymic and chemical reactions. Reduction in the storage temperature inhibits the multiplication of bacteria and other microorganisms and slows down the chemical and enzymic reactions. At normal refrigeration temperature, reactions are still taking place but at a much slower rate, and at frozen food storage temperatures (–20ºC approx.) nearly all reactions cease. A temperature of 0–3ºC does not give a storage life comparable to frozen food but it does produce a good product.

It is generally accepted that, even when high standards of fast-chilling practice are used and consistent refrigerated storage is maintained, product quality may be acceptable for a only a few days (including day of production and consumption). The storage temperature of 0–3ºC is of extreme importance to ensure both full protection of the food from microbiological growth and the maintenance of maximum nutritional values in the food. It is generally accepted that a temperature of 10ºC should be regarded as the critical safety limit for the storage of refrigerated food. Above that temperature, growth of microorganisms may render the food dangerous to health.

Finishing kitchens

Finishing kitchens can consist of purpose-built regeneration equipment plus refrigerated storage. Additional equipment, such as a deep fat fryer for chips, boiling table for sauces and custards and pressure steamer for vegetables and so on can be added if required to give greater flexibility.

Where chilled food is produced to supply a service on the same premises, it is recommended that the meals should be supplied, stored and regenerated by exactly the same method as used for operations where the production unit and finishing kitchens are separated by some distance. Failure to adhere to just one procedure could result in disorganised production and reduce productivity. Once a decision is taken to sever production from service this method should be followed throughout the system.

Microsteam technology

Used for food production in hospitals and schools, microsteam is a fast, healthy cooking system, which maintains the freshness of food using steam cooking. It enables nutritious meals to be available in minutes without the need for full kitchen back up. The vacuum-packed polymer packaging allows cooking to near perfection, resulting in maximum flavour and minimal nutritional loss.

Microsteam is a unique value control system that regulates the pressure throughout the cooking process. As soon as the pack goes into the microwave, energy waves create steam from the water in the raw ingredients which gradually builds up in the container. The pack expands as it cooks which is where the smart valve comes in releasing the pressure gradually so that it stays at just the right level to cook the food perfectly.

The most important point about microsteaming is that it is not about reheating pre-cooked, but is about cooking the freshest ingredients from raw. The micro-steam system is space saving. It reduces the need for bulky equipment allowing kitchen systems to be simplified. This system is easier to manage. It facilitiates the bulk production and cooking of fresh vegetables and other items for large scale banqueting and industry events. The technology can also be used for vending machines, is suitable for people working off-peak hours, for airports, call centres, trains and any environment where it is difficult to have full kitchen backup.

◼ Cook-freeze system

Blast freezers have increasingly been introduced with success into foodservice operations. The ability to freeze cooked dishes and prepared foods, as distinct from the storage of chilled foods in a refrigerator or already frozen commodities in a deep freezer, allows a foodservice operator to make more productive use of kitchen staff. It also enables economies to be introduced into the staffing of dining rooms and restaurants.

The cook-freeze process

Cook-freeze uses a production system similar to that used in cook-chill. The reci-pes used have to be modified, enabling products to be freezer-stable and modified starches are used in sauces so that on reheating and regeneration the sauce does not separate. Blast freezers are used in place of blast chillers. The freezing must be carried out very rapidly to retain freshness and to accelerate temperature loss through the latent heat barrier, thus preventing the formation of large ice crystals and rupturing of the cells.

Blast freezing takes place when low-temperature air is passed over food at high speed, reducing food in batches to a temperature of at least −20°C within 90 minutes. Blast freezers can hold between 20 and 400kg (40–800lb) per batch, the larger models being designed for trolley operation.

■   Overall benefits of cook-chill and cook-freeze

For the operation

- Good portion control and reduced waste
- No overproduction
- Central purchasing – bulk-buying discounts
- Full utilisation of equipment.
- Full utilisation of staff time
- Savings on equipment, space and fuel
- Fewer staff with better conditions – no unsocial hours, no weekend work, no overtime
- Simplified delivery to units – less frequent
- No need to move hot food (EC regulations forbid the movement of hot foods unless the temperature is maintained over 65°C (149°F). Maintaining 65°C is regarded as very difficult to achieve and high temperatures inevitably will be harmful to foods.)

For the customer

- Increased variety and selection
- Improved quality, with standards maintained
- More nutritious foods
- Services can be maintained at all times, regardless of staff absences
- Thawing time is eliminated
- Smaller-capacity storage is required: 3–4 days' supply as opposed to up to 120 days
- Chiller storage is cheaper to install and run than freezer storage
- Blast chillers are cheaper to install and run than blast freezers
- Cooking techniques are unaltered (additives and revised recipes are needed for freezing)
- All foods can be chilled so the range of dishes is wider (some foods cannot be frozen). Cooked eggs, steaks and sauces such as hollandaise can be chilled (after some recipe modification where necessary)
- No system is too small to adapt to cook-chill.

■   Sous vide

Sous vide is a form of cook-chill: a combination of vacuum scaling in plastic pouches, cooking by steam and then rapidly cooking and chilling. The objective is to rationalise kitchen procedures without having a detrimental effect on the quality of individual dishes. Vacuum pressures are as important as the cooking temperatures with regard to weight loss and heat absorption. The highest temperature used in *sous vide* cooking is 100ºC and 1000 millibars is the minimum amount of vacuum pressure used.

As there is no oxidation or discolouration it is ideal for conserving fruits, such as apples and pears, for example pears in red wine, fruits in syrup. When preparing meats in sauces the meat is pre-blanched and then added to the completed sauce.

Sous vide is a combination of vacuum scaling, tightly controlled *en papillote* cooking and rapid chilling. Potential users are brasseries, wine bars, airlines, private hospitals and function foodservice operators seeking to provide top quality with portion convenience.

The advantages of the sous vide process

- Long shelf-life, up to 21 days if refrigerated
- Ability to produce meals in advance means better deployment of staff and skills
- Vacuum-packed foods can be mixed in cold store without the risk of cross-contamination
- Reduces labour costs at point of service
- Beneficial cooking effects on certain foods, especially moulded items and pates. Reduced weight loss on meat joints.
- Full flavour and texture are retained as food cooks in its own juices
- Economises on ingredients (less butter, marinade)
- Makes pre-cooking a possibility for à la carte menus
- Inexpensive regeneration
- Allows a small operation to set up bulk production
- Facilitates portion control and uniformity of standards
- Has a tenderising effect on tougher cuts of meat and matures game without dehydration.

Its disadvantages

- Extra cost of vacuum pouches and vacuum packing machine
- Unsuitable for some meats (for example, fillet steak) and vegetables which absorb colour
- All portions in a batch must be identically sized to ensure even results
- Most dishes require twice the conventional cooking time
- Unsuitable for large joints as chilling time exceeds 90 minutes
- Complete meals (for example, meat and two vegetables) not feasible – the meat component needs to be cooked and stored in separate bags
- Extremely tight management and hygiene controls are imperative
- Potentially adverse customer reaction (boil in the bag syndrome).

■   ## Water bath cookery

Many chefs have adopted a technique of vacuum packing ingredients and cooking them at low temperatures in a water bath. This is a slow and gentle process. Moisture is not expelled and flavour is retained. Some meat is cooked from 6 to 46 hours at temperatures of 55–68ºC.

Caution must be taken as this is not a *sous vide* system and environmental health officers like a minimum core temperature of 65°C for red meats and 80ºC for poultry. It must be remembered that some harmful bacteria will survive or even grow at 50°C. It is strongly advised that if chefs use this system, there should be a regular system of food safety and analysis to establish the type of microbiological count.

5.4   Volume in food production

The food production process may be seen in the general model for food production as was shown in Figure 5.1. That model identifies seven stages in the general food production process. These are:

1 Foods in

2 Storage

3 Preparation

4 Cooking

5 Holding

6 Regeneration

7 Presentation.

Each of these stages has an effect on the potential volume of the operation, and differing operations will route foods in different ways. The generic process was identified in Figure 5.2. This model can be adapted for all of the nine production processes identified in table 5.3. For instance, a fast food process will flow from **foods in** to **store** to **preparation** or **cooking**, then to **holding** then to **presentation**. A cook-chill process will flow from **foods in** to **store** to **preparation** to **holding** or **cooking** then to **holding**, then to **regeneration** and then to **presentation**. However, it is difficult to determine the key process in any food production system that limits the potential volume (Cousins, 1994), as each of the stages has a separate effect on the capacity of food able to be processed at any time, as follows:

1   Foods in

The availability of food and the frequency of delivery clearly have an impact on the maximum food capacity of the operation. Greater and more frequent delivery opportunities increase the potential capacity. In addition the variety of foods being bought either in terms of food type or supplier source will also affect food capacity.

2 Storage

The storage space and type of storage available determine the type of food that can be bought and the quantities that can be available at a given time. Capacity can be increased by altering the nature of foods being bought, for instance from fresh to convenience, and/or by increasing the delivery frequency.

3 Preparation

The extent to which food has to be prepared also impacts on capacity. High preparation requirements increase the space and the layout required. This stage can be greatly affected by increasing the use of ready prepared foods and by the use of equipment for bulk preparation activities.

4 Cooking

The availability of cooking space and the time cooking takes can limit capacity. Again this can be affected by variations in the needs for cooking and the type of cooking required. In addition the type of equipment used for the cooking processes can be altered to increase the volume of cooking that can be done at a given time.

5 Holding

Food capacity is limited by the type and availability of holding space. Variations in the need for holding in a given operation can vary the potential food capacity.

6 Regeneration

This stage follows from holding and has similar characteristics. However, the regeneration potential can be less than the full holding potential depending on the nature of demand at a given time.

7 Presentation

The food capacity at this stage is usually determined by the speed of the service process. This assumes that a critical path analysis approach has been used to ensure that the full range of foods required at a given time is available at the same time.

Overall the need to meet the demands of the presentation stage is determined by the expected volume of business at a given time. Each of the previous stages, through the application of careful critical path analysis approaches, should be able to be planned and operated to meet the presentation demand.

5.5   Purchasing

Once a menu is planned, a number of activities must occur to bring it into reality. One of the first and most important stages is to purchase the food (often also referred to as provisioning) and other items; and to receive the materials needed to produce the menu items. Skilful purchasing with good receiving procedures can do much to maximise the results of good menu planning. Six important steps must occur if purchasing and receiving functions are to be successful:

1 Know the market

2 Determine purchasing needs

3 Establish and use specifications

4 Design the purchase procedures

5 Ensure accurate receiving

6 Evaluate the purchasing task.

A market is a place in which ownership of commodity changes from one person to another. This could occur using the telephone, on a street corner, in a retail or wholesale establishment or at an auction. Since markets vary considerably, to do a good job of purchasing a buyer must know the characteristics of each market.

It is important also that the purchaser for a foodservice operation has knowledge of the items to be purchased. For example:

■ Where they are grown

■ Seasons of production

■ Approximate costs

■ Conditions of supply and demand

■ Laws and regulations governing the market and the products

■ Marketing agents and their services

■ Processing

■ Storage requirements

■ Commodity and product, class and grade.

■   Classification of markets

The primary market

Raw materials may be purchased at the source of supply, the grower, producer or manufacturer or from central markets such as Smithfield, Covent Garden, or Nine Elms in London. Some establishments or large organisations will have a buyer who will buy directly from the primary markets. Also, a number of small establishments may adopt this method for some of their needs, i.e. the chef patron may buy his fish, meat and vegetables directly from the market.

The secondary market

Goods are bought wholesale from a distributor or middleman; the foodservice establishment will pay wholesale prices and obtain possible discounts.

The tertiary market

The retail or cash and carry warehouse is a method suitable for smaller companies. A current pass obtained from the warehouse is required in order to gain access. This method also requires the user to have his or her, own transport. Some cash and carry organisations require a VAT number before they will issue an authorised card. It is important to remember that there are the added costs of:

- Running the vehicle and petrol used, and
- The person's time for going to the warehouse.

Cash and carry can often be an impersonal way of buying as there are often no people to discuss quality and prices with.

■ The buyer

The buyer is the key person who makes decisions regarding quality, amounts, price, what will satisfy the customers and allow a profit to be made . The wisdom of the buyer's decisions will be reflected in the success or failure of the operation. The buyer must not only be knowledgeable about the products, but must have the necessary skills required in dealing with sales people, suppliers and other market agents. The buyer must also be prepared for hard and often aggressive negotiations.

Unscrupulous suppliers can also subject buyers to bribes and other inducements. Many suppliers will use pressure in order to get the buyer to purchase from specific sources. It is important to remember to treat the company's money as if it were your own. Use firm, friendly tactics and only socialise if it means that it will improve your buying position or benefit the company in some way. A buyer must always retain the right to be a free agent.

Buying demands integrity, maturity, bargaining skills and an even disposition. Buying associations have ethical codes to which members subscribe. They require a high standard of ethical relationship between buyer and seller.

A buyer must have knowledge of the internal organisation of the company, especially the operational needs, and be able to obtain the product needs at a competitive price. The buyer must also be acquainted with the procedures of production and how these items are going to be used in the production operations, in order that the right item is purchased. For example, the item required may not always be of prime quality; for example, tomatoes for soups and sauces, to be cost-effective, do not need to be grade A or class I. Another example is certain types of nuts which do not have to be whole prime quality nuts for certain pastry goods or salads. Therefore, to reduce costs it is better to purchase broken nuts.

A buyer must also know the storage requirements for each item and the space available, and the ability of the operation to finance special purchases in order to make good use of market conditions. For example, if there is a glut of fresh salmon at low cost, has the organisation the facility to make use of the extra salmon purchases? Is there sufficient freezer space? Can the chef make use of salmon, by creating a demand on the menu? The buyer must also have a knowledge of yield testing procedures and know how to work closely with the chef and food production team to establish a specification so the right item is obtained.

■ Buying methods

These depend on the type of market and the kind of operation. Purchasing procedures are usually formal or informal. Both have advantages and disadvantages. Informal methods are suitable for casual buying, where the amount involved is not large and speed and simplicity are desirable. Formal contracts are best for large contracts for commodities purchased over a long period of time. Prices do not vary much during a year, once the basic price has been established. Using informal methods, prices and supply tend to fluctuate.

Informal buying

This usually involves oral negotiations, talking directly to salespeople, face to face or using the telephone. Informal methods vary according to market conditions and include:

- *Quotation and order sheet method:* This uses a list of particular commodities always wanted in quantity and quality. Columns are provided to record prices from different suppliers. Prices are compared and orders given.

- *Blank cheque method:* This is when there is an extreme shortage of a commodity or some other market condition exists where the buyer must get the commodity at any cost. This usually only operates in extreme circumstances.

- *Cost plus method:* This is used when prices are not known or the market is unstable. Many suppliers like this arrangement, so that they do not have to add a safety factor to take care of risk, if commodities fluctuate considerably in price. They are free to buy at the most favourable price and then add on what they require to cover costs and give a profit. The amount over and above the cost paid for the item charged to the buyer is usually a standard percentage. Thus a supplier may buy fruit and vegetables and charge the buyer the price paid, plus 10%.

Formal buying

This is known as competitive buying, giving suppliers written specifications and quantity needs. Negotiations are normally written. Methods are detailed as follows.

- *Competitive bid method:* The sellers are invited to submit bids through written communications. The suppliers then send prices and other information on the commodities to the buyer. Bids are opened at a specified time to determine awards. Only those sellers able to meet the established purchase conditions of the buyer will be considered in awarding bids. The invitation to bid usually contains certain conditions. These will include:

☐ Terms of payment

☐ Discounts

☐ Method of delivery

☐ Invoice requirements.

■ *Negotiated method:* This is used when suppliers are hesitant to bid because of time restrictions, fluctuating market conditions, or a high perishability of the product. Negotiations may occur using the telephone and later confirmed in writing. Several suppliers are usually contacted to compare prices. This method is useful in that it allows competitive bidding while giving flexibility.

■ *Futures and contract method:* This is used by large organisations who have sufficient capital and staff to contract for future delivery of commodities at an established bid price. The advantage is that it ensures an adequate supply at an established price and avoids shortages and price fluctuations that affect prices.

Sometimes this system is used to establish a buying agreement for only a week or month for commodities such as meat, fresh fruits and vegetables, but arrangements can also extend to a short season. For items more stable in price such as canned goods, baked beans, tomato purée, canned potatoes, potato powder, tea and coffee, and frozen goods such as ice cream, gateau, sausage rolls, vol-au-vents and pies, they are often placed on contract for long periods, up to one year.

The quantity under contract may vary and the amount purchased will depend on the amount used over a period. Contract and industrial foodservice operators are able to forecast fairly accurately how much of each commodity they are likely to consume. A price is agreed along with quality and the quantity may also be set. For example, the price of baked beans may be dependent on the number of cases a buyer is guaranteeing to take over a period. Frequencies of delivery of the baked beans will also be determined. The maximum stock of baked beans held at any one time is determined by the buyer according to what was needed over a period of time. This is directly related to the operational need, how many food outlets have baked beans on the menu and the sales forecast of baked beans over a given period. When the stock diminishes to the reorder level, the buyer will contact the supplier for a new delivery. In some cases the supplier's salesperson may visit the company regularly to bring the inventory of the operations up to an established point. Whichever the case, such an arrangement is often called par stock supplying. This ensures that a safety stock level on the quantity of the items to be used between the time of reorder and delivery, be maintained. A reserve stock (or safety stock) is essential in case the delivery is late.

■ Selecting suppliers

Selecting suppliers is important in the purchasing process. Firstly, consider how a supplier will be able to meet the needs of your operation. Consider:

■ Price

■ Delivery

■ Quality/standards.

Information on suppliers can be obtained from other purchasers. Visits to suppliers' establishments are to be encouraged. When interviewing prospective suppliers, you need to question how reliable a supplier will be under competition and how stable under varying market conditions.

Suppliers are also selected on experience. A buyer soon gets to know the reliable suppliers. New suppliers are often tried and tested: some are retained. Considerations leading to a decision to continue to do business with a supplier include:

■ If the supplier anticipates the needs of the organisation through monitoring market conditions and informing the company buyer of product and market information.

■ Willingness to break quantities down as and when required rather than the buyer having to take a minimum quantity, which may be far more than the quantity offered.

■ Maintenance of adequate stocks to meet potential demand.

■ Provides credit terms and discounts relevant to the buyer's business.

■ Required access to premises and other delivery conditions such as timing.

■ Potential for purchasing a wide range of products from one supplier that can lead to considerable savings.

Many suppliers now offer fresh fruit and vegetables, part-prepared fresh vegetables. For example, peeled and turned potatoes, peeled and sliced carrots, prepared fresh beans. They will also offer a full range of frozen vegetables and speciality goods.

■ Three types of needs

Within a foodservice operation there can be identified three types of purchasing and stock needs. These are:

■ *Perishable:* Fresh fruit and vegetables, dairy products, meat and fish. Prices and suppliers may vary. Informal means of buying are frequently used. Perishables should be purchased to meet menu needs for a short period only.

■ *Staple:* Supplies of canned, bottled, dehydrated, frozen products. Formal or informal purchasing can be used. Because items are staple and can be easily stored, bid buying is frequently used to take advantage of quantity price purchasing.

- *Daily use needs:* Daily use or contract items are delivered frequently on par stock basis. Stocks are kept up to the desired level and supply is automatic. Suppliers may be daily, several times a week, weekly or less often. Most items are perishable, therefore supplies must not be excessive, only sufficient to get through to the next delivery.

Quantity and quality

Determining quantity and quality of items to be purchased is important. This is based on the operational needs. The buyer must be informed by the chef, or other authorised members of the production team, of the products that are needed. The chef and his/her team must establish the quality and they should be encouraged to inspect the goods on arrival. The buyer with this information then checks out the market and looks for the best quality and best price. Delivery arrangements and other factors will be handled by the buyer. In smaller establishments the chef may also be the buyer. When considering the quantity needed, certain factors should be known:

- The number of people to be served in a given period
- The sales history
- Portion sizes, determined from yield testing a standard portion control list drawn up by the chef and management teams.

Buyers need to know about food production, often to be able to decide how many portions a given size of order may yield. He/she must also understand the factors that can affect yields; for example cooking shrinkage may vary, causing problems in portion control and yield. Determining yields from the range of commodities in use, as this will be the basis for determining the cost per unit. Yield testing indicates the number of items or portions that can be obtained and helps to provide the information required for producing purchasing specifications. Yield testing should not be confused with product testing, which is concerned with the physical properties of the food texture, flavour and quality. In reality, tests are often carried out which combine both of these requirements.

The chef must inform the buyer of quantities. The buyer must also be aware of different packaging sizes, such as jars, bottles, cans and the yield from each package. There must be an indication of grades, styles, appearance, composition, varieties and quality factors such as:

- Colour
- Texture
- Size
- Absence of defects
- Braising
- Irregular shape
- Maturity.

The chef and management team should establish quality standards when the menu is planned. Menus and recipes are developed using standardised recipes that directly relate to the buying procedure and standard purchasing specifications.

The standard recipe

Standard recipes are a written formula for producing a food item of a specified quality and quantity for use in a particular establishment. It should show the precise quantities and qualities of the ingredients together with the sequence of preparation and service. It enables the establishment to have a greater control over cost and quantity.

The objective of the use of the standard recipe is to predetermine the following:

- The quantities and qualities of ingredients to be used, including the purchase specification
- The yield obtained from a recipe
- The food cost per person
- The nutritional value of a particular dish.

And to facilitate:

- Menu planning
- Purchasing and internal requisitioning
- Food preparation and production
- Portion control.

In addition, the standard recipe will assist new staff in preparation and production of standard products – which can be facilitated by photographs or drawings illustrating the finished product.

Standard purchasing specification

Purchasing specifications have two functions:

1 They communicate to a supplier what the specifier wishes to have supplied in terms of goods and service.
2 They provide criteria against which the goods and services actually supplied can be compared.

The main advantages of specification buying are:

- Drawing up the specifications requires careful thought and a review of the buyer's needs. This frequently results in a simplification of the variety of products purchased and often reveals the possibility of using less expensive commodities. Both factors result in economies.
- Buying according to specifications frequently induces more suppliers to bid on an order, because all suppliers know exactly what is wanted and that their

chances are as good as those of other suppliers because they are bidding on identical items. This increased competition for the business often results in lower prices.

- Specifications ensure the identical nature of items purchased from one or two sources. When the purchaser has more than one supplier of an item, this identity is essential and specification buying is a virtual necessity.

- Purchasing to specifications gives the person receiving the order an exact standard against which to measure the incoming materials and results in accurate inspection and a uniform quality of commodities.

- If specification buying is combined with quality control on the part of the supplier, it may be possible for the buyer to save money by doing a less complete inspection.

- Specification buying is a necessary step towards industry-wide standardisation and standardisation programmes hold the promise of substantial savings.

The main disadvantages of buying by specifications are:

- It is not economical to prepare specifications for small-lot purchases. This rules out the possibility of specification buying for many items.

- Specification buying adds to the purchaser's responsibilities. They must be able to state precisely what they want and the supplier's obligations extend only to complying with those terms. If the product does not live up to expectations, the liability rests with the buyer.

- In specification buying, the cost of inspection is greater than in purchasing by brand-name where you are guaranteed a standard through experience. Items purchased to specification must be examined, whereas branded items need little more than a casual check and count.

- There is always the danger of becoming over-defined in preparing specifications and as a consequence, paying more than necessary for items.

- There is also a danger of assuming that after specifications are established, the characteristics of the item have been permanently set. Unless specifications are periodically reviewed, there is a chance that the buyer will lose out on product improvements.

The content of a specification varies according to whether it is written for a user, designer, manufacturer or seller. A simple item may only require a brief description, whereas in the case of a complex assembly, the specification will be a comprehensive document, perhaps running to several pages. It is also convenient to write them in a standard form. An example of information to be included is:

- *Definition of the item:* Care must be taken so that a common catering term used by the buyer means exactly the same thing to the supplier; for example, whole sirloin means with bone and strip loin, without the bone; washed and sliced potatoes means after they have been peeled and of a thickness of no more than the specification.

- *Grade or brand-name:* For example, apples – grade extra class, or Granny Smiths; Lea and Perrins Worcestershire Sauce; where available it should state the desired variety and next acceptable substitute.
- *Weight, size or count:* For example, pounds, kilos; A2s or A10s; lemons 120s, pineapples 12s. Counts vary from country to country; therefore desired country of origin should be quoted against the count and the substitute country with the alternative count noted.
- *Unit against which prices should be quoted:* For example, per pound, per case, per box, per sack, each.
- *Special notes for the commodity:* For example, for meat it could contain details of the preparation of a particular cut of meat, or details of special packaging and delivery requirements.

■ Centralised purchasing within a company operating a number of units

There are advantages for large organisations in establishing a specialist department through which all purchasing is channelled. These include:

1 Economies of scale enabling the use of bargaining power and resources to the best effect. This is done thus:

☐ A consolidation of quantities can take place resulting in quantity discounts.

☐ Suppliers dealing with a central purchasing department have the incentive of competing for the whole or substantial proportion of the requirements.

☐ Cheaper prices may result since the fixed overheads of the supplier can be spread over longer production runs; however, as food is a perishable commodity this may not have a major impact.

☐ Specialist purchasing staff can be employed for each of the major categories of purchase.

☐ Cheaper prices may be achieved by going directly to the grower and not via the marketplace, e.g. buying the whole crop of one farm at a negotiated rate.

☐ Lower administrative costs apply; for example, it is cheaper to process one order for £10,000 than ten each of £1000.

☐ The use of computerisation can be used to facilitate the collection, summary and analysis of data, which in turn can improve purchasing efficiency.

2 Co-ordination of the activity:

☐ Uniform policies can be adopted.

☐ Uniform purchasing procedures can be followed.

☐ Standardisation is achieved by the use of company specifications.

☐   Back-up services, especially stock control, can be co-ordinated.

☐   Staff training and development can be undertaken on a smaller scale with better results.

☐   Research into sources, qualities and supplier performance can be achieved.

☐   It is more convenient for the supplier to approach a central purchasing department.

3   Control of the activity:

☐   The performance of the purchasing department can be monitored by fixing objectives and comparing actual results with predetermined standards.

☐   Stock rotation is achieved and loss of wastage due to out-of-date stock can be minimised.

☐   Uniform pricing is achieved and assists in standard costings nationwide.

A centralised role in a company such as foodservice retail (chain of restaurants) can work very well, as each of the restaurants has a set menu and therefore is limited to the commodities it requires, perhaps 200 at most. In a unit that where there is a contract foodservice operator the requirement varies from unit to unit. A directors' dining room will require fillet steak and smoked salmon, a school kitchen would never order such commodities. Therefore a centralised purchasing department would have to order many thousands of different commodities due to the diversity of the business.

Purchasing may be completely decentralised with each unit undertaking its own purchasing, although unit buyers are given some guidelines upon which to purchase. It is at this level that food specifications are most needed to give the non-specialist food purchasers some technical guidelines upon which to buy.

A combination of centralisation and decentralisation may apply. It could be said that the function of the purchasing administration is already done centrally under the purchasing director, but no physical purchasing is done at this level. It is necessary to have central administration to ensure the achievement of company purchasing standards.

However, it is possible for non-perishable goods and commodities with an extended shelf life, to be bought centrally and delivered to the unit on a weekly basis. This would improve the effectiveness of this area. But the perishable items, i.e. bakery goods, dairy produce, fresh meat and fish, fresh fruit and vegetables, would be purchased straight into the unit. Alternatively, there could be a system whereby the unit informs a central office, operated by purchasing specialists, of their requirements, who then place the order and organise delivery to the unit.

No matter which system is adopted, there is always a need for purchasing specifications to assist in the task. Even specialists with technical training need to know the standard that the company expects its suppliers to reach. A standard indicated in a specification lends itself to the ultimate standard which a company wants to achieve. Good specifications aimed at the right standard will ensure:

- Quality products
- Quality service
- Acceptable prices.

An important factor in finding suppliers interested in selling commodities to a specification prepared by a foodservice operator is that of the purchasing power of the foodservice operator. If a foodservice operator is large enough, he is able to influence the supply trade quite easily. The small foodservice operator has a problem of purchasing only what suppliers have readily available to sell, as he has only a low purchasing power. To find suppliers to prepare commodities to his specification is rare and if fortunate enough to find any interested, extremely costly. Sometimes the difficulty can be overcome by finding suppliers who are already producing an item for a larger concern to a similar specification and who therefore can accept a compromise that will go towards the needs of the small foodservice operator's specification.

5.6   Operational control

Food is expensive and efficient stock control levels are essential to help the profitability of the business. The main difficulties of controlling food stocks include:

- Food prices fluctuate because of inflation and falls in the demand and supply, through poor harvests, bad weather conditions, etc.
- Transport costs, which rise due to wage demands and cost of petrol.
- Fuel costs rise, which affects food companies' and producers' costs.
- Changes in approaches to government food subsidies.
- Changes in the amount demanded by the customer; increased advertising increases demand.
- Changes in taste and fashion influence demand from one produce to another.
- Media focus on certain products, which are labelled healthy and unhealthy, will affect demand, e.g. butter being high in saturated fats. Sunflower margarine is high in polyunsaturates.

Each establishment should devise its own control system to suit the needs of that establishment. Factors that adversely affect the establishment of an efficient control system include:

- Regular changes in the menu
- Menus with a large number of dishes
- Dishes with a large number of ingredients
- Problems with assessing customer demand
- Difficulties in not adhering to or operating standardised recipes
- Raw materials purchased incorrectly.

Factors assisting in the establishment of an efficient control system include:

■ Constant menu, e.g. McDonald's, Harvester
■ Standardised recipes and purchasing specifications
■ Menu with a limited number of dishes.

With some of all these factors present in a foodservice operation, stock control is often easier and costing more accurate.

In order to carry out a control system: food stocks must be secure; portion control must be accurate, and a record keeping system must be developed to monitor the daily operation.

The process for food production control can be summarised as shown in Figure 5.3, which shows it as a five-stage process. Each of these stages is considered in turn below.

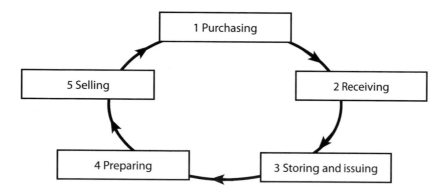

Figure 5.3: The food production control cycle of daily operation

Purchasing

Requisition and inventory control must be implemented. The purchasing transaction can be shown diagrammatically as in Figure 5.4. Control begins with the calculation of the amount and the writing of the specification. Orders are usually placed through a purchase order. This states the item or items required, amount, size, weight and other pertinent information.

All purchase orders have numbers so that they can be quickly identified. Only an authorised person should sign purchase orders. The individual issuing it normally holds one copy, one may go to the accounting department, and another to the receiving rooms. Copies are sent to the supplier. In some cases, it may be a requirement to have the purchase order signed and returned by an identified individual in the supplier's company, so it is then known that the order will be honoured.

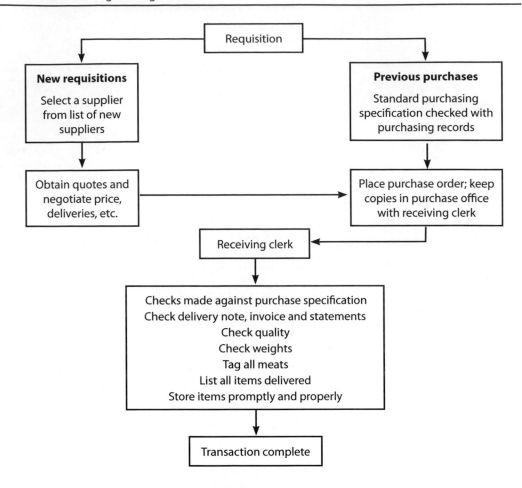

Figure 5.4: Summary of the purchasing transaction

Regular purchase orders are for one single order to be delivered at a specified date. 'Open delivery' purchase orders establish the purchase of items over a period of time. Items needed daily or weekly are often purchased by open delivery orders.

A purchase record may be maintained. This record may indicate what was ordered and from whom, as well as any other information that may be needed to be maintained. A purchase price record usually is maintained on cards to keep information on the price paid for a particular item.

■ Receiving

Receiving practices vary with different organisations. The general principles of control are:

1 Check delivery note to see if the products delivered agree with it.

2 Inspect products/raw materials to determine if they are in agreement with the purchase order and specification.

3 Tag all meats with date of receipt, weight and other information needed to identify the delivery properly.

4 List all items received on the daily receiving report.

5 Accept the products/raw materials by signing the delivery note and returning the copy to the driver/delivery person.

6 Store or deliver to the correct place.

In large organisations, receiving is a specialised job. This job may be combined with the storeroom job. Authority and responsibility must be given to the individual receiving. This must include jurisdiction over those who help receive and store. The various approaches to receiving include:

- **Invoice receiving:** If the invoice accompanies the delivery with the delivery note, check the invoice against the delivery and check with the purchase order or the quotation and the order sheet, or other documents. Note any discrepancies. Check quality and quantity against documentation.

- **Blind check receiving:** For blind receiving, the clerk is given a blank invoice or purchase order listing the incoming products/raw materials. The quantities, quality, weights and prices are omitted. The receiving clerk must add these in when the products/raw materials are delivered. This enforces a formal checking system and not merely a glancing job to see if the goods agree with the figures on the invoice. The receiving clerk must weigh items to record their correct weight. A count is required in addition to a quality check. Another invoice with quantities, weights, quality and prices is sent to the finance office. This is checked against the invoice of the receiving clerk and the figures verified. Blind receiving is an accurate method of checking merchandise and verifying deliveries. It does take more time and costs more since it requires the clerk to prepare a complete record of all incoming products/raw materials.

- **Partial blind receiving:** This is a combination of invoice receiving and blind receiving. The receiving clerk has itemised purchase orders, delivery notes and invoices with the quantities omitted. When the goods, products and raw materials are checked, the quantity of each item is listed in the space provided. This is not as accurate as the previous method, but is faster and less costly. It is essential in both methods that the supplier's invoice does not accompany the goods, products or raw materials. If it does, the information on quantity must be omitted or made invisible by a blank area where such information would appear.

Good principles of receiving are important for control. These are:

1 Being ready and prepared for the delivery.

2 Checking the incoming goods thoroughly against the purchase order and the purchase specification. Open cases if they appear to be damaged or tampered with. Date all canned goods before storing.

3 Weigh items separately. When receiving bulk items, remove excess paper, ice, etc.

4 Weigh meats and tag them. The practice prevents disputes with the supplier about over- and under-weights. Tagging also reduces the chance of spoilage or excess weight loss. It also simplifies calculation of food costs, since a good record of meat withdrawals can be obtained from the tags taken from meat as it comes from the inventory.

Recording incoming deliveries is as important as checking quality and quantity. The form or style of doing this may vary but the intended principles are the same.

■ Storing and issuing

Raw materials should be stored correctly under the right conditions, temperature, etc. A method of pricing the materials must be decided and one of the following should be adopted for charging the food to the various departments. The cost of items does not remain fixed over a period of time; over a period of one year a stores item may well have several prices. The establishment must decide which price to use:

- Actual purchase price
- Simple average weight
- Weighted average price
- Inflated price (price goes up after purchase), or
- Standard price (fixed price).

■ Preparing/production

This is an important stage of the control cycle. The cost of the food consumed depends on two factors:

1 The number of meals produced

2 The cost per meal.

In order to control food costs the operation must be able to:

- Control the number to be catered for
- Control the food cost per meal in advance of production and service by using system of pre-costing, using standardised recipes, indicating portion control.

■ Selling

In order to be able to sell well, it is necessary to be able to predict the volume of sales for a future period. In order to be of practical value the forecast must:

- Predict the total number of covers (customers)
- Predict the choice of menu items.

Therefore, it is important to:

- Keep a record of the numbers of each dish sold from a menu
- Work out the average spend per customer
- Calculate the proportion, expressed as a percentage, of each dish sold in relation to total sales.

Forecasting is in two stages:

1 Initial forecasting – this is done once a week in respect of each day of the following week. It is based on sales histories, information related to advance bookings and current trends and when this has been completed, the predicted sales are converted into the food/ingredients requirements. Purchase orders are then prepared and sent to suppliers.

2 The final forecast – this normally takes place the day before the actual preparation and service of the food. This forecast must take into account the latest developments, e.g. the weather and any food that needs to be used up; if necessary suppliers' orders may need to be adjusted.

Sales forecasting is not a perfect method of prediction, but does help with production planning. Sales forecasting, however, is important when used in conjunction with cyclical menu planning.

Storekeeping

Keeping a properly run and efficient storeroom is essential in order to maintain the unified process of control throughout the establishment/organisation. A clean, orderly food store, run efficiently, is essential in any foodservice establishment for the following reasons:

- Stocks of food can be kept at a suitable level, so eliminating the risk of running out of any raw material.
- All food entering and leaving the stores can be properly checked; this helps to prevent wastage.
- A check can be kept on the percentage profit of each department of the establishment.

■ Control and profitability

A summary of the key factors that will help the profitability of the foodservice operation is as follows:

- Ensuring correct cooking of food to minimise portion loss

- Efficient preparation of raw materials

- Correct portion control

- Minimising wastage, sufficient use of raw materials, utilising left-over food

- Reducing theft

- Accurate ordering procedures

- Adequate checking procedures

- Reference marks to standardised recipes and yield factors

- Sufficient research into suppliers

- Accurate forecasting

- Sound menu planning.

6 Beverage provision

Aim

This chapter considers beverage provision within foodservice operations.

Objectives

This chapter is intended to support you in:

- Promoting safe, sensible drinking
- Identifying types of wine and drinks lists
- Developing wine, drink and other beverage lists
- Developing skills in operating and managing the purchasing, storage and control of beverage stocks.

6.1   Safe, sensible drinking

There is increasing concern about higher levels of alcohol consumption and the health risks associated with it. Various initiatives are being tried such as improving information on labels, alcohol exclusion areas at certain times, restrictions on price promotions and also on licensing. Those who sell and serve alcoholic beverages, as well as being the subject of various licensing arrangements (see Chapter 1, page 42) are also being giving far greater encouragement to become more responsible.

The majority of the population drink alcohol for many reasons: to quench a thirst, as a relaxant or simply because it is enjoyable. A small amount of alcohol does no harm and can even be beneficial. However, the more you drink and the more frequently you drink, the greater the health risks.

Alcohol depresses the brain and nerve function, affecting a person's judgement, self-control and skills. The four general stages of becoming drunk are:

Stage 1: Happy (relaxed, talkative and sociable).

Stage 2: Excited (erratic and emotional; movement and thinking affected).

Stage 3: Confused (disorientated, loud, out of control).

Stage 4: Lethargic (unable to stand, talk or walk).

It is important that members of the service staff are aware of these stages so that potential problems can be identified and handled properly before they become more serious. This can include refusing to serve more alcohol to intoxicated persons, which is either required under the law or may be undertaken as a safety precaution – such as with people on aircraft.

■   Alcoholic strength

The two main scales of measurement of alcoholic strength may be summarised as:

- OIML Scale (European): range 0% to 100% alcohol by volume.
- American Scale (USA): range 0° to 200°.

The Organisation Internationale Métrologie Légale (OIML) Scale, previously called Gay Lussac Scale, is directly equal to the percentage of alcohol by volume in the drink at 20°C. It is the universally accepted scale for the measurement of alcohol. The by volume measurement indicates the amount of pure alcohol in a liquid. Thus, a liquid measured as 40% alcohol by volume will have 40% of the contents as pure alcohol (under the American Scale 80° (80 degrees proof) is equal to 40% alcohol by volume). The alcoholic content of drinks, by volume, is now almost always shown on the label. Table 6.1 gives the approximate alcoholic strength of a variety of drinks

Table 6.1: Approximate alcoholic strength of drinks (OIML scale)

0%	Non-alcoholic
not more that 0.05%	Alcohol free
0.05–0.5%	De-alcoholised
0.5–1.2%	Low alcohol
1.2–5.5%	Reduced alcohol
3–6%	Beer, cider, FABs* and 'alcopops'** with any of these being up to 10%
8–15%	Wines, usually around 10–13%
14–22%	Fortified wines (liqueur wines) such as sherry and port, aromatised wines such as vermouth, vin doux naturels (such as Muscat de Beaumes-de-Venise) and Sake***
37.5–45%	Spirits, usually at 40%
17–55%	Liqueurs, very wide range

Notes

* FABs is a term used to describe flavoured alcoholic beverages, for example, Bacardi Breezer (5.4%).

** 'Alcopops' is a term used to describe manufactured flavoured drinks (generally sweet and fruity) which have had alcohol, such as gin, added to them. They are also known as alcoholic soft drinks or alcoholic lemonade. Usually 3.5 to 5% but can be up to 10%.

*** Sake is a strong (18%), slightly sweet, form of beer made from rice.

■ Sensible limits

Most of the alcohol consumed passes into the bloodstream from where it is rapidly absorbed. This absorption may be slowed down somewhat if drink is accompanied by food but the amount of alcohol consumed will be the same. The liver must then burn up almost all the alcohol consumed, with the remainder being disposed of in urine or perspiration. It takes approximately one hour for the liver to burn up one unit of alcohol; if it has to deal with too much alcohol over a number of years, it will inevitably suffer damage.

So what are the sensible limits to avoid damaging our health? Of course, not drinking alcohol cuts out any risk. However, medical opinion in the United Kingdom has set the limit at 21 units spread throughout the week for men, and 14 units spread throughout the week for women (excluding pregnant women where the advice is for no alcohol). Drinking in excess of these limits is likely to be damaging to health.

One unit of is equal to 10 millilitres (liquid) or 8 grams (weight) of alcohol. This is roughly equivalent to:

■ Half a pint of ordinary beer or lager

■ One glass of wine (125 ml)

■ One glass of sherry (50 ml)

■ One measure of vermouth or other apéritif (50 ml)

■ One measure of spirits (25 ml).

However, it is also important to take into account:

- Some extra strength lagers and beers have up to two or three times the strength of ordinary beers. Remember too that many low-calorie drinks can contain more alcohol than their ordinary equivalents.

- The number of units required to reach the maximum permitted levels for driving varies between individuals but it can be as little as three units. Some alcohol remains in the bloodstream for up to 18 hours after consumption. This should be considered in relation to the legal limits for alcohol in the blood when driving.

- There are about 100 calories in a single unit of alcohol. The amount of calories quickly adds up and can lead to weight gain. However replacing food with alcohol as a source of calories denies the body essential nutrients and vitamins.

Calculating alcohol intake

The amount of alcohol being consumed is a measure of both the strength of the alcoholic drink and the amount or volume of the drink being consumed.

To calculate the alcohol unit intake for wines:

Wine at a specific percentage of alcohol by volume multiplied by the amount in litres equals the units of alcohol per bottle. For example:

Wine at 12% alcohol by volume × 0.75 litre bottle = 9 units per 0.75 cl bottle.

Therefore this 75 cl bottle of wine will give 6 × 125 ml individual glasses of wine and each glass will therefore contain 1.5 units of alcohol (9 units in the whole bottle divided by the 6 glasses).

Other examples for calculating the alcohol unit intake for other drinks are:

Lager at 5% alcohol by volume × 0.50 litre measure = 2.5 units per half litre measure.

Spirit at 40% alcohol by volume × 0.025 litre (25 ml) measure = 1 unit per 25 ml measure.

Sherry at 18% alcohol by volume × 0.05 litre (50 ml) measure = 0.9 unit per 50 ml measure.

(For further information on safe sensible drinking visit the *Drink Aware* website at http://www.drinkaware.co.uk)

6.2 Types of wine and drink lists

Wine and drinks lists are primarily a selling aid. The lists identify for the customer what is on offer, the price of the item and details such as the measure in which the item is to be sold.

The service staff should have a good knowledge of all the wines and other drinks available and the main characteristics of them. They should also have a good knowledge of wines or other drinks that are most suitable to offer with different foods.

■ Bar and cocktail lists

These may range from a basic standard list offering the common everyday apéritifs, a selection from a basic standard list offering the common everyday apéritifs, a selection of spirits with mixers, beers and soft drinks together with a limited range of cocktails, to a very comprehensive list offering a wide choice in all areas.

When setting up a cocktail bar or preparing a bar and cocktail list, it is necessary to consider the availability of the specialised equipment, preparation requirements and stocks which are necessary for presentation including specialised glass ware and garnishes, etc. Additionally in order to profit from yield management techniques, it is imperative that the majority of beverages have standard recipes and measures.

■ Apéritif lists

These can be combined with the restaurant wine list – although they are more frequently today presented as a separate apéritif list as are digestif and liqueur lists. For apéritif lists it is common to include lighter, drier styles in wines and fortified drinks although drinks with some acidity are useful to enhance appetite. The contents might include:

- Champagne – non-vintage, vintage, premier cuvées, champagne rosé,
- Kir Royale
- Other sparkling wines, sparkling rosé
- Dry sherry – fino, manzanilla through to dry oloroso
- Dry white wine – for example, Muscadet and New Zealand Sauvignon Blanc
- Lighter Mösel, Austrian and Swiss wine styles
- Pineau des Charentes
- Sercial Madeira, Rainwater, Verdellho
- Ratafia
- Vermouths
- Bitters
- White port
- Dry Marsala
- Tawny port (served chilled).

■ Restaurant wine lists

Customers can tell a lot about a restaurant from the content and presentation of the wine list. The list must inform although too much information is just as bad as having none. Careful consideration also needs to be given to the extensiveness of the wine list as it can cost a vast amount of money to maintain.

Examples of types of wine list include:

- A full and very comprehensive list of wines from all countries, but emphasis on the classic areas such as Bordeaux/Burgundy plus a fine wine/prestige selection;

- A middle of the road, traditional selection, e.g. some French, German, Italian together with some New World wines;

- A small selection of well-known or branded wines, or

- A prestige list predominantly with wines of one specific country.

After-meal drinks lists (*digestifs*)

These are more frequently presented as a separate digestif or liqueur list. Digestif lists should comprise soothing, mellowing, heavier, sweeter and richer styles of beverages, for example:

- Really good sweet wines such as sweet German, Austrian, Loire and Jurançon wines can refresh the palate

- Fortified wines such as port (vintage and LBV), Sherry, Madeira, Marsala, Malaga, rich and liqueur muscats

- Cognac, Armagnac and brandies and/or a specialist range of malt and 'older malt' whiskies

- A range of liqueurs

- A range of speciality liqueur/spirit coffees might also be included.

Banqueting wine lists

For banqueting wine lists:

1 The length of the list is generally according to size and style of operation.

2 There should be a range of prices from house wines to some fine wines to suit all customer preferences.

3 In some instances the banqueting department will draw wines from the restaurant wine list – this reduces the need for double stocking.

4 There is usually a selection of popular wine names/styles on offer.

Essentially an operation is endeavouring to achieve ease of availability, strong gross profit margin and high recognition. Some considerations in drawing up banqueting wine lists are:

- Ensuring that the list will allow suitable pairing with the menu(s) on offer – especially if there is a range of suggested standard menus.

- Because banqueting lists are often sent out months in advance of an event, care needs to be taken to ensure ongoing supplies.

- A disclaimer might be useful which advises that an alternative may be necessary, or substitutions may be made if the client does not request that wines be set aside for their event.

- Ensuring that the presentation of the sales mix data is able to distinguish between banqueting lists sales and from restaurant sales, as wines may appear to be performing more strongly simply through an order placed for a banquet.

■ Room service drinks list

These lists tend toward less formality. However:

- They usually offer a limited range of wines and other drinks although it can be helpful if the customers can purchase from the main lists if required.

- There may be a mini-bar/refreshment centre or choice from a standard bar list.

- In some instances a fixed stock in sealed decanters is provided for VIP and other customers.

■ Hot beverages

The three main hot beverages are teas, coffee and chocolate. Increased travel and growing numbers of European tourists have impacted on tea, coffee and chocolate service in no small way. The impetus is towards ever-higher standards of fresh preparation and an accelerating demand for more international styles. More recently far greater attention has been given to hot beverages with even the simplest of foodservice operations offering a broad range of teas, coffees and chocolate. The 'barista' movement has also contributed substantially to this increased impetus.

Coffee being offered includes filter, cafetière, espresso and cappuccino as standard. Single estate coffees are also entering the market with exceptional taste profiles. Iced coffee is also becoming popular. Other offerings can also include traditionally made Turkish coffee. By far the most popular are the espresso-based coffees such as:

- *Ristretto* – intense form of espresso, often served with a glass of water in Europe

- *Caffè crème* – regular coffee prepared from fresh beans ground fresh for each cup, resulting in a thick cream coloured, moussy head

- *Espresso macchiato* – espresso spotted with a dollop of milk foam

- *Espresso con panna* – espresso with a dollop of whipped cream on top

- *Caffè latte* – shot of espresso plus hot steamed milk, with or without foam as desired

- *Flat white* – double shot of espresso topped with frothed milk which has been stirred together with the flat milk from the bottom of the jug, to create a creamy rather than frothy texture.

Teas offered can range from general basic teas to more specialise teas such as:

- *Assam* – full, rich and malty served at breakfast usually with milk
- *Darjeeling* – delicate and light usually served in the afternoon or evening with lemon or a touch of milk
- *Earl Grey* – blended Darjeeling and China teas scented with oil of bergamot. Served with lemon or a touch of milk
- *Jasmine* – fragrant and light green tea dried with jasmine blossom
- *Kenya* – refreshing and light tea served with milk
- *Lapsang Souchong* – smoky tarry highly aromatic tea, delicate on the palate with a rewarding acquired taste. Can be served with lemon
- *Sri Lanka* – golden tea from a Ceylon blend served with lemon or milk
- Iced teas may also be offered.

Included under teas are also flavoured teas (tisanes) such as blackcurrant, cherry, etc.

Hot chocolate has become very popular. It is often served in glassware or in a pot or jug so it can be served as required by the customer into a teacup or mug. It may come sweetened or non-sweetened and as a powder or soluble granules and is mixed with hot water or hot milk. Whipped cream, from a whipped cream dispenser, marshmallows or a sprinkling of powdered chocolate may be added upon request.

6.3   Developing wine and drink lists

Wine and drinks lists come in a variety of different styles usually reflecting the type of establishment. The factors affecting wine and drink lists are similar to those for menus (Chapter 5, page 106). As well as taking those factors into account the compiling of wine and drink lists should also take account of:

- The overall presentation and style, including the colour scheme, being in keeping with the style of operation
- The size and shape of the list in order to make it easy to handle and use for both customers and staff and have the required durability
- Flexibility in design and construction so as to be able to make changes as vintages change and for the inclusion of special promotions
- The length of time that the list will be in operation
- The overall design and legibility of the lists which can include illustrations, or inclusion of a contents page if the list is extensive
- Ensuring that the information included assists the customer as well as meeting legal requirements
- How decisions are to be made on the actual content of the list

- Considering the availability of supply, storage capacity and the capital investment required
- The inclusion of bin numbers which will simplify inventory and reordering for wine lists, so assisting both internal personnel and customers.

The wine and drink lists are part of the expression or character of the operation. Presentational style can mark one operation out as special even though there may be very similar content to other operations within the local area. Poor presentation can adversely affect the customers' judgement of the business and the food and beverage product.

The contents of wine and drink lists are commonly listed in the order in which they may be consumed, for example:

5 Apéritifs – which alongside sparkling and still wines can include a range of aromatised wines, fortified wines and natural spring and mineral waters.

6 Cocktails and other mixed drinks (including non-alcoholic drinks).

7 Spirits and associated mixers such as aerated waters.

8 Wines – sparkling and still wines, alcohol-free, de-alcoholised and low-alcohol wines.

9 Beers, cider, perry and non-alcoholic drinks including natural spring and mineral waters, aerated waters, squashes, juices and syrups.

10 Digestifs – which as well as liqueurs may also include various spirits, such as brandy, malt whiskies, and also ports, other fortified wines, sweet table wines, and vin doux naturels.

11 Hot beverages including speciality coffees.

Listing of wines

Wines are usually listed in three main ways:

- By place of origin (geographical)
- By type (sparkling, still), or
- By the grape variety.

Geographical listing for wines

The traditional approach is to list wines by geographical area. Within this approach the wines are presented country by country or region, such as for instance France, or Australia, and then area by area within that country It is also usual to have the wines presented under each country, region or area with the white wines first, followed by the rosé wines and then the red wines. Using this approach the listing of wines within a wine list might be:

1 Champagne and sparkling

2 France

3 Germany

    4 Italy

    5 Spain

    6 Portugal

    7 England

    8 Other European wines

    9 Australia

    10 The Americas (Canada, USA and South America)

    11 New Zealand

    12 South Africa

    13 Other world wines

    14 House wines

Listing wines by type

A modern approach is to have wines listed by type:

- Sparkling wines
- White wines
- Rosé wines
- Red wines
- Dessert (sweet) wines.

The wines can then be listed under each type of wine in three main ways:

- Country by country
- Region by region (similar to the geographical listing described above)
- By the style of the wine.

If the wines are to be listed by type and by style, then the wines could be presented under the following headings:

- Sparkling wines
- Rosé wines
- White wines
  - ☐ grapy whites
  - ☐ grassy-fruity whites
  - ☐ richer whites
- Red wines
  - ☐ fruity reds
  - ☐ claret style reds
  - ☐ herby-spicy reds.

To help the customer choose a wine and to enable staff to make recommendations, it is also useful for each of the groups of wines to be listed in order from the lighter wines to the more full wines.

Listing wines by grape

If the wines are to be listed by grapes then one approach could be to list the grapes in alphabetical order as follows:

White grapes	Red grapes
Chardonnay	Cabernet Sauvignon
Chenin blanc	Gamay
Gewürztraminer	Merlot
Pinot Blanc	Pinot Noir
Pinot Gris/Pinot Grigio	Sangiovese
Riesling	Shiraz/Syrah
Sauvignon Blanc	Tempranillo
Sémillon	Zinfandel
Other white grapes	Other red grapes

Under each heading the wines made with that grape are listed, as well as the principal blends that are made with that grape as the predominant grape. When the wines are listed under the headings 'Other white grapes' or 'Other red grapes', then the grape(s) of the wine should also be listed next to the name of the wine.

Again, to help the customer choose a wine and to aid staff in making recommendations, it is useful for each of the groups of wines to be listed in order from the lighter wines to the more full wines.

■ General information for wine and other drinks

It is usual to give information on wine and drink lists that help the customer in making decisions and also the staff in making recommendations. This information is shown below:

Wines

- ☐ Bin number
- ☐ Name of wine
- ☐ Country and area of origin
- ☐ Quality indication (e.g. AOC, Qmp etc.)
- ☐ Shipper
- ☐ Château/estate bottled
- ☐ Varietal (grape type(s))
- ☐ Vintage
- ☐ Alcoholic strength
- ☐ ½ bottle, bottle, magnum
- ☐ Price
- ☐ Supplier
- ☐ Descriptive notes as appropriate

Other drinks

- ☐ Type of drink, e.g. juices, whisky, gin, sherry
- ☐ Brand name if appropriate, e.g. Martini
- ☐ Style (sweet, dry, etc.)
- ☐ Description, e.g. for cocktails
- ☐ Alcoholic strength as appropriate
- ☐ Descriptive notes as appropriate

6

6.4 Pricing of wines and drinks

Restaurant wine and drink pricing tends to be based on three basic methods of pricing:

- **Cost plus pricing** – the selling price of a drink is determined by the addition of specific percentage, of the cost price, to the cost of the drink in order to achieve a predetermined percentage gross profit (gross profit = sales less the cost of sales). In practice, percentages are varied to achieve standard pricing for similar groups of products, e.g. all spirits or all minerals.

- **Rate of return** – the total costs of the business are determined for a given business level and from this the percentage of the cost price required to be added to the cost price is determined in order to ensure that the business will be viable.

- **Market orientated** – the selling prices are determined by considering both what the customer is likely to pay as well as what others in similar operations, locally are charging. It is also worth considering that there is a certain naivety on the part of some consumers who expect restaurant prices to reflect those of the retail market.

In practice, a combination of these methods is used. For drinks other than wine, it is usual to find that similar products will have the same prices. This avoids each item having a different price and it makes it easier for staff to remember prices. In addition, the percentage of cost prices that is added will vary in order to achieve a balance of selling prices between various items. This is to ensure that the selling prices are in line with what the customer is likely to expect. Thus, lower-cost items such as minerals tend to have a higher percentage of the cost price added to them whereas higher-cost items such as spirits have a lower percentage of the cost price added.

For wines, the simple cost-plus approach (aiming for a gross profit of 66% for instance) tends to be used as well as various formula approaches. One such formula approach is 'double the cost plus'. This takes the cost price of the wine, doubles it and then adds a fixed amount. The difficulty with both the cost plus and formula approaches is that the more expensive wines tend therefore to have a disproportionately higher selling price on the wine list and this does not encourage the sales of these higher priced items.

An alternative to the cost plus and formula approaches is to recognise that the gross profit cash contribution derives from the total number of sales of an item multiplied by the cash profit that the item provides. Thus, the most profitable item is the one that gives the highest total cash contribution. In this approach, the pricing of wines achieves a potential profit irrespective of the cost price of the wine. Prices in this method are determined by adding a fixed amount to the cost price. In some cases a banding system is used where the fixed amount is increased slightly the higher the cost price of the wine. With this approach, the higher-priced wines look more attractive to the customer and this encourages sales.

■ BYOB and corkage charges

Some establishments allow customers to 'bring your own bottle' (BYOB). This can be for various reasons including cases where the premises are unlicensed for the sale of alcoholic beverages. Other examples are where the operation is offering this as a special promotion or, for example, bistro operations that are located within wine stores. These operations then charge a set amount per bottle for allowing this and the operation will also provide the glassware for customers to use. This charge is known as a 'corkage charge'.

Another example of where this can happen is for events. The organiser can negotiate with the venue to be able to supply their own wines and other alcoholic beverages. Again a set corkage charge is applied. This can be per bottle but more often now it is charged per person attending the event. The reason for this is because of the difficulties in determining exactly how many bottles have been brought to the venue and then how many bottles have actually been consumed.

6.5   Purchasing

6

The objective of good purchasing is to achieve the right amount of stock, at the right quality, at the right level and at the right price. In contrast to food, beverages generally have longer shelf lives with the exception of cask and keg beers. However, all items do have a limited life although in the case of good wines this could be several decades.

Although longer shelf life will mean that greater stocks can be held, the cost of storage both in fuel and space costs has to be taken into account. In addition, the holding of high value stock ties up capital that could be used for other purposes.

For tied house premises, where the establishment is linked to a particular brewer, the sources for purchasing beverages are determined by the brewer. It is common for brewers to own or have links or associations with specific suppliers of spirits, minerals and other drinks. In these cases, the opportunities for selective purchasing are limited.

For free house premises, the establishment can determine whom they wish to buy from. Some considerations are as follows.

- **Using one main supplier** – The advantage is buying from one supplier rather than many, which reduces administrative costs. Deliveries will be regular and will cover all items. There are also additional benefits from the support that can be had from suppliers in producing wine and drinks lists and menu covers and from discounts that are available depending on amounts purchased. On the other hand, the range of beverages may be limiting in some way, thus reducing the potential range of beverages on offer in a particular establishment. In addition, using one main supplier can make the establishment overly dependent on that source.

- **Using a variety of suppliers** – The advantage for the establishment of being to buy to achieve a particular range of beverages on offer and reduces dependency on any one particular source. It also means that advantage can be taken of special promotions or discounts at particular times and from differing sources. Potential disadvantages are that this approach increases the number of separate deliveries, increases paperwork and can lead to inconsistencies in the range of beverages on offer.

Generally, establishments use a combination of the two approaches above: on the one hand, using one main supplier but with additional purchases coming from other sources. Depending on the particular policy of the establishment, the buying of wines needs some further consideration. Buying wines for laying down and service at some future time can build up a good stock of fine wines which can, when sold, produce good profits. However, the downside is the initial capital required and storage costs together with the risks to the stock through spoilage and breakage that could be associated with this approach.

The costs of purchasing

There are three areas of cost associated with purchasing. These are:

1   The costs of acquisition:
   ☐ Preliminary costs including, preparation and specifications, supplier selection and negotiation
   ☐ Placement costs including order preparation, stationery, postage, telephone
   ☐ Post-placement costs including order progressing, receipt of goods, inspection of goods, payment of invoices and other clerical controls.

2   The holding costs:
   ☐ Financial costs, e.g. interest on capital tied up in inventory, cost of insurance
   ☐ Losses through deterioration, pilferage
   ☐ Storage costs including space, handling and inspection, stores lighting, heating/refrigeration, clerical costs, e.g. stores records and documentation

3   The cost of stockouts:
   ☐ Cost of alternatives including buying at enhanced prices and or/using more expensive substitutes.

Determining stock levels

Stock levels may be determined by using past sales data. A formula that can be useful is:

$$M = W (T+L) + S$$

Where:

M is the maximum stock

W the average usage rate

T the review period

L the lead time and

S the safety stock (buffer or minimum stock level).

An example using this formula could be:

W	=	24 bottles per week
T	=	4 weeks
L	=	1 week
S	=	1 week's usage, e.g. 24 bottles

Therefore:

M	=	W (T+L) + S
	=	24 (4+1) +24
	=	144 bottles

Minimum stock (buffer or safety stock) may also be calculated as follows:

$$L \times W = 1 \times 24 = 24 \text{ bottles}$$

ROL (reorder level) may also be calculated as follows:

(W × L) +S	=	(24 × 1) + 24
	=	48 bottles.

Using this type of approach can enable operations to determine the appropriate stock holding to meet the needs of the establishment whilst at the same time minimising the amount of capital tied up in the amount of stock being held. Good stock control can be used to apply just in time approaches to stock holding, rather than stock levels being determined through just in case approaches.

6.6   Further consideration on wine provision

There are basically two types of commercial wine cellar: the 'restaurant cellar' and 'long-term investment cellar', in some cases the two are combined.

Restaurant cellars usually stock three categories of wine:

- Inexpensive well-made wines for everyday casual consumption
- Moderately priced well-crafted wines from known producers
- Special occasion expensive wines from known producers such as premium older vintage and rarer vintages.

The centre of activity within the wine cellar will alter with the seasons. In winter months, investment in hearty reds matching heavier dishes produced during this period will increase. In warmer months it may be necessary to invest in more light wines, rosé and sparkling wines. These will be refreshing indoors and outside.

The **long-term investment cellar** ensures supply as well as value. It is often found in fine dining restaurants and hotels, and houses specific styles of wines (for laying down) whose value will potentially increase over time. Although techniques in vinification have changed enormously in the last two decades, proportionately in response to consumer demand for quicker maturing wines, great wines if stored correctly will have the potential to achieve more harmony over time, and, as other individuals consume these vintages prematurely the remaining stocks will increase their value. However high levels of capital invested in fine wines and spirits can seriously affect the cash flow of a business, so it is important for management to know what beverages to purchase and where and what optimum stock levels should be kept for the specific type of operation.

■ Purchasing wines

How wine will be purchased and from where will depend on the scale of the operation, the level of interest, purchasing freedom, specialisation, location and how much time can be devoted to sourcing wine. The range of options open to the foodservice operation is listed in Table 6.2.

Table 6.2: Sources for wine purchasing

Fine wine merchant/ distributor	Most frequently used by establishments seeking best quality wines from well-known, well-established producers
(Branded) wine merchant/ distributor	Most frequently used by small, medium and many large businesses
Wine division of a brewery company	Purchasers may be locked into purchasing only from a designated supplier
Direct from producer	Usually dependent on your proximity to producers and volume requirements
En primeur	Where ageing cellar space permits, this can prove profitable. See 'Brokers' below.
Wine retailers	Much less likely in larger establishments, but can be very effective
Wine clubs	Rarely used by larger businesses
Internet	Some good finds can be had
Wine fair	Rarely used by the largest businesses. Good for the small and medium-sized business
Auction rooms	Good for small and medium-sized businesses
Brokers	Good for small, medium and large-sized businesses. The bulk of en primeur purchasing is now being managed through brokers
Tastings	Held by wine merchants and can invigorate sales as hoteliers and restaurateurs have ample opportunity to sample a broad range of wines

Many businesses will be purely interested in the price of specific wines. However the purchasing decisions will be better shaped if serious consideration is given to value for money and obtaining the return that an operation feels is justified for a particular outlay. Most suppliers do not surmise that operations select simply on price and operate with the understanding that there has to be a price–value balance.

Using merchants

Good merchants can steer buyers towards added value options but also assist in the composition of award-winning wine lists. This should be their objective when talking to a quality establishment. Writing wine lists should be the merchants' main area of expertise, but the merchant should also be both food and marketplace aware. They should be able to propose the right level of wine list and the right quality of wine, which will be in keeping with the level of the establishment within the marketplace.

Larger hotels and restaurants tend to use more than one supplier and especially if they are part of a group, there may be one nominated supplier for the basic stock. The best merchants supply bespoke services for wine list printing and consultancy services in wine and these services are part of the merchant's main added value. They should be specialists in constructing wine lists, even to the extent of putting together a wine list with the wines from perhaps two other suppliers. Reputable wine merchants can also provide information suggesting food and wine combinations, but it should be remembered they are not absolute experts (no one is) as this is such a subjective area. The wine buyer must certainly be knowledgeable enough to detect bluffers and weaknesses/gaps in the merchant's knowledge or portfolio.

When a merchant is reviewing a list or suggesting a list to a client, they must be able to suggest wines for current drinking, and be able to state clearly that 12 months from that period he/she will review the wines listed in terms of a development statement on the list. However, it may perhaps be more appropriate to change some of the wines completely at this stage. Wine merchants should also be able to undertake on-site promotions, and contribute to merchandising, training, tasting events, and be speakers at gastronomic events.

Many individuals agonise over the profitability of wine on their lists and many more get it completely wrong. The merchant can offer advice in this area if requested:

- The merchant can do many of the calculations, both suggesting a total open margin, a total margin across the list and individual margins for each of the wines
- The merchant should also be able to give advice if the operation is perhaps a little too aggressive (greedy) in pricing some of the finer wines.

■ Maintaining the quality of wine stock

Wine is a living thing and the development of it must be periodically checked through systematic and regular tasting. This process is to ensure that wines are sold at their optimum condition and within expected the lifespan of the wine. In addition the wine waiter, or sommelier, must have an extensive knowledge of the contents of the wine list. He or she should also have a good knowledge of the characteristics of the different wines and other drinks offered. To develop these skills and knowledge a professional approach to tasting must be adopted. The tasting, or evaluation, of wine and other drinks is carried out to:

- Develop learning from experience
- Help in the assessment of the quality of a wine in terms of value (the balance between price and worth) when making purchasing decisions
- Monitor the progress of a wine which is being stored, to determine the optimum selling time and as part of protecting the investment
- Assist in the description of a wine when explaining its qualities or deficiencies to customers
- Provide a record of wines tasted, which also helps to reinforce the experience and the learning.

When undertaking professional tasting it is important to be logical in the approach and to always follow the same sequence. The professional tasting, or evaluation, of wines includes three key stages:

1 Recording the details of each individual wine
2 Looking at, smelling and tasting the wine
3 Recording the findings.

Whenever wine is being evaluated a written record must be kept. These notes should be made at each stage of the process; otherwise it is possible to become muddled and confused. The process of writing down the findings helps to reinforce the discipline of the approach and leads, over time, to the development of greater confidence and skill. This process also provides a record of wine tastings so that there can be greater confidence in the quality of the wines being sold.

6.7 Storage and beverage control

The cellar is the focal point for the storage of alcoholic and non-alcoholic liquor. The key factors that will determine good cellar management are:

- Good ventilation
- High levels of cleanliness
- Even temperatures of 13–15°C (55–59°F).
- Strong draughts and wide fluctuation of temperature should be avoided.

■ Storage

For beers, good practices are:

- On delivery all casks should be placed immediately upon their stillions.
- Casks remaining on the floor should have the bung uppermost to withstand the pressure better.
- Ensuring the correct humidity.
- Spiling should take place to reduce any excess pressure in the cask.
- Tappings should be carried out 24 hours before a cask is required.
- Pipes and engines should be cleaned at regular intervals.
- Beer left in pipes after closing time should be drawn off.
- Returned beer should be filtered back into the cask from which it came.
- Care should be taken that the cellar is not overstocked.
- All spiles removed during the service should be replaced after closing time.
- All cellar equipment should be kept scrupulously clean.
- Any ullage should be returned to the brewery as soon as possible.
- All beer lines should be cleaned weekly with diluted pipe-cleaning fluid and the cellar floor washed down weekly with a weak solution of chloride of lime (mild bleach).

6

For wines, good practices are:

- A subterranean northerly aspect is ideal where possible.
- Excessive temperature variation should be avoided – a constant cool temperature of 7–12.5°C (45–55°F) should be maintained which will assist the wines to develop gradually.
- Wine should be stored away from the likes of excessive heat, hot water pipes, heating plant or hot unit.
- Excessive dampness should also be avoided and a relative humidity of between 55–70% be maintained. Humidity assists in keeping the cork from drying out, but the very important labels require protecting in the cellar (this can be achieved by spraying with ordinary hair spray which provides years of protection).
- Draughts and unwanted odours should be avoided, so the cellar should be clean and well ventilated.
- Fluorescent light (it does not give off heat) can be used in a cellar area. otherwise 20–40 watt maximum lighting should be used throughout. Wine can lose its colour followed by its flavour if exposed to too much light. Some wines are partially protected from light however, by their coloured glass bottles. Bright light however, especially sunlight or ultra-violet light should be avoided, especially with champagne and chardonnay.

- Table wines should be stored on their sides in bins so that the wine remains in contact with the cork. This keeps the cork expanded and prevents air from entering the wine – a disaster which quickly turns wine to vinegar.

White wines, sweet wines and champagne are more fragile than reds. White, sparkling and rosé wines should be kept in the coolest part of the cellar and in bins nearest the ground (because warm air rises). Red wines are best stored in the upper bins.

Some red burgundies, which are not filtered – in efforts to preserve their full flavour characteristics – are more likely to suffer from adverse cellarage. Syrah and Cabernet Sauvignon wines are more resilient than Pinot Noirs.

Special refrigerators or cooling cabinets can keep sparkling, white and rosé wines at serving temperature. These may be stationed in the dispense bar (a bar located between the cellar and the restaurant) to facilitate prompt service.

If fine wines cannot be cellared effectively in-house, location of the cellarage at a wine merchants should be considered. There are also self-storage systems around the UK, which provide temperature-controlled vault storage.

Storage of other drinks

Spirits, liqueurs, beers, squashes, juices and mineral waters are usually stored upright in their containers, as are fortified wines. If screw caps are used stand the bottles upright, if in cork, lay the bottles on their sides. Stopper caps and served caps are generally used for sherries and most ports, which are also stored upright once opened. Vintage and crusted ports are stored horizontally but require time upright to allow sediment to settle at the bottom prior to decanting. Sherries rarely improve in bottle. Finos and manzanillas and tawny ports are best consumed as soon as possible after purchase.

■   Beverage control

In any foodservice establishment where income is received from the sale of wine and drink, a system of control and costing must be put into operation. The system used will depend entirely on the policy of the establishment. Some or all of the books necessary, depending upon the requirements of the particular foodservice operation, are listed in Table 6.3 together with a statement of their purpose. Although referred to as books here, most modern-day systems are computer-based. However, the basic processes are the same whatever the method being used to record the data.

When any alcoholic or non-alcoholic beverages need to be purchased, for an establishment to keep up the level of stock, the person responsible for the cellar will carry this out. The order should be written in duplicate on an official order form. The top copy is then sent to the supplier and the duplicate remains in the order book for control purposes when the goods are delivered. In many operations there may be three copies of the order sheet. If so they are distributed as follows:

- Top copy: supplier
- Duplicate copy: control and accounts department
- The third copy: remains in the order book.

Table 6.3: Examples of control books used in beverage control

Book	Used to record
Order book	Orders made to suppliers
Goods inwards/received book	Goods received from suppliers
Goods returned book	Goods that are sent back to suppliers
Returnable containers book	Returnable containers sent back to suppliers
Cellar stock ledger	Stock movement in and out of the cellar
Bin cards	Stock of individual lines in the cellar
Requisition book	Re-stocking orders for individual service areas
Daily consumption sheets	Usage of stock in individual service areas
Ullage book	Breakage, spillage and wastage
Off-sales book	Items sold at the off-sale prices
Transfers book	Movement of stock between different service areas

When the goods are delivered to an establishment, either a delivery note or an invoice should accompany them. Whichever document it may be, the information in the document should be exactly the same, with one exception: invoices show the price of all goods delivered whereas delivery notes do not. The goods delivered must first of all be counted and checked against the delivery note to ensure that all the goods listed have been delivered. The individual responsible for the cellar may carry out an extra check. This is done by checking the delivery note against the copy of the order remaining in the book. This is to ensure that the items ordered have been sent and in the correct quantities and that extra items have not been sent which were not listed on the order sheet, thereby incurring extra cost without immediately realising it. At this stage all information concerning the goods delivered must be entered in the necessary books for control purposes.

Goods received book

All deliveries should be recorded in full detail in the goods received book. Each delivery entry should show, basically, the following:

- Name and address of the supplier
- Delivery note/invoice number
- Order number
- List of items delivered
- Item price
- Quantity

- Unit
- Total price
- Date of delivery
- Discounts if applicable.

The amount and deposit cost of all containers such as kegs, casks and the number of CO2 cylinders delivered can also be recorded in this book or in a separate returnable containers book.

Cellar stock ledger

The cellar stock ledger (see Figure 6.1) may be used as either an extension of, or in place of, the goods received book. It shows movement of all stock into the establishment and issues out to the bars or dispensing points. All movement of stock in and out of the cellar is normally shown at cost price.

Name of drink	Bin no.	Opening stock	Received	Total	Closing stock	Consumption stock	Price per unit	£

Figure 6.1: Cellar Stock Ledger

Bin cards

Bin cards (see Figure 6.2) are used to show the physical stock of each item held in the cellar. The movement of all stock 'in and out' of the cellar is recorded on each appropriate bin card.

Stock item		Bin no.	
Date	Received	Balance	Issued

Figure 6.2: Heading for a bin card

The bin cards are also often used to show the maximum and minimum stock. The minimum stock determines the reordering level, leaving sufficient stock in hand to carry over until the new delivery arrives. The maximum stock indicates how much to reorder and is determined by such considerations as storage and space available, turnover of a particular item and to some extent by the amount of cash available within one's budget.

No items should be issued from the cellar unless it is being accounted for by the top copy of an official requisition form, correctly filled in, dated and signed by a designated person from each of the departments concerned. It can be helpful if all requisitions are handed in before a set time each day so that the issues can be prepared together. In certain instances, however, depending on the organisation of an establishment, it may be necessary to issue more than once per day. All requisition sheets are written in duplicate. The top copy of the requisition comes to the cellar for the items required to be issued, and the duplicate remains in the requisition book for bar personnel to check drink on receipt from the cellar.

Requisitioning from the cellar

Each separate unit dispensing alcoholic and no alcoholic beverages should use some form of requisition to draw items from the cellar. These requisitions may be controlled either by colour or serial number, and are normally in duplicate or triplicate. The copies are sent as follows:

- Top copy to the cellar
- Duplicate to the beverage control department
- The triplicate would be used by each unit to check its goods received from the cellar.

Computer-based systems are now more commonly used for requisitioning but underlying principles are the same. Information listed on the requisition would usually be:

- Name of dispensing unit
- Date
- List of items required
- Quantity and unit of each item required
- Signature of authorised person to both order and receive the goods.

The purpose of the requisition is to control the movement of items from the cellar into the dispensing unit and to avoid too much stock being taken at one time, thus overstocking the bar.

The level of stock held in the bar is known as par stock. The amount ordered on the requisition, each day, should bring your stock back up to par. The amount to reorder is determined simply by taking account of the following equation: opening stock plus additions (requisition) less closing stock equals consumption (the amount to reorder, each item to the nearest whole unit).

In the outlets, as all drink is checked before issue, a daily consumption sheet (see Figure 6.3) is completed each day after the service by copying down the sales shown on the top copy of the wine checks or from electronic point of sale control systems.

Name of drink	Bin no.	Mon	Tue	Wed	Thu	Fri	Sat	Sun	Total

Figure 6.3: Daily consumption sheet

At the end of the week the consumptions are totalled up, thereby showing the total sales for that period. These totals may then be transferred on to a bar stock book for costing purposes. Where drink consumed is not checked in any way then either a daily or weekly stock is taken so that the amount to be requisitioned from the cellar may be noted. This then brings the bar stock up to its required level, which is the par stock. The daily or weekly consumption (sales) would then be costed and the cash total for sales arrived at would be related to the daily or weekly income.

Ullage, allowance, off-sales book

Each sales point should have a suitable book for recording the amount of beer wasted in cleaning pipes, broken bottles, measures spilt, or anything that needs a credit.

Either in the same book or in a separate one, the off-sales book, must be recorded the number of bottles, whether beer or spirits, at off sales prices and the difference in price. This difference will be allowed against the gross profit.

Transfer book

This book is used in multi-bar units to record movement of stock between bars.

■   Analysing sales

In order to make decisions about the beverage provision over time there is a need to consider the analysis and evaluation of a number of factors. These include:

- Gross profit margin
- Beverage sales per customer
- Average number of bottles sold per customer
- Sales mix data such as how much white to red wine has been consumed as a percentage amount
- Assessing the average price per bottle sold per period

- Making stock considerations and changes to the lists based on popularity and profitability of items
- Logging requests for wines not on the list
- Monitoring the competition.

Chapters 9 considers in detail the whole range of issues involved with the appraisal of performance and making strategic decisions is considered in Chapter 10.

Determining the cost of beverage sales

The traditional approach to determining usage, or cost of sales, is to take the value of the opening stock, add to it the value of the purchases during the period and then deduct the value of the closing stock. This value is usually the cost price. For outlets with differing gross profit mark-ups, the issue to the various outlets are also costed at selling price to ensure that the revenue is reconciled with that expected from the issue records. This is a very laborious process.

An alternative method is as follows: the beverage stock of an establishment is located in two main areas, the cellar and the outlet or outlets. The outlet stock is usually set at a par level and returned to this level at a set time. This could be each day or each week. All, for control purposes, that is really important is the cost of actual sales. Therefore, only the cost of goods issued to the outlets needs to be calculated.

For the cellar, all that is really important is the physical stock. Its actual value is only required for the end-of-year accounts. If this is true then the stock control of the cellar can be undertaken as follows.

For each stock item, a bin card or entry in the stock book is drawn up including:

- Item – the name of the item
- Quantity – the stock unit, this could be a dozen, six or single
- Reorder level – the level of stock at which a new order is placed; this is predetermined for all items as is the quantity of the stock to be ordered
- Opening stock – in unit terms
- Deliveries – in unit terms
- Issues to outlets – in unit terms
- Closing stock – in unit terms
- Current cost price.

From this record for each trading period, the cost price of issues can be determined. This is the consumption as issued from the cellar to the outlets. In addition, stock levels can be first determined from the book and then physically checked against what is actually in the cellar.

The advantage of this system is that it is only the cost of the issues that needs to be calculated.

For each bar or outlet, a similar system exists. There is a par stock and each day or week this is returned to the par levels. Over a period of time it will be found that the stock value of the outlet, at selling price, will be more or less constant. Thus the cost of goods issued to this outlet, at selling price, should equal revenue.

This approach does require the predetermining of the stock levels; the reorder levels and ensuring that issues to the outlets within the operation are only in whole units (single, dozen etc.).

7 Food and beverage service

Aim

This chapter considers various aspects in the management of food and beverage service.

Objectives

This chapter is intended to support you in:

- Developing your understanding of the service sequence and the service process
- Identifying and categorising food and beverage service methods
- Exploring the relationship between levels of customer service and resource productivity
- Developing approaches to the maintenance of good customer relations
- Dealing with the management of the volume in food and beverage service
- Identifying and applying sales promotion principles
- Managing the stages of the service sequence
- Controlling revenue.

7.1 The nature of food and beverage service

Food and beverage service is a difficult job. Whilst there have been changes in food and beverage service, with less emphasis on the high level technical skills (mistakenly bemoaned by some as deskilling) what wasn't initially being recognised was that other parts of the job are just as, if not more, important. The other thing that wasn't initially recognised was that the provision of high quality service was not confined to a particular type of restaurant and a particular type of service style. In other words excellence in food and beverage is not defined by the inclusion of a narrow range of high-level technical skills.

For food and beverage service the key requirements for staff are:

- Sound product knowledge
- Competence in technical skill
- Well-developed social skills
- The ability to work as part of a team.

Good food and beverage service is achieved where management continually reinforces and supports service staff in the maintenance of good standards of achievement in these aspects. Additionally the provision and maintenance of good service is primarily dependent on teamwork, not only among service staff but also amongst and between staff in other departments.

For managers within the foodservice operations, skills in marketing, staff management, team development, training, customer relations, financial management and operational management are necessary for the management of the service sequence and ultimately for the survival of the business.

7.2 Food and beverage service systems

Food and beverage service had traditionally been seen as a delivery system. However, as we saw in Chapter 1, food and beverage service actually consists of two separate systems, which are being managed at the same time. These are:

1 **The service sequence** – which is primarily concerned with the delivery of food and beverages to the customer
2 **The customer process** – which is concerned with the management of the experience the customer undertakes to be able to order, be served, consume and have the area cleared.

Separating the service process into two systems provides for a better understanding of the processes as well as providing an indication of the potential options for the organisation of food and beverage service.

■   The service sequence

The service sequence is essentially the bridge between the production system, beverage provision and the customer process (or customer experience). The service sequence may consist of eleven or more stages (Lillicrap and Cousins 2010) as summarised in Table 7.1.

Table 7.1: Food and beverage service sequence

1	Preparation for service
2	Taking bookings
3	Greeting and seating/directing
4	Taking food and beverage orders
5	Serving of food
6	Serving beverages
7	Clearing during service
8	Billing
9	Dealing with payments
10	Dishwashing
11	Clearing following service

Within these stages, there are a variety of alternative ways of achieving the service. The choices on how the service sequence is designed, planned and controlled are made taking into account a number of organisational variables. These include:

- Customer needs
- Level of customer demand
- The type and style of the food and beverage operation
- The nature of the customers (non-captive, captive or semi-captive)
- Prices to be charged
- Production process
- Volume of demand
- Volume of throughput
- Space available
- Availability of staff
- Opening hours
- Booking requirements
- Payment requirements, and
- Legal requirements.

7

■   The customer process

If food and beverage service is viewed as primarily a delivery process, then the customer can often be seen as a passive recipient of the service. As a result, systems and procedures tend only to be designed from the delivery perspective. However, as has been discussed in Chapter 3, a customer service specification cannot be achieved if it does not take account of both the infrastructure supporting the specification as well as the ability to implement standards within the interactive phase.

If the whole issue of quality is to be taken seriously, then the customers' involvement in the process must be considered. Customers are not passive but provide the impetus for the operations in the first place. In addition, the customer receiving the food and beverage product is required to undertake or observe certain requirements. It must therefore make sense to ensure that this process that the customer has to go through is also considered and managed.

For food and beverage operations, 15 separate service methods can be identified within the industry if the delivery system, or service sequence approach, is taken. However, this number is reduced when the analysis of the various service methods is taken from the customer process perspective. Four basic customer processes can be identified based on what the customer has to be involved in. These are:

- **Service at a laid cover**: the customer is served at a laid table. This type of service, which includes plated service or silver service, is found in many types of restaurant, cafés and in banqueting.

- **Assisted service**: the customer is served part of the meal at a table and is required to obtain part through self-service from some form of display or buffet. This type of service is found in carvery type operations and is often used for meals such as breakfast in hotels. It may also be used for functions.

- **Self-service**: the customer is required to help him or herself from a buffet or counter. This type of service can be found in cafeterias and canteens.

- **Service at a single point**: the customer orders, pays and receives the food and beverages, for instance at a counter, at a bar in licensed premises, in a fast food operation or at a vending machine.

In these four service processes, the customer comes to where the food and beverage service is offered and the service is provided in areas primarily designed for the purpose. However there is then a need for a fifth customer process where the customer receives the service in another location and in an area not primarily designed for the purpose. This can be called:

- **Specialised service or service in situ**: here the food and beverages are taken to and served where the customer is located. This includes tray service in hospitals or aircraft, trolley service, home delivery, lounge and room service.

A summary of the five *customer processes* is shown in Table 7.2.

Table 7.2: Simple categorisation of the customer processes in food and beverage service

Service method	Service area	Ordering/ selection	Service	Dining/ consumption	Clearing
Table service	Customer enters and is seated	From menu	By staff to customer	At laid cover	By staff
Assisted service	Customer enters and is usually seated	From menu, buffet or passed trays	Combination of both staff and customer	Usually at laid cover	By staff
Self-service	Customer enters	Customer selects items onto a tray	Customer carries	Dining area or take away	Various
Single point service	Customer enters	Orders at single point	Customer carries	Dining area or take away	Various
Specialised or in situ service	Where the customer is located	From menu or predetermined	Brought to the customer	Served where the customer is located	By staff or customer clearing

Within this simple categorisation, all of the fifteen modern food and beverage service methods can then be grouped within the five customer processes as set out in Table 7.3, together with the descriptions for the service methods.

With the exception of Group E, the customer process within each of the other four groups is similar for the different service methods that are found within each group. Additionally the skills, knowledge, tasks and duties required are similar within each group, with Group A being the most complex and Group D being less complex. Group E has a specialised set of requirements, some of which are different from those found in the other groups. To identify the commonality of tasks and duties, and therefore organisational needs as well as staff development needs, within each of the service method groups, the service sequence for each group can be examined in detail.

Viewing food and beverage service from the customer process approach on the one hand ensures a customer service-based perspective but on the other hand it also enables the management to consider alternatives. It is possible, for instance, to alter the delivery of the service without essentially changing the customer process, by moving between the service methods within each of the first four groups. Thus within Group A, the change from full silver service to a plate service delivery system does not essentially alter the customer process. It will, however, affect the way the service sequence is organised and possibly the production system. On the other hand, changing between the service method groups will substantially changes the customer process. If, for example, the service method changes from one in group A to one in group C, the effects on the requirements placed on the customer are very different, as can be appreciated from Table 7.2 above.

Table 7.3: Food and beverage service methods

Group A: Table service

Service to customers at a laid cover

1 Waiter	Silver/English	Presentation and service of food by waiting staff, using a spoon and fork, onto a customer's plate, from food flats or dishes
	Family	Main courses plated (or silver served) with vegetables placed in multi-portion dishes on tables for customers to help themselves; sauces offered separately
	Plate/American	Service of pre-plated foods to customers. Now also widely used for banqueting
	Butler/French	Presentation of food individually to customers by food service staff for customers to serve themselves
	Russian	Table laid with food for customers to help themselves (may also be used to indicate Guéridon or Butler service)
	Guéridon	Food served on to customer's plate at a side table or trolley; may also include carving, jointing and fish filleting, the preparation of foods such as salads and dressings, and flambage
2 Bar counter	Service to customers seated at bar counter (often U-shaped) on stools	

Group B: Assisted service

Combination of table service and self-service

3 Assisted	Carvery	Some parts of the meal are served to seated customers; other parts are collected by the customers. Also used for breakfast service and for banqueting
	Buffets	Customers select food and drink from displays or passed trays; consumption is either at tables, standing or in lounge area

Group C: Self-service

Self-service of customers

4 Cafeteria	Counter	Customers queue in line formation past a service counter and choose their menu requirements in stages before loading them onto a tray (may include a 'carousel' – a revolving stacked counter, saving space)
	Free-flow	Selection as in counter (above) but in foodservice area where customers move at will to random service points; customers usually exit area via a till point
	Echelon	Series of counters at angles to the customer flow within a free-flow area, thus saving space
	Supermarket	Island service points within a free-flow area

Note: some 'call order' production may be included in cafeterias.

Group D: Single point service

Service of customers at single point – consumed on premises or taken away

5 Takeaway	Takeaway	Customer orders and is served from single point, at a counter, hatch or snack stand; customer consumes off the premises; some takeaway establishments provide dining areas
	Drive-thru	Form of takeaway where customer drives vehicle past order, payment and collection points
	Fast food	Term originally used to describe service at a counter or hatch where customers receive a complete meal or dish in exchange for cash or ticket; commonly used nowadays to describe type of establishment offering limited range menu, fast service with dining area, and takeaway facility
6 Vending		Provision of food service and beverage service by means of automatic retailing
7 Kiosks		Outstation used to provide service for peak demand or in specific location; may be open for customers to order and be served, or used for dispensing to staff only
8 Food court		Series of autonomous counters where customers may either order and eat (as in 2 Bar counter, above) or buy from a number of counters and eat in separate eating area, or takeaway
9 Bar		Term used to describe order, service and payment point and consumption area in licensed premises

Group E: Specialised (or in situ)

Service to customers in areas not primarily designed for service

10 Tray	Method of service of whole or part of meal on tray to customer in situ, e.g. at hospital beds; at aircraft seats; at train seats; also used in ODC
11 Trolley	Service of food and beverages from a trolley, away from dining areas, e.g. for office workers at their desks; for customers at aircraft seats; at train seats
12 Home delivery	Food delivered to customer's home, or place of work, e.g. pizza home delivery, or sandwiches to offices
13 Lounge	Service of variety of foods and beverages in lounge area, e.g. hotel lounge
14 Room	Service of variety of foods and beverages in hotel bedrooms or in meeting rooms
15 Drive-in	Customers park their motor vehicle and are served at their vehicles

Note: Banquet/function is a term used to describe catering for specific numbers of people at specific times in a variety of dining layouts. Service methods also vary. In these cases banquet/function catering refers to the organisation of service rather than a specific service method – see Chapter 8, *Events*, page 212.

Source: Cousins and Lillicrap, 2010

One further issue to come out of this analysis is to note, that apart from for fast food operations, there is no particular link between a specific service method and a specific food production method (for food production methods see Chapter 5, page 113). It is also possible that the food production and beverage provision may be separated from the service by distance or by time, or by both, as for example in off-premises catering.

7.3   Customer service vs resource productivity

On the one hand, a food and beverage operation is designed to provide customer services and on the other the achievement of profit is largely determined by the efficiency of the use of resources. Customer service can be defined (as discussed in Chapter 3), as being a combination of five characteristics. These were presented alongside the resources being managed, as shown again here in Figure 7.1.

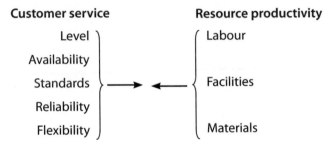

Figure 7.1: Customer service versus resource productivity

In determining the customer service specification for a particular operation, it is necessary to consider the effect that the achievement of the service specification will have on the productivity of the resources.

The effects of variation in the five customer service characteristics and the resource utilisation can be considered as follows:

- **Service level**: as the level of personal service increases, the labour costs will increase as the number of staff required will increase as well as the level of staff professionalism. Mealtimes are likely to become longer and therefore the potential capacity of the operation will reduce. In addition in the higher levels of food and beverage service, the equipment used tends to be of higher quality and the amount of equipment needed increases.

- **Availability of service**: increasing the availability of the service will potentially increase labour and material costs and will reduce the efficiency of the facilities used. In these cases it is necessary to endeavour to match the labour and materials being used to the expected volume of business which will vary over a given period.

- **Level of standards:** increasing the level of standards in the food and beverage operation will increase the cost of materials as better grade materials are used and will increase the cost of labour as the level of staffing and the staffing professionalism will need to be higher. In addition, the provision of the facilities will also have a higher cost again because of the higher grade of finishes being used.

- **Reliability of the service**: in order to ensure a high reliability in the provision of the service, again the labour and material costs will increase because, in order to protect the reliability of the product, it will be necessary to have a higher proportion of equipment, labour and materials available.

- **Flexibility of the service**: moving away from a limited standard range of products and services will increase material and labour costs and will reduce the efficiency of the facilities being used.

Reduced resource utilisation is often associated with the provision of a more individually tailored or personal service. There is therefore an expectation of a higher level of revenue being obtained from the higher prices that can be changed for the service. This higher level of revenue will compensate for the reduction in the efficiency of the use of the resources. A further development of this approach is that it is then potentially possible, through changes in the service process, to effect greater efficiency without fundamentally altering the customer process: moving from full silver service to plate service, for example.

On the other hand, and in all cases, the opposite of the examples given above will potentially increase the efficiency of the resources being used. This approach is often associated with more standardised levels of service together with reduced levels of personal service. Consequently this lower cost provision is then associated with potentially lower revenue due to lower prices being able to be charged. However lower cost provision and greater standardisation is also associated with potentially higher volumes of customers so revenue matches the required profit levels required by the operation.

In summary then, the development of the customer service specification should always take account of the five customer service characteristics identified above in order to be able to predetermine the level of resource utilisation and therefore the level of efficiency that is possible. This then also has implications for the revenue that will be required to meet the cost of the provision of the service. (Developed from the original text in Cousins, 1994.)

7.4   Customer relations

The existence of good customer relations is as much a part of the food and beverage product as any other aspect. Developing and maintaining good customer relations can be achieved if people working in the food and beverage operation have:

- The ability to recognise the **symptoms** of a deterioration in customer relations
- The ability to **minimise the causes** of customer relations problems.

The **symptoms** of potential customer relations problems are:

- Increasing number of complaints generally
- Increasing number of complaints specifically about staff
- Increasing number of accidents
- Regular mistakes by staff in orders, etc.
- Customers arriving without previous bookings being noted
- Increases in breakages
- Shortages of equipment
- Arguments between staff
- Poor morale of staff
- High turnover of staff.

Minimising the causes of customer relations' problems is concerned with ensuring that the conditions members of staff work under are likely to support the maintenance of good standards of interpersonal skills. There are four requirements to be considered when attempting to achieve this:

- The existence of agreed procedures for dealing with a range of customer service issues
- The customer service specification being able to be supported by the physical capabilities of the operation
- The customer service specification being able to be supported by the technical, interpersonal skills, product knowledge and team working abilities of the staff
- The identification of the likely customer satisfaction or otherwise that customers are likely to receive from the food and beverage experience.

These four requirements are examined further below.

■ Agreed procedures

Example of situations where there is a need for agreed procedures are:

- Addressing customers
- Wrong orders
- Complaints about food and beverage items or other matters
- Lost property
- Customer illness
- Unacceptable customer behaviour
- Alcohol over-consumption

- Enforcement of dress codes
- Enforcement of mobile phone and non-smoking codes
- Dealing with children (and lost children)
- Dealing with customer who:
  - ☐ Have limited mobility
  - ☐ Are blind or partially sighted
  - ☐ Are deaf or dumb
  - ☐ Do not speak English
- Emergencies such as power cuts, fire alarms and bomb threats

Procedures for all these types of situations must be agreed and consistently applied by all staff. These procedures should then be reviewed and reconsidered on a regular basis as part of training sessions and staff feedback sessions.

■ Physical capabilities of the operation

Limitations in the physical capabilities of the operation to meet the requirements of the customer service specification will always be the cause of difficulties. This is why the customer service specification itself should only be agreed by taking account of the physical capabilities of the operation.

■ Abilities of the staff

Limitations in the capabilities of the staff to be able to support the intended customer service specification will also always be the cause of difficulties. Again there has to be a balance between the technical and interpersonal skills, product knowledge and teamworking capability of the staff and the requirements of the customer service specification. As well as interaction with customers, service staff also are interacting with staff outside of the service areas, e.g. kitchen staff, bill office staff, dispense bar staff, stillroom staff. It is important that the provision of the food and beverage product within an establishment is seen as a joint effort between all departments, with each department understanding the needs of the others in order to meet the customers' demands. If there is imbalance, then either the staff capabilities have to be modified or customer service specification altered so that the two are in harmony.

■ Customer satisfaction

Knowing what the potential for customer satisfaction is from the food and beverage product can help to ensure that there are procedures in place for dealing with any difficulties that might arise.

The potential for satisfaction should already have been built into the design of the product so that it meets the needs the customers have at the time. There is also, though, the potential for dissatisfaction. In Chapter 1 we identified that the potential dissatisfactions fall into two categories: those which are controllable by the establishment, such as scruffy, unhelpful staff, or cramped conditions; and those which are uncontrollable, such as behaviour of other customers, the weather, or transport problems. Being able to identify all of these possibilities will enable an operation to have procedure in place to deal with them when they occur (see also Chapter 9 page 233 for further information on reviewing performance and on obtaining customer feedback, page 255).

In minimising the potential for customer relations problems then, there has to be equal concern over the physical aspects of the service, the way in which the service is operated, and with the interpersonal interaction between customers and staff.

7.5 Managing volume

Business volume inevitably varies throughout any trading period whether this be a year, a month, a week or even an hour. Operating at under full capacity for any period can lead to a disproportionate increase in costs and therefore a reduction in the overall profit contribution. The management of foodservice operations therefore is also about matching the ability of the operations to provide services to the expected volume of demand.

Kotler *et al.* (2010) identify specific dimensions that should be taken into account when considering the hospitality product (see Chapter 1, page 18). One of these dimensions is the 'perishability' of the product. This is a key dimension of the food and beverage product. It cannot be stored. For instance, seats in a restaurant, which are not sold at one mealtime, cannot be compensated for by additional sales at another time. In other words, the sale of food and beverage is limited by the capacity of the operation at the time. Therefore, in food and beverage operations, it is necessary to consider how the capacity of the operation for customer sales can be managed in order that the goals of the business may be achieved.

■ Measuring capacity

The capacity of a food and beverage operation is measured not only by considering the maximum capacity of customers at a given time but also the capacity that can be achieved over time. For example, a restaurant operation with a maximum seating of 100 covers can achieve a much higher actual capacity for a given meal period if the seats can be used more than once during the period. The potential for this will, however, vary according to the type of operation. A banqueting room, for example, can usually only be filled once during a meal period and therefore the size of the function in terms of covers served will determine the capacity achieved at that time. (For examples of how customer throughput may be determined for different types of operation, see Chapter 4, page 92.)

Volume and service organisation

One of the key differences between the management of food and production and the management of food and beverage service is that as the volume of business increases, it requires fundamental alterations in the food production process, whereas the service process may simply be multiplied (Cousins, 1988). As the volume of food production increases, the way in which the production is organised has to change. This change can be either where the process is separated into various parts of the menu required, which is the basis of the 'partie' system, or where the production system is based on the type of processes being used. For food and beverage service, as the volume increases additional service is provided through, for instance, increasing the number of stations in a restaurant. This is much the same as the opening of additional checkouts in a supermarket or increasing the number of tellers available in a bank, as the level of demand increases.

Although in foodservice operations there is the possibility of changing the service methods, such changes are usually driven by needs to improve resource efficiency rather than by the need to provide for higher volumes of business. An example is breakfast service. This can be provided through conventional table service at any volume of business but the need to reduce costs, especially staff costs, is often the main reason behind moving to a buffet system.

Increasing throughput

There is a relationship between the volume of customers to be served and the length of time they stay on the premises. The time customers take in different types of operation varies. There are various norms, which exist for seating/consumption times. Examples of there times for various types of foodservice operation are given in Table 7.4.

Table 7.4: Seating/consumption times in various types of foodservice operation

Operation	Consumption time (minutes)
Restaurant	60–120
Carvery	45–90
Popular catering	30–60
Cafeteria	15–40
Wine bar	30–60
Pub (food)	30–60
Takeaway with seating	20–40
Fast food with seating	10–20

There is also a relationship between the potential volume of customers and the opening times of the operation. For example, in a full service restaurant, the seating time of customers might average one and a half hours. If the restaurant is open for four hours, then it might be possible to fill the operation twice. If, however, the opening hours were only two and a half hours, then this would not be possible.

Opening times are determined by the consideration of:

- Local competition
- Local attractions, such as a theatre
- Location of the premises, e.g. city centre/country/suburb
- Transport systems Staffing availability
- Volume of business anticipated
- Local tradition.

A way of increasing the potential volume of demand that can be accommodated is to consider ways of increasing the throughput of the number of customers. The desirability of this, and the extent to which it can be achieved, varies with the type of operation. Some approaches to increasing throughput might be as follows:

For bar operations efficient clearing will encourage further sales or discourage lingering. People feel uncomfortable sitting at an empty table or bar. This approach can also be adopted in lounge areas and for cafeterias.

For areas where table meals are served, the type of operation will have an effect on the potential to increase the throughput. The higher the level of service – and usually the higher the price – customers can have seriously negative reactions to attempts to limit the length of the meal, especially where the meal out is the sole purpose of an evening. Initial alternatives could be to extend opening hours, set sitting times or be able to separate the customer who might accept this approach from those who won't. Combinations of these approaches are often found.

Both brighter lighting and less comfortable seating, used in appropriate settings, can have the effect of encouraging increased throughput.

For some operations, encouraging customers to share tables can also be a way of increasing throughput. However the acceptability of this to customers substantially decreases in operations with higher levels of service and higher prices. However this possibility is also becoming far less acceptable in any type of operation.

Other approaches include limiting the need for increasing the throughput of customers, such as setting minimum charges for peak demand periods thus attempting to ensure maximum revenue from the customers who are being accommodated. Reduced menu alternatives with quick service promises can also be considered. Additionally for restaurant operations offering an alternative location for coffee and drinks can free up tables in a restaurant earlier.

Limiting demand

Where the actual demand is significantly higher than the capacity of the operation, consideration must be given to methods of limiting the volume of demand.

Depending on the type of operation, this issue varies in significance. An à la carte restaurant operating at a high customer service specification will tolerate fluctuations in demand and seek to ensure availability and flexibility to meet all the expected demand. On the other hand, a cafeteria operation will seek to maximise demand during the service period.

Limitations in demand can be achieved through pricing policies. In city-centre hotels for instance, the demand for full breakfast is limited in this way through disproportionately higher pricing for a full breakfast compared to other alternatives. Meal packaging is also a way of reducing the variations in the range of demand being met.

Using queues

In addition though, there is the use of queues to ensure that the operation is working to a full capacity. Examples of this approach are found in, for instance, fast food operations where although the queue is controlled by a time limit for the customers to queue, it does provide constant demand at the service point. Another example is, for instance, TGI Fridays, where the queue for food service is the central bar area. In this operation, the queue becomes part of the meal experience and also provides for revenue from the queue, through drink sales, while waiting for meal service. In managing the queue requirement there are a number of factors to be taken into account so that the process of waiting in the queue does not become a negative part of the service process from the customers' perspective. The factors, which affect customer satisfaction, and some of the actions that the foodservice operation can consider, are summarised in Table 7.5.

Table 7.5: Service considerations in minimising queuing dissatisfaction

Factor	Service consideration
Unfair versus an fair wait	Try to ensure that the wait the customer undertakes is perceived as fair; design queuing systems to ensure service to customers is strictly in the order of the queue
Uncomfortable versus a comfortable wait	Consider the impact of the waiting environment; seek to maintain a high level of comfort
Unexplained versus an explained wait	Provide reasonable explanations for the wait and update regularly; try to avoid the customers' seeing underused capacity
Unexpected versus an expected wait	Accept responsibility; provide reasonable explanations for the wait and update regularly
Unoccupied versus an occupied wait	Provide distractions, which either increase the efficiency and effectiveness of the service sequence or involve the customer more in the service sequence

Initial versus a subsequent wait	Design the service sequence so that the customer has early contact with the servers; try to spread the total wait time across a number of the stages of the service sequence
Anxious versus calm wait	Assess the general level of anxiety of the customers; be aware of the need of customers for staff contact and reassurance
Individual versus a group waiting	Recognise that an individual waits feel longer than a group waiting; consider ways of ensuring that the wait is more pleasant through providing distraction
Valuable service versus less valuable service	Recognise that customers will wait longer the higher the perceived value of the service being offered; but still try to minimise the wait time
New or infrequent users versus regular users	Recognise that new or infrequent users will perceive that waiting times are longer than frequent users who will have become accustomed to waiting; always provide information and reassurance to all customers

Source: developed from proposals by Maister (1985), Davis and Heineke (1994) and Jones and Peppiatt (1996).

■ Banquet/function operations and capacity

In the organisation of banquet/function operations, there are special considerations in respect of capacity issues. Clearly the capacity of the function rooms will determine the maximum numbers that can be accommodated at a particular time. However, variations in the service methods and the dining lay outs can alter both the maximum numbers which can be served and also the volume which can be achieved over time. Selling functions that are similar in service method and layout, for instance, can reduce the preparation for service and the clearing after service periods.

In addition, the capacity of function rooms is affected by the combination of the bookings taken. The taking of certain types of functions will reduce or preclude the taking of others. Noisy presentations will for instance limit the use of adjoining rooms. If the intention of the operation is to be flexible, then this is inevitable. If the operation wants to specialise (and therefore reduce the flexibility) it is possible to increase the volume throughout. This supposes however that the volume of business requiring more standardisation is available.

■ The complexity of managing capacity

Managing capacity in food and beverage operations is not a simple issue. The provision of food and beverages is highly complex with a variety of stages both in the production and the service processes, all of which have an effect on the volume of business that can be met. In addition, the limitations posed by the physical facilities are not always the key determinant of the potential capacity that can be achieved. In many cases the customer service specification will determine that inefficiency in the use of the facilities will be outweighed by the need to provide a certain level of service. In addition, the control of labour and material costs must be taken into account in determining the potential volume of business which can be handled within the predetermined customer service specification.

7.6   Sales promotion

Sales promotion is about offering short-term incentives, which are designed to change the buying habits of customers and increase the revenue of the operation (Kotler *et al.*, 2009). In order to do this sales promotions are geared to directly encourage the customer to purchase, often through short-term improvements in the cost–value ratio.

Sales promotions as a marketing tool require planning, monitoring and careful evaluation, so that mistakes are not repeated, successes are, and these are then built upon. Additionally by their very nature sales promotions are designed to attract attention, consequently the operation must be geared up to meet the additional demand that the promotion is likely to generate.

Sales promotions are oriented toward changing the customer's short-run purchasing behaviour through:

- Increasing average spend and therefore sales revenue
- Invigorating slow-moving product(s)
- Promoting a new menu, product or product range
- Influencing impulse purchasing in a certain fashion
- Amalgamating items for sale
- Attracting attention to the business in shoulder months
- The celebration of special event(s)
- Increasing customer visits
- Adding variety and interest to bars, restaurants, etc.
- Establishing or enhancing awareness in potential customer's minds of the business and its products
- Stimulating purchasing by facilitating communication of product/business features and benefits
- To positively alter customers' opinions and attitude
- To inform in order to entice business
- To increase product/service profile.

The essential feature of sales promotions is to move, or incentivise, the sale of the product today, or for a specific period and not at some future point. This is achieved through offering additional value, financial inducement to purchase and try, advertising campaigns, etc. Sales promotions can also be linked to public relations and sponsorship strategies. Examples of tactical approaches than can be used to help to increase sales include:

- **Never discount**: it does not make good business sense to discount as a general approach. Once discounted, which customers get used to, it is difficult to then justify why the full price should be paid later for the same product. Discounting should really only be considered if the customer is also required to fulfil other additional conditions, such a buying a certainly number of products at the same time, or over a period of time with the promise of a future discounted product once the conditions have been satisfied.

- **Package**: instead of discounting it is often more beneficial to make up a package deal such as providing two courses at a reduced price or providing a drink with a special meal.

- **Special promotions**: these are often time–based, e.g. at a certain time outside of the main meal service periods to encourage trade during that period. This is used, for example, by restaurants wanting to encourage trade from theatre goers, where special limited choice menus are offered (which also provide for quicker service) before and/or after performances only.

- **Seek customer loyalty**: there are many ways of encouraging loyalty. Examples are: having good records of regular customers and targeting them with special promotions; giving vouchers each time a meal is taken so that a free course of drink can be gained once a certain number are collected; having a paid-for loyalty scheme where customers register, pay a fee and then are entitled to regular benefits, or promoting special offers through on-line booking systems, such as that operated by TopTable (http://www.toptable.com). (For more information on loyalty see, for example, *The Loyalty Guide*, 2010.)

- **Concentrate on value:** anything that assists in customers perceiving that they are receiving good value can be beneficial. This can be things such as including potatoes and vegetables with the price of a dish, or including a drink (also see notes in Chapter 2 on price, cost value and worth, page 32).

- **Reposition**: this is about reviewing the market(s) being targeted. Often this is a result of a downturn or a change in business from the customers that have traditionally been coming to the operation. If there are clear sign of these changes then it is time to reconsider the product on offer. (See also, Chapter 2, 'Concept development' and Chapter 3, 'Product development'.)

- **Cash profit maximisation**: in order for the business to survive, it is the cash gross profit that is important, not slavishly trying to achieving a target percentage gross profit. In order words sales promotion needs to be targeted to encourage the highest revenue and also the highest cash gross profit contribution. (For further notes on cash gross profit see Chapter 9, page 238.)

■ Merchandising

Merchandising revolves around attempting to increase spend per head. The basis of it is often associated with heightening the values, beliefs, attitudes, ideas and other meaningful values adopted by customers. In food and beverage operations merchandising is about helping customers interpret and evaluate what is being sold through a variety of verbal and non-verbal reassurances of the quality of the offering. All of this has to be consistent with the expectations the intended market might have, especially where in attempting to be competitive, the food-service operation is increasing the likelihood of increasing competition from competitors.

The aims of merchandising are to:

- Identify real opportunities to promote sales
- Recognise and promote customer benefits
- Maximise the value and sales
- Appeal to the senses, and the customer's identification of 'self'.

The four principal ways of achieving this are through:

- Starting to appeal to more customers
- Charging existing customers more money
- Spurring existing customers to spend more money
- Investing what is sold with clearly expressed benefit(s) – thus enhancing perceived value.

In order to be able to adopt any of these approaches the food and beverage operation needs to attract customers to the business, encourage them to spend and also to encourage repeat business.

Merchandising can be most effective where it is based on a genuine understanding of customer needs. Merchandising, which is empathetic towards (in sympathy with) the customer, is based on having an awareness and understanding of the emotions and feelings of other individuals.

The aim of merchandising is to identify a range of opportunities to promote sales, maximise volume and revenue. If customer contact personnel are involved in conceiving approaches to merchandising, such approaches will be better targeted as they will utilise the depth knowledge that these staff have of their customers and their understanding of the specific needs and desires of their customers. Merchandising techniques developed in this way can provide 'targeted' quality products, which are more likely to lead to total satisfaction and repeat business.

In effect, operations are then able to recognise and promote specific customer benefits from a position of depth knowledge. In empathetic merchandising the operation is more able to target merchandising to communicate social and economic status and worth, group affinity and distinction, symbolic association, self-image, and shared value. Table 7.6 provides a summary of merchandising approaches and possible sample outcomes.

Table 7.6: Merchandising activities and sample outcomes

Merchandising activities	Sample outcomes
Marketing	Identifies demand with the ultimate aim of expanding the customer base and in creating and keeping customers.
Advertising	Attracts the customer through visual merchandising, sensory merchandising and service merchandising.
Selling	Through point-of-sale materials and active promotion of product.
Profitability	Ensures business success and strengthens and prolongs the lifecycle of the business.
Perception, experience and mood – staff recognition of immediate needs through reading the customer	Recognition that no two people are the same and perceive stimulus differently at differing times.
Using design	Building strong emotional and psychological links between the business environment and the customer.
Personality – traits, behaviours and experiences making the customer distinctive and unique	Recognition of customer traits or characteristics reflected back ensuring the customer realises they are in the right environment.
Emotional value and connectivity	Ensures customers are valued and have an orientation with the businesses success.
Customer satisfaction and self-actualisation need	Ensures the continuation of the process and meets the customers' esteem needs (rising from notions of 'wise choice' and other positive character elements).

Menu and beverage list merchandising

The menu and beverage lists are vitally important sales tools. Menu and beverage list merchandising is concerned with the way in which the menu and beverage lists can be utilised most efficiently as a catalyst for optimising sales. It is necessary therefore for all menus and beverage lists to be correct against a checklist of operational compatibility, overall design and layout, clarity of expression, legibility, size, cleanliness and of course legality.

Creative merchandising

Displaying products in an effort to enhance sales applies as much to food and beverage operations as it does in general retail operations. The illuminated fascias above fast food service counters, which graphically exhibit the menu, illustrate this well. However it is equally important to for example, fine dining restaurants to set the scene with display materials. These can include own brand merchandising like champagne, wines, or the chef's own chocolate truffles, sauces, preserves, etc.

Merchandising stimuli for foodservice operations can include:

- Aromas
- Audio visual displays
- Bulletin/blackboards/floor stands
- Directional signs
- Display cards/brochures/iPads
- Displays of food and drinks
    - ☐ Trolleys (sweet, liqueurs etc.)
    - ☐ Buffets/salad bars
- Self-service counters – bar displays, flambé work, etc.
- Drink mats and placemats
- Facia boards
- Illuminated panels
- Other customers' food/drink
- Posters
- Production areas being able to be seen
- Tent cards, and
- Using service storage, as for instance in wine racks, as part of the design concept

Merchandising should not be difficult. In promoting sales, the basis of the promotion should be on providing customers with well-researched quality products which will potentially match the customer's perceived value of those products and their need for them. This is an extension of the development of the consumer–product relationship (as discussed in Chapters 2 and 3), which the foodservice operation is intending to develop and maintain.

Personal selling

In order for merchandising to be successful it has to be supported by corresponding well-developed personal selling and interpersonal skills of the staff. If staff training includes the examination of the profiling of the operation's target groups of customers then staff will be aware of:

- The nature of the demand being met
- The people and organisations buying the product
- The frequency of their custom
- Their use of other businesses and why
- Their use of disposable income
- Their desire to express their unique identity
- Their desire for greater variety tailored to their individual needs.

Personal selling refers specifically to the ability of the staff in a food and beverage operation to contribute to the promotion of sales. This is especially important where there are specific promotions being undertaken. The promise of a particular type of menu or drink, a special deal or the availability of a particular service can often be devalued by the inability of the staff to fulfil the requirements as promised. It is therefore important to involve service staff in the formulation of particular offers and to ensure that briefing and training are given so that the customer can actually experience what has been promised.

Members of staff will feel more confident about selling if they have information about the products on offer. If staff can tell well they can sell well. Examples of the type of information staff will need to know include:

- A description of what the item is (food, wine or other drink) and an explanation of how it is served
- Where the produce comes from
- What the local animals are fed on
- Where the fish are caught
- Where the local fruit and vegetables are grown
- How the produce is delivered
- Where and how the local drinks are made
- What the specialities of the establishment are and their origin.

There are various ways of providing opportunities for enhancing the product knowledge of staff, such as:

- Arranging for staff visits to suppliers
- Arranging visits to other establishments that use local produce
- Seeking out supplier information
- Allowing staff to taste products
- Arranging for staff to visit local trade fairs
- Organising training and briefing sessions for staff.

Within the context of personal selling, the service staff should be able to:

- Describe the food, wines and drinks on offer in an informative and appealing way, that makes the product sound interesting and desirable
- Use the opportunity to promote specific items or deals when seeking orders from the customer
- Seek information from the customer in a way that promotes sales, for example, rather than asking *if* a sweet is required, ask *which* sweet is required
- Use opportunities for the sales of additional items such as extra garnishes, special sauces or accompanying drinks, such as a dessert wine with a sweet course

- Provide a competent service of the items for sale and seek customers' views on the acceptability of the food, drinks and the service.

Ability in personal selling is necessary for all aspects of successful food and beverage service. The contribution of service staff to the meal experience is vital. The service staff contribute to the customers' perception of value for money, hygiene and cleanliness, the level of service and the perception of atmosphere that the customer experiences. Good food and beverage service staff therefore must have a detailed knowledge of the food and beverages on offer, be technically competent, have well developed interpersonal skills and be able to work as part of a team.

7.7   Managing the service sequence

In developing the customer service specification, the capability of the operation needs to be considered. Similarly, once the customer service specification has been determined, then the service sequence can be designed or redesigned and managed in order to ensure that the customer service specification is achieved. Aspects of the managing the service sequence are considered below.

Preparation for service

Within the service areas, there are a variety of tasks and duties which need to be carried out in order to ensure that adequate preparation has been made for the expected volume of business and the type of service which is to be provided. These include:

- Housekeeping duties
- Setting out dining/consumption areas
- Preparing serving equipment, cutlery, crockery, glassware and disposable service ware
- Preparing linen, other cloths and paper items
- Preparing counters and trolleys
- Stocking bar areas and stillroom areas
- Preparing and stocking workstations.

Preparation for service should also include the briefing of staff to ensure that they have adequate knowledge of the product.

One of the preparatory tasks is the taking of bookings. Systems need to be developed to ensure that bookings are taken in a way that ensures the efficiency of the operation. This includes consideration of overbooking systems in operations where bookings are taken. There are, however, risks with this approach. It is also necessary to take into account the law on contract. Bookings for larger parties and events are discussed in Chapter 8.

■   Taking food and beverage orders

Taking orders from customers for the food and drink they wish to have, takes time. Limiting the choice can reduce this time but this possibility depends on the particular operation. The order-taking process, though, is part of a longer process, which feeds information to the food production or bar areas and provides information for the billing method. Whatever type of system is used, whether manual or computer based, it will be derived from one of four basic order-taking methods. These are:

1 **Duplicate**: order taken and copied to supply point and second copy retained by server for service and subsequent billing.

2 **Triplicate**: order taken and copied to supply point and cashier for billing, third copy retained by server for service.

3 **Service with order**: taking order and serving to order, as used for example in bar service and takeaway methods and also for self-service (where the customer self-selects from a counter).

4 **Pre-ordered**: individually, or for groups of people such as for events.

Even the most sophisticated electronic system is based upon either the triplicate or duplicate method. Checks can be written by staff on check pads or keyed in on handheld terminals. Customers can also hand write orders (as in some bar operations) or use electronic systems such as iPads. There are also systems where the menu is projected onto tabletops enabling the seated customer to select their order from these interactive displays. The written order is then communicated by hand to the food production or beverage provision areas, or, for computer based systems, electronically to visual display units (VDUs), or printout terminals, in those areas.

When taking food and beverage orders it is important to identify which customer is having which item on the order. This helps to ensure that the right customer receives their correct order. There are check pads available that are specially designed to support this requirement; and electronic order-taking systems are easily able to record this information.

In addition to the standard order-taking process, there is also a need to make provision for orders to cover particular incidents such as:

■ **Follow on** – to indicate that one order has already been taken for that particular table or customer.

■ **Supplement** - indicating that a portion of something is being ordered, which is additional to that which has already been served.

■ **Return/Replacement** – for when a member of staff has ordered a wrong item and the order has to be sent back to the kitchen or bar and then be replaced.

■ **Accidents** – for when an item has to be replace because of, for example, the spillage of a drink. Usually this is also noted as a no charge order.

- **No charge** – for when an item or meal is being given on a complimentary basis.

Within the order-taking procedure there are also many opportunities to the promotion of additional sales (sometimes referred to as up-selling) through exploiting the potential for personal selling by the service staff (for more information on personal selling, see pages 183 to 185).

■ The service of food and beverages

The various service methods available to the foodservice operator are listed in Table 7.3. The choice of service method will depend as much on the customer service specification as on the capability of the staff, the operation and the equipment available. Differing service methods will also determine the speed of service and the time the customer takes to consume the meal, which in turn will have an impact on the throughput of customers.

Within food and beverage service there are traditional ways of doing things that have become established over time. These are known as the 'service conventions' (Cousins and Lillicrap, 2010) and they have proved to be effective and efficient ways in which to carry out the service. Having agreed service conventions for the operation ensures standardisation in the service sequence and the customer process (see page 164 for the definition of these terms), both for staff and for customers. These are often also used as the basis for the compilation of standards of performance manuals. Examples of service conventions, and the rationale for them, are given in Table 7.7.

For food and beverage service to operate efficiently and smoothly, it is important that all members of the staff follow the same service conventions. Different establishments may adopt variations on the service conventions exampled here but whatever service conventions are used it is essential that all members of staff follow the same ones. Otherwise the service will be inefficient and potentially chaotic. It will be unpleasant for the staff working in the establishment and the customers will also perceive that the operation is not well managed and coordinated. (For a more extensive listing of service conventions see Cousins and Lillicrap, 2010.)

7

Table 7.7: Examples of service conventions

Service conventions	Rationale
Always work as part of a team	All members of the team should know and be able to do their own job well, to ensure a smooth, well-organised and disciplined operation.
Work hygienically and safely	For the protection of other staff and customers from harm and to avoid accidents.
Pass other members of staff by moving to the right	Having an establishment rule about each member of staff always moving to the right (or left) avoids confusion and accidents.
Use checklists for all aspects of service	These help to ensure that all information is complete and that all managers and staff carry out procedures in the same way.
Prepare service areas in sequence	Ensure service areas are laid out and housekeeping duties have been completed before the preparation for service begins. This can save time and unnecessary duplication of effort afterwards.
Hold glasses or cups at the base or by the handle	This is hygienic practice. Service staff should not hold glasses or cups, etc., by the rim.
Hold cutlery in the middle at the sides between the thumb and forefinger	This is safer, makes for more accurate placing of items on the table, and also helps to prevent finger marking on the clean cutlery items.
Lay table place settings (covers) from the inside out	This makes table laying easier. Place a centre to the cover (e.g. a table mat or side plate) then lay tableware in order from the inside outwards. When laying a number of covers it is more efficient to lay each piece of tableware for all covers in sequence, i.e. all side plates, then all side knives, etc.
Take food, wine and drink orders through hosts	This is common courtesy – agreement needs to be obtained for any items that are to be served. For larger parties, where there may be a choice, orders may be taken individually but it is useful to confirm what has actually been ordered with the host as this may save any disagreements later.
Use order notation techniques	Use of such techniques helps any server to identify which member of a party is having a particular item of food or beverage.
Be aware of customers who may have additional needs	Look out for, and be prepared to deal with, people with sight, hearing, speech, mobility and language difficulties. Also be able to deal with children.
Avoid leaning over customers	This shows courtesy and respect for physical space. Remember that no matter how clean service staff members are, food and beverage smells do tend to cling to service uniforms.
Serve wine before food	Similar to above. Customers will wish to enjoy the wine with their meal. They will not want to wait for the wine service, as their hot food will go cold.
Use underplates (liners)	These are used (cold) for four main purposes: to improve presentation on the table; to make carrying of soup plates, bowls and other bowl-shaped dishes easier; to isolate the hand from hot dishes; to allow cutlery to be carried along with the item.
Use service salvers or service plates (with napkins or mats on them to prevent items slipping)	Service salvers or service plates are used for five main purposes: to improve presentation of items to be served; to make carrying of bowl-shaped serving dishes easier and more secure (also avoids the thumb of the server being inside a service dish); to allow for more than one serving dish to be carried at a time; to isolate the hand from hot dishes; to allow service gear to be carried along with the item(s).

Hold flats, food dishes and round trays on the palm of the hand	This is safer and ensures that the food items are best presented for the customer. It also makes for easier carrying and avoids the server's thumb or service cloths being seen on the edge of flats, dishes and round trays. If the flats or dishes are hot then the service cloth can be underneath, folded and laid flat onto the palm to protect the hand.
Use doilies/dish papers on underplates (liners)	Doilies, dish papers (or linen or paper napkins) on underplates are used to improve presentation, to reduce noise and to prevent the dish from slipping on the underplate. Use doilies for sweet food items and dish papers for savoury food items.
Serve cold food before hot food	When the hot food is served the service is complete and customers can enjoy the meal without waiting for additional items to be served. For the same reason, accompaniments should be automatically offered and served at the same time as the food item.
Start service from the right-hand side of the host, with the host last	Honoured guests are usually seated on the right of a host. And are served first. The convention then is to serve a table by moving anti-clockwise for silver service, or clockwise for plated service, as this ensures that members of the serving staff are always walking forwards to serve the next person.
Serve women first	Often done if it does not slow the service. Particular care needs to be taken so as not to confuse things when the host is a woman. A host of either gender is still the host and should always be served last.
Silver serve food from the left-hand side of a customer	Ensures that the service dish is nearer the plate for ease of service and to prevent food being spilt onto the person. Customers can more easily see the food being served and make choices if necessary, and members of the service staff are also able to see and control what they are doing.
Serve plated foods from the right-hand side of a customer	Plates can be placed in front of the customer with the right hand and the stack of other plated food is then behind the customer's chair in the left hand. If there is an accident, the plates held in the left hand will go onto the floor rather than over the customer. Plated foods should be placed so that the food items are consistently in the same position for all customers.
Serve all beverages from the right-hand side of a customer	Glasses are placed on the right hand side of a cover and the service of beverages follows from this. For individual drinks and other beverages, the tray is held behind a customer's seat in the server's left hand. Other beverages such as coffee and tea are also served from the right. All beverages should also be cleared from the right.
Clear from the right-hand side of a customer	Plates can be removed from in front of the customer with the right hand and the stack of plates is then behind the customer's chair, in the server's left hand. If there is an accident, the plates held in the left hand will go onto the floor rather than over the customer. The exception to this is for side plates, which are on the left-hand side of the cover. These are more easily cleared from the left, thus avoiding stretching in front of the customer.
Use trays	Use trays to bring foods and beverage items to the service areas and to clear during and following service. Trays can be brought to, or removed from, sideboards or service tables and also to serve plated foods from (or to clear plates onto) with service staff working as a pair
Separate the serving at table from food/drink collection and sideboard/ workstation clearing	Ensures that there is always someone in the room to attend to customers and to monitor the overall service, while others are bringing in food and beverage orders or clearing items away from the service station. This approach also allows for the training of new staff and ensures that customer contact is primarily through experienced staff.

7

■ Billing

The various billing methods found in foodservice operations are as follows:

- **Bill as check**: second copy of order used as bill
- **Separate bill**: bill made up from duplicate check and presented to customer
- **Bill with order**: service to order and billing at same time, e.g. bar or takeaway methods
- **Prepaid**: customer purchases ticket or card in advance either for specific meal or specific value. This can also include pre-loaded cash balances onto cards that can also be topped up.
- **Voucher**: customer has credit issued by third party, e.g. tourist agency voucher for either specific meal or specific value
- **No charge**: customer not paying
- **Deferred**: refers to functions and events where bill paid by organiser.

The actual choice of billing method will be dependent on the type and style of the operation. However, the billing system is also part of a longer process linked first to the order-taking method and second to the revenue control procedures (see the notes on Revenue Control on page 192). In managing the billing method, it is necessary therefore to ensure that the method chosen supports both the order-taking method and the revenue control requirements. The range of acceptable payment methods, for example, needs to be predetermined, as well as the level of discretion, which is to be allowed to different individuals or groups of staff. Consideration also needs to be given to the use of electronic point of sale control (EPOS) systems.

■ Clearing

The various clearing methods found in foodservice operations may be summarised as follows:

- **Manual 1**: the collection of soiled ware by waiting staff to dishwash area
- **Manual 2**: the collection and sorting to trolleys by operators for transportation to dishwash area
- **Semi-self-clear**: the placing of soiled ware by customers on strategically placed trolleys within dining area for removal by operators
- **Self-clear**: the placing of soiled ware by customers on conveyor or conveyorised tray collecting system for mechanical transportation to dish wash area
- **Self-clear and strip**: the placing of soiled ware into conveyorised dishwash baskets by customer for direct entry of baskets through dishwash.

The choice of clearing method, whether manual by staff or involving customers, will be dependent not only on the type of operation but also on the nature of the demand being met. In captive situations, for instance, it is possible to have greater customer involvement.

■ Dishwashing

The capacity of the dishwashing system should always be greater than the operational maximum required. This is because slow dishwashing increases the amount of equipment required to be in use at a particular time and increases the storage space required in service areas.

The various dishwashing systems are as follows:

- **Manual**: the manual washing by hand or brush machine of soiled ware
- **Semi-automatic**: the manual loading by operators of dishwash machine
- **Automatic conveyor:** the manual loading by operators of soiled ware within baskets mounted on conveyor for automatic transportation through dishwash machine
- **Flight conveyor:** the manual loading by operators of soiled ware within pegs mounted on conveyor for automatic transportation through dishwasher.
- **Deferred wash:** the collection, stripping, sorting and stacking of ware by operators for transportation through dishwash at later stage.

Essentially, the potential volume that can be accommodated increases, as well as potential efficiency, from the manual method to the flight conveyor method, and the choice of method will be largely dependent on the scale of the operation. It is also often necessary to employ more than one method. The deferred wash system can be used as a cost-saving approach as wash-up staff do not have to be employed until the end of a service period especially when this is late at night.

■ Clearing following service

After the service periods, there are a variety of tasks and duties to be carried out partly to clear from the previous service and partly to prepare for the next. The efficient management of the clearing stage can have a dramatic impact on the potential reuse of an area.

Included in this stage of the service sequence is the requirement for the management of cleaning programmes. Detailed cleaning schedules need to be developed to ensure that all cleaning activities are coordinated. These can be daily, weekly, monthly and for other periods. Alongside these cleaning schedules, it is desirable to incorporate maintenance checks. These, together with the operation of cleaning schedules, can help to ensure that equipment and facilities are always available and in working order.

(More detailed information on the service sequence for differing service methods is set out in Lillicrap and Cousins, 2010.)

7.8   Revenue control

Revenue control encompasses the sale of all food and beverage and is essential to ensure maximum return. Particular attention must be paid to the key factors influencing profitability. Crucial controls have to be assigned for the main factors affecting the revenue of the business, such as the menu, wine list and other beverages, the total volume of food and beverage sales, the sales mix, the average spend of customers in each selling outlet at different times of the day, the number of covers served and the gross profit margins.

■   The control system

The revenue control system should be simple and manageable and ensure control:

- At all locations of the operation where selling takes places, and
- For all items internally issued from the various departments.

With the aims of:

- Reducing pilfering
- Eradicating wastage
- Protecting revenue.

The type of control system varies with the size of the foodservice operation. There needs to be accountability for what has been served to the customer and payment for what has been issued from the kitchen or the bar. Accurate billing should be standard and the outcome should be that the system can provide a detailed breakdown of sales and revenue sources in order that adjustments and improvements may be made.

The systems that are used to support the various order taking and billing methods (see pages 186 and 190 respectively) are summarised below:

- **Manual systems:** using hand-written duplicate or triplicate checks for ordering from kitchen and bar and for informing the cashier. Often used with a cash till or cash register. This system is found in many high class restaurants and in popular catering.
- **Pre-checking system:** orders are entered directly onto a keypad that then prints each order check with a duplicate and retains a record of all transactions. The keypad may be pre-set or pre-priced. This system may be found in many full-service restaurants and in popular catering.
- **Electronic cash registers:** allows for a wider range of functions including sales analysis. ECRs may be installed as standalone or linked systems. These systems are found in store restaurants, cafeterias and bars.
- **Point-of-sale control systems:** have separate keypad terminals in the various service areas, which are linked to remote printers or visual display units (VDUs)

in the kitchen, bar, etc. The terminals can be fixed or set in docking stations for hand-held use. In hotels, this equipment may also be linked to the hotel accounting systems. This system is also found in many modern restaurants.

- **Computerised systems:** enable a number of serving terminals, intelligent tills and remote printers to be controlled by a master unit compatible with standard computer hardware. Depending on software, the functions may also include a variety of performance measures such as planning and costing, sales analysis, gross profit reporting, stock control, re-ordering and forecasting, VAT returns, payroll, staff scheduling and account information. These systems are often found in hotels, fast food and chain restaurants.

- **Satellite stations:** remote terminals linked to a central processor to enable sales performance to be analysed (usually overnight) and reported back. These systems are found in fast food and chain restaurant operations.

All staff handling cash and other payment methods should be adequately trained in the policies of the operation and the procedures to be followed with the aim of ensuring that revenue security is efficiently carried out at all times.

The more sophisticated of the systems (point-of-sale, computerised and satellite) provide for increasingly efficient service at the point of sale, as well as improving the flow and quality of information to management for control purposes. The advantages vary from one system to another, but may be summarised as follows:

- **Fewer errors:** sales information entered will be more accurate because mistakes in the sequence of entries required for a particular transaction are not permitted. Automatic price look-up or pre-set keys are available rather than the potentially less reliable manual entry.

- **Faster processing:** transactions can be processed more quickly and this may be achieved by:
  - ☐ The automatic reading of price tags using a hand-held wand or moving the item over a fixed reader set in a counter top
  - ☐ Single key entry of prices, and
  - ☐ Eliminating any manual calculation or handwriting by the assistant

- **Training time**: may be reduced because many systems have a sequencing feature, which takes the user through each transaction step by step, giving instructions on a VDU.

- **Instant credit checking:** a customer's credit rating can be checked by having terminals compare the account number with a central computer file or through online connections to debit and credit card providers.

- **Detailed management information:** electronic systems provide more direct information, which improves both the detail and quality of computerised stock control and accounting systems and also makes them more economic for relatively small establishments.

- **Additional security features:** includes such things as:

☐ Locks which permit the ECR to be operated only by authorised personnel and totals that can only be altered and reset by supervisors and managers, and

☐ Not disclosing at the end of the day the sum of the receipts that should be accounted for.

■ **Advanced calculating facilities:** systems can be programmed to calculate the total price when a number of items of the same price are purchased, there are a number of items at various prices or if VAT has to be added.

■ **Improved printouts:** in terms of quality and the amount of information contained on the customer's receipt. This may also include facilities where:

☐ Receipts may be overprinted with sales and VAT

☐ Both alphabetic and numeric information can be presented in black and white or colours, and

☐ The receipt can contain the names of the goods purchased as well as, or instead of, a simple reference number.

■ **Improved appearance:** modern systems are styled to fit in with the décor of present-day foodservice environments.

Individual foodservice operators will determine which system best suits their needs and gives them the information they require. Whatever revenue control system is used, it should be able to generate information for a variety of performance measures. These include:

■ Reconciliation of total payments against orders served

■ Average spend per head on food or beverages

■ Average bill

■ Sales mix data

■ Payment method breakdowns

■ Seat turnover – the number of times a seat is used in a service period

■ Sales per member of service staff

■ Sales per period – can be monitored on an hourly basis such as in fastfood operations or in bar operations

■ Sales per seat

■ Sales per square metre or square foot.

The nature of, and the relationship between, revenue, costs and profits are explored in detail in Chapter 9 together with an examination of the various performance measures. Operational and financial ratios are detailed in Appendix B.

■ Common malpractices

Although the aim of control systems is often to completely eliminate dishonesty, this cannot always be achieved. But the control systems can make it much more difficult. When designing control systems it is worth investigating possible malpractices. Some of the common ones are listed in Table 7.8 together with advice on detection and also a rating of the difficulty of detection: rated 1–3 with three being the hardest to detect.

Table 7.8: Examples of common malpractices in food and beverage operations

Malpractice	Detection	Rating
Dilution of liquor	A hydrometer will detect dilution, but a control test should also be performed from a new bottle as air temperature can affect the result. However this test is easy to make.	1
Short measures	Cocktails and other mixed beverages are vulnerable here. Can be detected by Protective Services, (Weights and Measures) Agents. Usually signalled by a complaint.	3
Overcharging of customers	Not easily checked in a busy bar or restaurant. If done frequently enough, the thief can end up with spare bottles or other items of unrecorded stock. Nowadays a receipt should always be proffered.	2
Undercharging of friends	Not easily checked in a busy bar or restaurant. If this appears to be taking place a careful watch is necessitated. General control procedures should detect this with checking systems and under due diligence a camera can be focused on cash registers.	3
Management pilferage	Difficult to detect as management have greater freedom of access. Missing produce/product can be written off as waste without ever being detected as pilferage. All management should have ledger accounts for all entertaining, comping and writing off. The existence of this type of control provides for open identification of potential abuse.	3
Kickbacks to managers	Here it is necessary to know what was purchased know what was bought, etc. Suppliers can make kickbacks directly to manager(s) ensuring their product is adopted above others. Free products, which could reduce operational costs, may be kept as incentive for buying goods from one supplier over another. Goods offered as 'incentive' may never actually arrive at the property and may be delivered to the member of staff or manager's home address. Kickbacks are always brought to light by lengthy and in-depth analysis.	3
Part-time banqueting personnel removing food, beverages and light equipment from the establishment	Utilise establishment security personnel to have a high profile presence and randomly search personnel. Provide clear polythene bags for all personal items brought into the premises, so as to be able to recognise the content on exiting the premises. In banqueting, for example, agreed limits of an average of 1/2 bottle per guest can still lead to whole bottles being misappropriated or creamed off the top. Corks could be counted back, although corks can also be stored and brought into the premises. Again, vigilance is important.	3

7

Cellar/stores personnel	Items can be booked out to bars and not be delivered. In this case they are lost at cost price. The blame can later be placed on the bars as having lost the items. Small and large amounts of food can also be lost through selling on to staff or others. Goods can be ordered as kickbacks and never recorded. Good control procedures should be able to detect this over time.	2
Cash registers taken off line	A register or point-of-sale machine may be taken off line, and assigned to only a couple of personnel to use it. The server's sales can be tracked off line, albeit the machine is still tied into remote kitchen printers. Sales are recorded separately and the proceeds stolen by the member of staff or manager. This individual can make the adjustments the next day or at close of shift. Good control procedures and random checks can detect this over time.	2
Complimentary meals	Managers can void bills by using their management keys on point-of-sales machines. They can also give complimentary meals – often called 'comping'. Transactions can be voided or recorded as complimentary and the revenue stolen by the Manager. See possible approach to control under management pilferage above.	2
Utilising differentiated gross profit percentages	Items can be recorded as being sold in a department where the gross profit is lower than the department where the items are actually sold. E.g. optic liquor as off-licence liquor sales. Can be detected over time through control procedures and by examining sales patterns for anomalies.	3

Information on possible malpractices should also be shared through trade and professional association meetings so that up-to-date knowledge of potential malpractices can be obtained and monitored.

8 Events, conferencing and banqueting

Aim

This chapter aims to provide a critical overview of the management and control of event operations.

Objectives

This chapter is intended to support you in:

- Determining the size and scope of the events industry
- Identifying the opportunities and challenges for operators
- Maximising yield and profit through the application of strategic techniques
- Identifying key organisational and staffing issues for events
- Managing the event process.

8.1   Overview and structure of the events sector

An event is the planned management of an occasion that takes place between a space provider and a customer. The sector is commonly referred to as MICE (Meetings, Incentives, Conferences and Exhibitions) but other names used can include catering, events, conferences and banqueting. A list of event categories and examples is given in Table 8.1.

Table 8.1: Event categories and examples

Event catagory	Examples
Personal	Weddings, bar mitzvahs, anniversaries, birthdays
Local	Village fairs, community quiz nights, local drama clubs
Commercial	Conferences, exhibitions, trade shows, product launches
Fairs/festivals	Book fairs, carnivals
Public	Festivals, exhibitions, concerts, galas
Civic	Anzac Day celebrations
Special	National Day celebrations, cultural performances
Expositions	World Trade Expo, boat shows
Sporting	Dubai tennis open, Singapore grand prix
Global	Royal weddings, Live Aid
Mega/hallmark	Olympic, Paralympic Games and FIFA World Cup

In most cases the sector can be divided into two main groupings, conference and banqueting. Conference events focus on providing space for more formal business activities, whereas banquet events concentrate on activities for clients who wish to celebrate an occasion. Table 8.2 presents a comparison between the two types of event group and their characteristics. A more extensive description of event types is presented in Table 8.3.

Table 8.2: Comparison of conference and banqueting characteristics

Conference	Banqueting
Focus on conducting business or training	Focus on celebration and enjoyment
Emphasis on equipment and technology	Emphasis on food and beverage
Attendees tend to be from outside local area	Attendees tend to be from local vicinity
Lower staff to customer ratio	Higher staff to customer ratio
Booking lead times tend to be shorter	Booking lead times tend to be longer
Greater demand for accommodation	Less demand for accommodation
Duration can last from half a day to one week	Duration tends to last hours
Events tend to be less seasonal	Events tend to be more seasonal

Table 8.3: Examples of event types

Type	Description
Congress	Large assembly of individuals to convene or discuss business, culture, religion or another topic.
Exhibition/ trade fair	Large event attracting thousands of people. Targeting or promoting a specific sector of industry or consumer. Usually run over several days and can be open to the public, specify consumers only, or trade only.
Forum	Group of individuals discussing a specific topic or theme which in most cases would be led by a host who would channel discussions between a panel and the audience. Often held in an auditorium with microphones being moved around by assistants for the audience to ask questions.
Interview	Small meeting which maybe an employment or appraisal interview.
Lecture	Delivered by an expert to a large audience from a podium with the use of audio-visual equipment. Usually theatre style seating.
Meeting	A general term for a get-together of individuals with a common purpose.
Retreat	Normally in an out-of-town location and is organised by companies or associations for employees or members to meet for the purpose of team building, training, coaching or personal development.
Road show	Businesses or organisations delivering a series of presentations in multiple locations for the purpose of promoting and selling products or services.
Seminar	Similar to lecture but for smaller groups who actively participate on a particular theme or topic being explored. Interaction is the main objective of most seminars. Can also be part of a series located at different venues.
Workshop	Small groups are divided and work on specific problems, challenges or case studies.
Off-premises events	Off-premises events are delivered in another location away from the home base of the main business. These can be large of small events. Good logistical planning is essential and include activities such as: • Visit the site first and check the layout, design and access • Consider equipment, transport, fuel, water, holding equipment • Evaluate what utilities are available • If the event is outside have a backup plan in case of bad weather • Obtain insurance, licences and equipment • Draw up a plan of operations – what you need and when you need it.

8

Events can be provided either on or off the premises. On premise is where the event is held on the physical premises of the establishment or facility producing and serving the function. With off-premises, or outside catering, refers to food, beverage, equipment and servers being transported to a location such as offices, homes, boats or open spaces, etc. The event planner may provide anything from canapés and champagne for a product launch to sit down banquets.

■ Size and scope of the industry

The events industry is a truly global industry with events being held each day around the world. Many major cities now feature large-scale conference and exhibition centres that host numerous events attracting local and international delegates. Events provide many benefits for destinations, which may include tourism, employment opportunities, publicity and financial growth. Table 8.4 shows top ranking countries for hosting meetings.

Table 8.4: Ranking for top international meeting countries in 2001

	Country	Number of meetings	Percentage of all meetings (%)
1	USA	1195	12.91
2	UK	615	6.64
3	France	600	6.48
4	Germany	544	5.88
5	Italy	414	4.47
6	Spain	340	3.67
7	Belgium	317	3.42
8	Australia	308	3.33
9	Netherlands	293	3.16
10	Switzerland	240	2.59
11	Austria	231	2.49
12	Japan	215	2.32
13	Canada	208	2.25
14	Sweden	194	2.10
15	Finland	184	1.99
16	China and Hong Kong	159	1.72
17	Denmark	152	1.64
18	South Korea	134	1.45
19	Singapore	120	1.30
20	Portugal	116	1.25
21	Greece	110	1.19
21	Norway	110	1.19
23	Poland	105	1.13
24	Hungary	99	1.07
25	South Africa	95	1.03

Source: Rogers, 2003

Examples of venues where events can be hosted include hotel function rooms, conference centres, community centres, restaurants, bars, church halls, academic institutions and community centres. The majority of space is multifunctional so can be used to accommodate different types of events. In most cases the venue will be responsible for the planning and delivery of the event. However, events can also be organised by event management companies (EMCs) or contract caterers. Bowdin *et al.* (2006) state: 'Event Management companies are professional groups or individuals that organize events on a contract basis on behalf of their clients'. Some of the services provided by event management companies include:

- Concept development
- Planning the event theme and decor
- Marketing and advertising
- Ticketing
- Screening venues
- Risk assessment
- Contracting entertainers, speakers and other artists
- Dealing with caterers.

Appraisal of event management

There are many benefits for hospitality operators in hosting events, examples include:

- Better utilisation of space and resources
- Flexible options for space
- Potential to capitalise on annual and local events
- Showcase facilities to large numbers with potential for return business
- Additional revenue streams
- Greater opportunity to achieve customer satisfaction as pre-booked and there-fore less opportunity for errors
- Savings through bulk food and beverage purchasing
- Less food waste due to fixed menu and numbers, and
- Reduced labour cost through using high quantity of part-time staff.

In addition to the many benefits of hosting events there are also challenges. Table 8.5 highlights some of these challenges and also provides potential solutions of how they may be managed.

Many hotel operations feature both restaurant and event space on the same premises. Table 8.6 presents a contrast of these two types of operation highlighting the impacts both can have on organisational profit. This table also indicates that event operations tend to yield more profit than restaurant operations.

Table 8.5: Hosting events: examples of challenges and potential solutions

Challenges	Potential solutions
Highly perishable product with pressure to fill space daily (for definition of perishability see Chapter 1, page 8)	Seek to maximise space utilisation through well-developed sales strategies and effective sales team
Competitive with many venue options	Conduct competitor analysis and differentiate
Large quantities of inventory and equipment to manage	Develop service standards, control, consider outsourcing equipment to reduce liabilities
Difficult to manage expectations of large numbers of customers	Conduct primary and secondary research with target markets to better meet their needs
Large events creates a challenge to manage satisfaction of all guests	Develop and implement quality controls, monitor customer satisfaction throughout
Often dependent on large quantities of casual labour	Selecting the right external agency, set strict criteria for casuals, develop close-knit team, induction and training 'treat as full-timers' (see also Table 8.11)
Heavily reliant on AV technology as part of event	Outsource audiovisual (AV) provision an support to third-party specialist also providing technical support
Many stakeholders in process	Select partners carefully, build relationships and treat well

Table 8.6: Contrast of restaurant and event operations

Restaurants	Events
Extensive list of menu items	Limited set menu
Uncertainty about which menu items will be selected	Minimal uncertainty – normally fixed menu
In most cases uncertainty about definite numbers that will visit restaurant	Minimal uncertainty – final numbers in most cases confirmed before event
Uncertainty about what time customers will arrive therefore difficult to schedule resources and staffing	Minimal uncertainty – customers arrive at prearranged time allowing better planning
Potential for food wastage due to difficulty in forecasting sales	Minimal food wastage as catered to confirmed numbers
Food production to consumption times shorter reducing time for quality control	Times longer allowing for a higher degree of quality control (e.g. cook–chill, cook–freeze)
Focus on fresh ingredients and which makes bulk ordering a challenge	Large customer numbers allow potential for bulk ordering and financial savings
Booking lead time times (if any) is shorter	Lead time is longer allowing for greater preparation of product and service
Difficult to practise yield management	Easier to practise yield management
Greater dependence on weather patterns	Less dependence on weather patterns
Simultaneous production/consumption provides challenges to standardise	Greater standardisation of product therefore less room for error
Combination of full and part-time labour	High percentage of part-time casual labour

8.2 Sales and marketing

Event space can range from a small social space in a church hall to a grand ball-room in a luxury hotel. Whatever the size of space it is a cost, and when it is not occupied it becomes an expense. It is therefore essential that event operators put in place clear strategies to ensure event space is sold as often as possible, achieving the greatest profit per square foot. Examples of some sales maximisation activities may include:

■ Marketing of venue to different customer segments
■ Maximising distribution channels and intermediaries
■ Effective sales teams
■ Event sales strategies.

■ Marketing of venue to different customer segments

Event operators have a diverse range of customer segments that they can target to fill their space. Table 8.7 shows a range of these segments and some of the potential opportunities they provide for venues.

Table 8.7: Examples of event segmentation

Segment or market	Opportunities
In-house customers	Customers visiting a hotel or other venue for another purpose should be made aware of event facilities available
Local businesses	Local businesses with no event facilities may require space for events
Local area residents	Local residents provide opportunities to cater for personal functions such as birthday parties, anniversaries and family get-togethers
Corporate companies	Large corporate companies often require space for business meetings, product launches and promotions and social functions
Charities or non-profit organisations	Providing event facilities to these organisations during low-demand periods can assist in raising the profile and image of the business
SMERF groups	Social, military, educational, religious and fraternal groups tend to be more price-sensitive, which can provide opportunities to sell event space during low-demand periods
Associations market	Many associations require event facilities to host meetings and other events
Incentives market	Incentives are in most cases organised by corporate companies to reward their employees who have achieved goals and sales targets
Exhibitions market	Generates revenue for hotels in terms of venue hire for using the function space and also potential to see accommodation and food and beverage services

8

■   Maximising distribution channels and intermediaries

Event operators can use a variety of intermediaries and distribution channels to maximise sales. Table 8.8 describes some examples of these channels.

Table 8.8: Examples of intermediaries and distribution channels

Example	Description
Company or department web pages	Allow clients to view details, availability and also has the potential for booking event rooms directly through on-line booking systems.
Central reservations system (CRS)	Some large hotel chains, where event revenues account for a large proportion of the total business, now operate a central reservations system solely for event reservations.
Event/meeting planners	Independent event management companies: either undertaking all of the organisation for a client or working on a commission basis, promoting specific venus and other services.
Destination management companies (DMC)	DMCs manage events (from small meetings to large incentive groups) on behalf of their clients. Hotels offer through commission on sales of accommodation and food and beverage, as incentives for the DMC to promote the hotel.
Convention bureaus	Bureaus promote the destination rather than the hotel. In most cases they send international leads for conventions/exhibitions/conference to hotel partners, e.g. the Dubai Convention Bureau.
Web-based software for meeting/events	Examples of these companies include Starcite, Cvent, and HotelPlanner. They are used by meeting planners to send proposals to hotels and other venus.

■   Effective sales teams

Different organisations will have different structures in relation to their sales teams. Smaller operations may just have co-ordinators who deal with incoming enquiries, whereas larger organisations will have larger teams with responsibility for different segments. What is important in a competitive marketplace is that sales should be proactive with sales personnel being allocated specific targets, given the right training and tools to meet these targets and monitored closely. It has the potential to achieve good results and sales incentives can be provided and rewarded accordingly. Sales personnel could be evaluated on the following criteria:

■ Number of telephone calls made, prospects or leads

■ Number of appointments, presentations or show-rounds made

■ Through appointments, presentations or show-rounds, what was the amount of revenue generated through these conversions.

■   Event sales strategies

Due to the competitive nature of the sector, various techniques are recommended to fill conference and banquet space achieving the greatest financial return. Some approaches may include:

- Utilising efficient event-booking software
- Applying effective sales techniques
- Creating venue generated events
- Developing high quality event collateral.

Event booking software

It is not sufficient to fill the event space with any customer, but to fill it with the right customer at the right price at the right time. In venues with large conference facilities a yield management technique is used to ensure the best financial return is achieved per room, per day. This is done with the use of automated room booking software (an example screenshot is shown in Figure 8.1). In addition, these systems can provide the venue with up-to-date information on function room availability, usage statistics, daily forecasts, actual yield per each event and room set-up configurations.

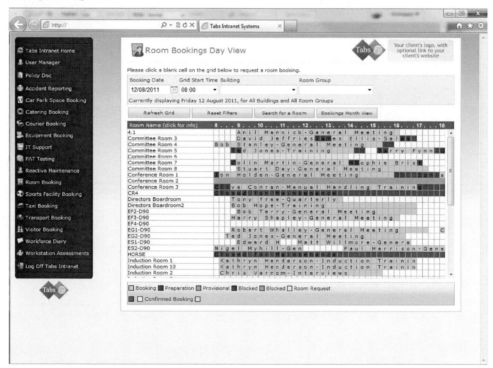

Figure 8.1: Example of automated room booking system (image courtesy of TabsFM)

Sales techniques

For those operations aiming to achieve a maximum yield on event bookings, Table 8.9 provides a list of possible techniques that can be adopted.

Table 8.9: Examples of event sales activities

Sales technique	Rationale
Forecasting high and low demand days for events throughout the year	Essential to be aware of when demand is high or low so that operators to set rates based on supply and demand and achieve the greatest yield per event booking.
Maintaining reservation records	Including records of booking enquiries, type of requests, cancellations, rejections and refusals. This can assist in budgeting and determining customer needs and potential demand for the next year.
Maintain past history records	Including booking behaviour, consumption preferences, delegate pick-up and shortages. This provides a more accurate estimate of their real potential when dealing with repeat bookings in the future.
Forecasting net yield per event booking	For operations with bedroom accommodation, when accepting event bookings consideration should also be give to potential for additional spend on food and beverage and room accommodation.
Booking pattern awareness	Keeping abreast of event booking patterns of target segments and market can assist operators to adjust marking approaches accordingly.
Future bookings	Operators should avoid confirming final details of bookings too far in advance as external changes can take place that could impact supply or demand, resulting in changes to costs.
Cancellations	Ensure cancellation procedures and controls are in place, including clear cancellation penalties.
Commissions for intermediaries	Consider methods of bookings and commissions paid to agents. Net yielded profit should always be calculated when dealing with intermediaries with the projected revenue minus fee.

Table 8.9 also indicates that it is important for event operators to be aware of high and low event demand days throughout the year as different approaches are needed at different times. Some high demand periods for event operators may include:

- Weddings and other social occasions
- National and religious holidays
- Annual cultural events
- End of financial year.

When demand is **high** for events, operations should not consider:

- Accepting subsidised corporate account bookings
- Accepting bookings from low income groups or segments
- Offering discounts or promotions
- Providing any complimentary products or services
- Having any out of order rooms or refurbishments.

When demand is **low** for events, operations should consider:

- Offering discounts and introduce promotions

- Never denying a booking if possible and be prepared to negotiate if necessary
- Creating venue generated events
- Providing upgrades
- Providing incentives for employees to maximise spend per head using positive selling techniques
- Providing familiarisation trips for potential clients
- Carrying out internal quality audits
- Carrying out deep cleaning and routine maintenance.

In addition, other potential ideas to fill event space may include:

- During period of low demand, operators consider giving some space free to local communities. This could be an excellent way to introduce the facilities, provide good will, network with local business and provides the potential to secure future event bookings.
- Consider making the event venue 'more green' in its operation and develop a corporate social responsibility (CSR) policy. This can then be built into marketing literature and appeal to more 'greener' customer segments.
- E-mail alerts at beginning of week to regular customers informing of room availability.
- When hosting residential conferences and exhibitions encourage and provide incentives for delegates to bring spouse or partners. This can result in additional spend by the partners in other outlets within the venue.
- Consider the impact of letting out large meeting rooms too far in advance for non-bedroom-related business as this may then turn away more lucrative residential business nearer the time.
- Develop ways how to reward loyal customers in a competitive marketplace. Complimentary accommodation, refreshments or gifts can make a difference.
- Consider how to embrace new media technology to promote the venue and communicate to existing and potential customers (see also Chapter 3, Table 3.3, page 70).

Creating venue generated events

When event operators are faced with the challenge of having few bookings and empty capacity, they may attempt to create demand through developing own generated events. Event managers should create ideas that can be developed into own events. The following questions may be considered when generating ideas for creating events:

- What is the event?
- Who is it targeting?
- How the target audience will be reached?
- What costs are involved?

- What are the forecasted revenues and potential profits?
- How it will be evaluated?

Some ideas for own events may include wedding fairs, themed nights, guest speakers, wine clubs and tastings and cookery demonstrations. Figure 8.2 provides an example of the process for developing venue-generated events from idea to sale.

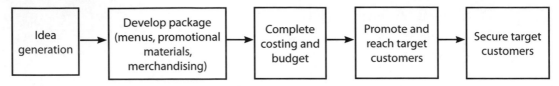

Figure 8.2: Venue generated events: the process

Event collateral

Marketing brochures are commonly used as a tool to advertise and promote the event facilities. These brochures can either be printed in the form of a folder, glossy flyer, supplied electronically on a compact disc or downloaded direct from the company website. The marketing information could include:

- Logo of venue or establishment
- Contact information (e.g. address, telephone, e-mail, website, Facebook or Twitter address).
- Geographic map of location with road, rail and other transport links
- An introduction to the venue (e.g. history, setting, atmosphere)
- Floor plans or blueprints of rooms detailing dimensions
- Details of different room set-up configurations, with numbers accommodated in various styles
- Professional photographs showcasing different events catered
- List of products and services offered (e.g. bedroom accommodation, car parking, leisure club, 24-hour security)
- Unique selling points of venue (e.g. award-winning chefs, professional service team, largest room in area, high-tech audio visual equipment, environmentally aware)
- Testimonials from satisfied customers and companies
- Examples of a range of menus for different events and prices
- Residential and non-residential delegate packages
- Prices of rooms and accommodation
- Classifications, star rating and awards.

■   Outsourcing and events

In the planning, preparation and delivery of the event, venues often need to outsource services and products with many different third parties to make the event a success. This may be done for several reasons including

- The venue prefers to outsource that specific product or service due to its specialisation, cost or convenience
- The customer has requested a specific external company to deliver a particular product or service, or
- The venue does not provide the particular product or service so needs to outsource.

Examples of third parties include suppliers of:

- Staffing
- Audio visual and lighting equipment
- Furniture (tables, chairs, dance floors)
- Decoration
- Marquees
- Linen
- Staffing (waiters, bar staff, chefs, toastmaster)
- Entertainers (disc jockeys, musicians, croupiers, children's entertainers)
- Professional caterers (for example kosher or halal caterers)
- Interpreters
- Transportation providers.

The outsourcing of services and products is a growing trend within hospitality. Some of the drivers of outsourcing are:

- Poor job markets
- Pressure to reduce costs
- Greater demand for quality
- Greater competition
- Fast growth of information technology.

Outsourcing of services is now being considered as a strategic move by organisations as it allows for greater specialisation, the ability to focus on core product and subsequently gain a competitive advantage.

8

8.3   Staffing considerations

The organisational structure of event operations can differ depending on:

■ Size of event operation

■ Sales turnover

■ Standards

■ Management structure

■ Geographic location of operation.

As events can be hosted in many different venues the internal structures can vary from a large sophisticated structure in a conference centre to a restaurant owner hosting an event in a small independent pizzeria. Regardless the structure, some of the main skills and qualities for any operator hosting an event are:

■ Welcoming and friendly approach

■ Good personal presentation

■ Flexibility in accommodating customers' needs

■ Ability to sell products and services to add value to the event

■ Planning and co-ordination skills

■ Visible to staff and existing and potential clients

■ Hard working and creative.

A typical conference and banqueting operation in a four-star hotel is detailed in Figure 8.3. Table 8.10 then details some examples of the key positions and highlights some of their main responsibilities.

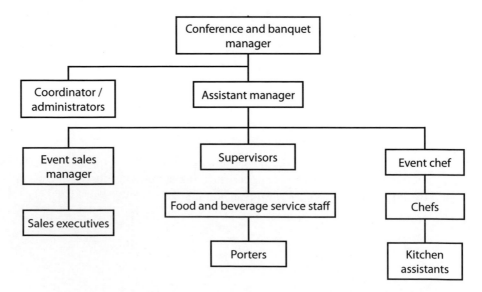

Figure 8.3: Example of organisational chart for conference and banquet department in a four-star hotel

Table 8.10: Examples of event staffing and responsibilities

Role	Responsibilities
Chef	Discuss event menu options with customers, create menus, food preparation and production
Supervisor	Oversee and supervise events, train employees, book casual employees, manage stocks, manage customers' expectations, monitor departmental performance standards
Sales manager	Create sales and marketing plan for events department, monitor the external environment, implement and monitor marketing plan, manage the sales and marketing team, set sales executives' targets and ensure maximum function room occupancy and rates are achieved, conduct market research within marketplace, develop promotions to increase demand
Sales executive	Conduct sales calls with event clients and prospects, make presentations, conduct show-rounds and follow up leads with prospects
Event coordinator	Take reservations and maintain the events diary, send out event brochures or CDs, create contracts and event order, liaise with departments when planning events
Servers	Set up events and carry out preparation tasks, serve customers, attend to customers' needs, break down rooms
Bar staff	Requisition beverages, carry out preparation tasks, serve customers, complete payment transactions if cash bar is operating
Porters	Transport and set up furniture and equipment, assist event servers, break down rooms, general cleaning

Agency staff

As the demand for events is very variable, it is common for event operators to use agency personnel as and when required. This allows for greater flexibility when staffing events and brings subsequent labour savings. However, when using large quantities of casual labour it can also create challenges in their management. Table 8.11 details some of the potential challenges when using casual labour, also some impacts, solutions and suggestions on how to manage them.

Table 8.11: Casual event personnel: potential challenges, impacts and solutions

Challenges	Potential impacts	Potential solutions
Many casual staff are transient and may not have the right skills	Service errors More responsibility on venue to train More monitoring required Greater potential for customer complaints	Provide job descriptions to agencies Consider using students from local hospitality schools, colleges or universities Inductions, training and detailed briefings
Different staff are supplied for events	Staff not aware of required standards Service inconsistencies More training required by venue Lack of team harmony Difficult to form a team	Try to use the same personnel each time, this will assist in building a team and greater efficiency will be achieved Provide standards of performance to agency to ensure the training of personnel. Only when potential staff demonstrated the required competence should they be supplied to venue.

In event operations that use a large proportion of casual personnel, it is also good practice in the event of an emergency to have a team of personnel from other departments who are trained in basic customer service and food and beverage service skills to assist as and when required.

(For more information on staffing considerations generally see Chapter 4 and Lillicrap and Cousins (2010) Chapter 11, Events.)

8.4   Managing the event process

As detailed by Getz (2007) all events, by definition, have a beginning and an end. With each event, be it small or large, it is recommended that operators follow a series of key steps to ensure the event runs efficiently and profitably. This can be brought together in the event process as shown in Figure 8.4. The event process can be divided into three main stages that include the pre-event, event and post-event. Each of the three stages comprises of a set of tasks to ensure a successful event is achieved. At each stage, event operators must put in place standards to ensure that both financial and quality control is achieved.

Stage	Task
Pre-event	1 Customer enquiry
	2 Event proposal
	3 Event contract
	4 Event order
Event	5 Event set-up
	6 Event quality
	7 Team briefing
	8 Customer welcome and service
Post-event	9 Event break-down
	10 Event billing
	11 Event evaluation

Figure 8.4: The event process

■   Pre-event

1 Customer enquiry

The enquiry is the initial stage of the event process. Prospective customers who require a venue for an event would in the first instance contact the venue by either telephone or e-mail. Most enquiries would be dealt with by an individual in the events office, or by the manager if a smaller independent operation. It is good practice for customers to have one point of contact from first visit through to the end of the event. This way, the communication between customer and event planner is enhanced. If the customer is dealing with different personnel throughout, miscommunication, delays and frustration may take place leading to dissatisfaction. As this may be the first impression, it is imperative that a friendly, professional and helpful image is conveyed from the start. When enquiries are received the initial details required by the venue from the prospect would be type of event, date/s required and numbers attending. On obtaining this information the staff member would then be able to determine if they can help the prospect with their enquiry. Most event offices would use a diary, usually computer based, to keep track of room bookings and availability throughout the year. Enquiries can be received from either intermediaries, prospective first time customers or returning customers. For examples of where potential enquiries may originate see Table 8.7.

Site visit

If the caller is a first-time customer and is local, it is good practice to invite them to the venue, as this is an opportunity to:

- Showcase the facilities
- Establish their specific needs for the event
- Recommend products and services.

When there are geographic restrictions and the customer is not able to view the venue they would in most cases be directed to the venues website or sent marketing information with all the particular details (see *Event marketing collateral*, page 208).

Showcase facilities

As many cities have several venues offering event facilities it is imperative that the appointment is well planned and executed. Where possible it is good to invite the prospect into the venue when rooms are already set up as this allows them to get a better picture of the products and services available. Some event operations make it a standard to always have rooms set up for any viewings that may take place and that prospects, where possible, should never been shown empty rooms. Furthermore, if an appointment is made every effort should be taken to ensure the rooms and surrounding facilities are clean and well presented. Poorly presented facilities can turn off prospects; therefore, it must be seen as a sales opportunity right from the start. If the venue is a smaller operation, photographs of past events can be a good way of displaying the type of events that can be delivered. Other more modern approaches being used to showcase facilities include websites, electronic presentations and iPad type devices.

Establish the specific needs for the event

Be it over the telephone or during a visit, event staff members are required to ask many questions to obtain all the details and requirements for the event. To

8

ensure that no question is forgotten, many establishments use a checklist or event booking form. Examples of details on a checklist may include:

- Organisers contact details (telephone, mobile, e-mail), also Facebook and Twitter in some cases
- Type of event (conference, workshop, wedding reception, anniversary dinner)
- Theme (if any)
- Information on attendees (e.g. quantity, age, children)
- Food requirements (e.g. breakfast, lunch, dinner, snacks)
- Food service method (e.g. silver service, buffet, cocktail, family service)
- Beverage requirements (e.g. cash bar, host bar, wines, liqueurs)
- Chronology of events and timings (e.g. arrival, breaks, meal times, speeches, departure)
- Room set-up style (e.g. classroom, theatre, cocktail, banquet)
- Audio and visual requirements (e.g. projector, microphone, speaker, handheld PowerPoint presenter (controller) or laser pointer)
- Telecommunication requirements (e.g. provision of Wi-Fi, telephones)
- Equipment (e.g. staging, lighting, dance floor, podium)
- Decoration (e.g. linen, flowers, red carpet)
- Financial (e.g. customer's budget, deposit, payment method)
- Accommodation (e.g. room bookings, complimentary rooms)
- Other (e.g. car parking requirements, disability, food allergies, deliveries, table plans, VIPs).

Recommend products and services

Another role during this enquiry stage is to recommend services and products that would add value to the customer's event. The staff member dealing with the enquiry should have a good knowledge of all services available and be able to advise, guide and up-sell whenever appropriate. Should a site visit take place it is good to involve key employees in the discussions. For example, if a customer is discussing the menu for a wedding, having a senior chef available to suggest and advise would be very helpful. During the enquiry a current trend is to become more client centric providing customers with exactly what they want from food to layout. Traditional marketing approaches tend to overload prospective customers with menus and packages. This has the potential to narrow the potential offer available to the customer and leaves little room for flexibility and scope.

Often a key requirement for even organisers is to be able to provide advice on event organisation, etiquette, order of precedence and standard customs and procedures. Publications such as the various Debrett guides are a valuable resource for venues. For more information see: *Debrett's Correct Form* (2010), *Debrett's Wedding Guide* (2007), *Debrett's New Guide to Etiquette and Modern Manners* (1999).

2 Event proposal

When all the information for the event has been gathered, the venue will create an event proposal to be sent to the client. The proposal will present a complete breakdown of how the event will run and the proposed charge of the event. It is common for clients to obtain several proposals from different venues to compare and contrast to get the best value. It is therefore essential that the proposal is prepared promptly, professionally and is competitively priced. A few days after sending out the event proposal the venue should conduct a follow-up phone call to discuss and finalise the proposal with the client. It is common at this stage to change arrangements to suit the client and the final charge may also be negotiated and confirmed. It is the objective of the event planner at this time to close the sale and create an event contract.

3 Event contract

The contract is the formal agreement between the event planner and the client. The contract will state the event details, prices, deposits, terms and conditions, responsibilities and legal clauses. Two copies of the contract would in most cases be created which both the venue and the customer will sign. Once the signed contract has been received from the client an event order will then be created.

4 Event order

The event order is an internal document and its purpose is to communicate details of the forthcoming event to the various internal parties, departments or personnel within the venue. The event order is prepared by the event coordinator and would be circulated, prior to the date of the event, to the different departments within the venue for their action or information. The different departmental managers are then required to familiarise themselves and their teams with the event and action any specific details relating to their department. For example, if a particular wine is required for a forthcoming event, then the stores would order accordingly. Examples of departments that may receive a copy of the event order may include kitchen, restaurants, bar, stores, reception, maintenance, housekeeping and finance. For event operators that have events taking place most days, it is good practice to hold weekly meetings to run through the event orders for the forthcoming week. These meetings should consist of key staff members involved in the preparation and running of the events such as the event coordinator, events manager, supervisors and a senior chef. The purpose of the meeting is to finalise arrangements, check progress, identify any concerns, resolve problems, and identify areas overlooked and action points. As illustrated in Figure 8.5 the event order is a detailed breakdown of the event, what is happening, how and when.

8

Date: Tuesday 16 August 2011	**Customer**: Regency Electronics *SAMPLE*
Event Type: Meeting	**Contact Details**: Miss Julie Parsons
Time: 9am – 5pm	**Telephone**: xxx xxxx xxxx **Fax**: xxx xxxx xxxx **Email**: Julie.parsons@xxxxx.com
Numbers: 120 Persons	

Timings	Lunch menu	Room set-up and equipment
9.00 – 9.15 – Coffee/tea on Arrival 11.00 – 11.15 – Coffee/tea break with Pastries 1.pm - Lunch in Restaurant 3.00pm – 3.20pm – Afternoon Tea 5.30pm - Finish	Carrot and Herb Soup Chicken Filet with Broccoli and Sweetcorn in a Mushroom Sauce Selection of Desserts from Buffet Tea or Coffee	Theatre style with top table for 3 persons Data Projector and PC Table Microphone and Speakers TV and CD Player 3 Flip Charts with Paper & Pens

Other Details

Reception: Event to go on lobby notice Board

No seating plan for lunch – Plate service

1 guest in wheelchair who will need assistance on arrival

Water cooler dispenser to be switched on and water levels monitored during the event

Figure 8.5: Example of an event order

■   The event

5 Event set-up

Each event needs to be set up for the event to take place. Some events are small and require minimal preparation however, some events are larger, for example a wedding which requires meticulous pre-planning to ensure all the preparations are achieved within the deadline. For larger events, a project management or 'base plan' approach is an effective way of meeting the set-up objectives. Tasks are broken down into smaller chunks, allocated a time for completion and put in the correct order of priority. Another method is to have a countdown plan which details what tasks are required to be carried out, by whom, each day counting down to the event. These methods would be used as management tools to brief service personnel beforehand and to delegate tasks accordingly. It is the supervisor's responsibility to ensure that all tasks are achieved in the right time and as requested. In addition, for large events pre-developed checklists are a good way of ensuring that all tasks have been completed and nothing has been forgotten. For example, forgetting to place champagne in the refrigerator for a large event could be disastrous. Whatever method is adopted good planning is essential. As presented in Figure 8.6, Gantt charts provide a visual presentation of the different timings of different tasks.

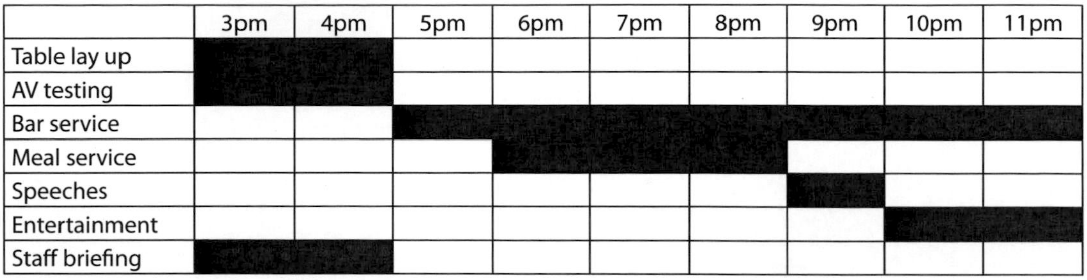

	3pm	4pm	5pm	6pm	7pm	8pm	9pm	10pm	11pm
Table lay up	█	█							
AV testing	█	█							
Bar service			█	█	█	█	█	█	█
Meal service				█	█	█			
Speeches							█		
Entertainment								█	█
Staff briefing	█	█							

Figure 8.6: Example of a Gantt chart for an event

An important part of any event is the preparation. Typical preparation tasks may include:

- Setting up tables, seating and side stations
- Laying tables for conferences (e.g. paper, pencils, glass, cordials)
- Laying tables for lunch or dinner
- Setting up front and back bars (e.g. glasses, beverages, accompaniments)
- Setting up of equipment (e.g. dance floors, projectors, staging), and
- General cleaning of the event area.

Room set-ups

Depending on the space available, there are a variety of room set-ups that event operators can use for events, as illustrated in Figure 8.7. When deciding on the most appropriate set up, consideration should be given to certain factors for example, objectives of event, atmosphere, numbers of people, room size, flow and time available. Some customers may on occasions pick room set-ups that would not be suitable so it is important for venues to guide the customer on the right set-up to achieve greatest customer satisfaction.

For further information on room set-ups, see Lillicrap and Cousins (2010) Chapter 11, 'Events'.

8

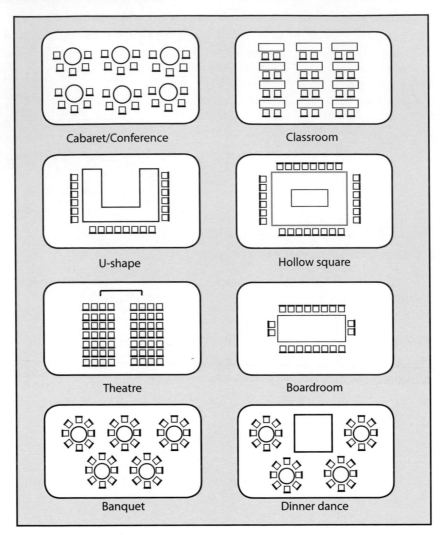

Cabaret/Conference   Classroom

U-shape   Hollow square

Theatre   Boardroom

Banquet   Dinner dance

Figure 8.7: Examples of room setups

6 Event quality

It is important for event operators to plan well and implement the necessary quality controls to ensure customer satisfaction is met. However, with any event the venue is confronted with challenges that need to be overcome. Tables 8.12 and 8.13 highlight some of the challenges when dealing with banqueting and conference events coupled with some recommended solutions.

To help to improve and maintain quality an event operation could apply to be accredited by a trade association. And example of this is the UK Meetings Industry Association, which conducts independent assessments of event operations and awards them at entry, silver and gold levels. For more information visit http://www.mia-uk.org. In addition thee are a wide range of potential industry awards.

Table 8.12: Banqueting: Potential challenges and recommendations

Potential challenges	Potential recommendations
Menu design – Ensure event menus are created considering the customer's needs and the operations resource capabilities.	A pre-cook-off menu with chefs and client will provide an opportunity to improve quality and identify any operational challenges. Avoid attempting complex menus.
Food safety – When dealing with large numbers the importance of food hygiene becomes even more important.	Enforce HACCP procedures (see Chapter 4 page 72) Prohibit customers bringing own food onto premises
Food quality – When dealing with large numbers it is a challenge to replicate the standard of fine dining, as time between food plating and consumption may be longer.	Develop dish specifications Select dishes that fit well with holding processes. Ensure effective kitchen supervision to maintain quality control
Food timing – A challenge when catering to large numbers is ensuring prompt food service delivery.	Gain a clear understanding of the time available for the meal and select the most appropriate food service method.
Flow of service – Bottle-necks/ queuing can cause dissatisfaction for both customers/service staff.	Ensure most appropriate service method is selected for numbers and space available.
Service quality – Future cost of dissatisfaction is always a concern when dealing with large quantities of guests.	Ensure service personnel are skilled Carry out thorough pre-service briefing Implement order of service Ensure effective supervision takes place
Diverse customer base – Events can be host to a diversity of guests with different dietary requirements.	During enquiry stage ask specific questions relating to demographic and potential dietary information of guests and recommend accordingly.
Intoxication – Over-consumption of alcohol can take place during some celebratory events.	Educate and train bar servers on sensible and responsible alcohol service to customers. Employ security for events where a large consumption of alcohol is forecasted (e.g. weddings, sports occasions) Conduct pre-event risk assessments
Event Crisis Planning – Even with pre-planning changes can take place outside the control of both the venue and the customer	Event operators and their management teams need to carry out crisis planning and attempt to predict uncertainties and how they can be minimised.

8

Table 8.13: Conferences: Potential challenges and recommendations

Potential challenges	Potential recommendations
AV delivery –Hi-tech audiovisual equipment are susceptible to whistling and interference during usage.	Ensure a qualified AV technician is on standby for full duration equipment is being used.
Keeping up to date with information technology – Technology is changing daily and keeping abreast can be costly.	Outsource technology to external companies to achieve a good standard of IT and reduce departmental equipment expenses.
Multiple contractors – With large conferences there could be multiple external contractors involved in the set up of the event.	Establish early on from the client contractors being used and obtain contact numbers to coordinate set-up times accordingly.
Additional revenues – It is common for groups of delegates to unexpectedly stay after an event and use other facilities such as bars or restaurants.	To avoid the potential for poor service maintain good customer history records of any groups that have done this in the past as it is possible it could recur.

For more information on quality management see Chapter 3, page 52 and Lillicrap and Cousins (2010), Chapters 1 and 2.

7 Team briefing

Shortly before the event is due to commence a final briefing should always take place by the manager with the service team. A briefing may include the following points:

- The company, type of event and number of guests
- How the event will run (e.g. chronology and timings of event)
- Order of service for event
- Communicate the details of organiser, host and any VIPs
- Inform of any special requests
- Allocation of tables to servers
- Menu briefing by chef
- Re-cap on any key standards.

8 Customer welcome and service

It is good practice when the guest arrives to run through the event order one final time. The reasons for this are:

- It puts the customer at ease
- It allows the customer to make any final last minute adjustments
- It eliminates any errors on behalf of the venue.

During the event a supervisors key responsibilities might include:

- Delivery of the event as per the details stipulated on the event order

- Ensuring departmental service standards are maintained, sales are maximised and costs are minimised
- Being visible and accessible to organisers, guests and staff throughout event.

■ Post-event

9 Event break-down

At the end of the event employees will break down the event, which may include duties for example:

- Collapsing furniture and equipment
- Clearing tables
- Taking cutlery, crockery and glassware to stewarding
- Transferring soiled linen to laundry room
- General cleaning
- Re-setting for next day's event or show rounds.

10 Event billing

At the end of the event the organiser or host would sign the bill to confirm all charges (room, food, beverage, miscellaneous) are correct. This would either be settled immediately or invoiced to the company. For more information on billing see Chapter 7, page 190.

11 Event evaluation

It is essential with at the end of any event that an evaluation is conducted with both with the customer and the event team. In addition to speaking to the customer at the end of the event, customer feedback can also be organised with either a follow-up telephone call, e-mail or mail questionnaire. It does not matter which method is used as long as it is conducted. With the event team it is good practice to discuss and measure how the event performed against planned budget, event order and departmental service standards. Further identifying what worked well and what areas need to be improved in the event delivery. It is imperative that all feedback is disseminated and circulated to the relevant department heads and any evaluation paperwork should be placed on the customer's file for future action.

8

9 Appraising performance

Aim

This chapter aims to identify and evaluate the techniques of measuring and appraising the performance of food and beverage operations.

Objectives

This chapter is intended to support you in:

- Considering the basis for performance appraisal

- Identifying the aspects of foodservice operations which are commonly appraised

- Developing skills in the application of a range of performance measures and appraisal techniques to revenue, costs and profits and the food and beverage product

- Determining the usefulness and limitations in the various quantitative and qualitative appraisal techniques and their application to foodservice operations.

9.1   Approaches to appraisal

In order to systematically appraise a food and beverage operation it is necessary to identify the component parts of an operation and appraise them separately before bringing them all together and appraising the operation as a whole. For a food and beverage operation the first component parts for performance appraisal are:

- Revenue
- Costs
- Profits
- The product.

The nature of revenue, costs and profits are complex. Each of these is considered in detail together with the approaches that might be used to appraise them. An identification of key points for each of these aspects is given at the end of the section where they are examined. The appraisal of the product is then considered taking account of the data, which the appraisal of the revenue, costs and the profits might provide.

The next stage, which is considered in Chapter 10, is to bring the various strands together in order to complete the appraisal of the operation as a whole and to make strategic decisions about the current and future operation and the business.

■   Fundamentals of appraisal

Appraisal is the action of placing a value on a measurement or collection of measurements. The measurements taken in a food and beverage operation are predominantly concerned with performance, and are therefore often referred to as 'performance measures'. However, a measure alone has no value. In order to be able to place a value on a performance measure, there will need to be an identified objective to measure it against. For example, an actual revenue measurement of £1200 has limited value until it is compared with a revenue objective of £1000. The revenue can then be appraised as surpassing the objective by £200, or 20% of the objective.

Other measurements and objectives are needed in order to explore or value the revenue measurement further. If cost objectives and actual costs are known, it is possible to explore or value the revenue measurement in a more meaningful way, i.e. the amount of profit (or loss) can be measured. Subsequently a profit objective can also be applied and a further value placed on the achievements of the operation.

In order to begin to appraise a food and beverage operation it is therefore a prerequisite to identify the goals and objectives of the operation. Knowing the operation's goals and objectives will enable the appraiser to focus on those parts of the operation which most significantly impact on the achievement of the goals and identified objectives.

In Chapter 2 we identified that:

- **Goals**, or aims, are the broad intentions of an organisation.
- **Objectives** are the measurable outcomes, which will indicate the progress being made by an organisation towards meeting its specific goals.

Operational appraisal then is concerned with measuring achievement against the objectives.

There may however be circumstances where the operation's objectives are not clear. In these situations it will be necessary for the appraiser to take a proactive role. This proactive role will vary depending on the responsibilities of the appraiser. For example:

- Area managers, managers, department heads and others with responsibility for revenue, costs, profits and product quality, who are unclear as to their objectives, need to be proactive by consulting with other members of their organisation (usually their immediate line manager), in an attempt to establish what the objectives are.

- An owner-operator with no clear objectives should consider what their objectives are. This can either be done by the owner or can be done in consultation with others: the staff and/or a consultant, for example.

The formulation of objectives is an important part of any business in order to try and ensure that resources are being directed efficiently and that the goals will be met. As objectives are dynamic and vary according to circumstances, the setting and revising of objectives is a continuous process. Appraisal is part of this process as it measures the extent to which the objectives are being met. The resultant appraisal will help in confirmation or revision of the appropriate goals for the organisation, which in turn will lead to the setting, or revising of the organisations objectives.

■ The basis for effective operational appraisal

Effective appraisal can only be achieved if there are established objectives for the food and beverage operation. These objectives are usually in the form of budgets and statements of other standards, against which actual performance can be measured and appraised. The time and resources devoted to identifying, establishing and communicating objectives will vary between operations, depending on the perceived importance of this process. In operations where the objectives are not clear, staff and management should be proactive in order to identify and establish what their objectives actually are.

Budgets

Some of the measurable objectives of a food and beverage operation are commonly expressed in the form of 'budgets'. Examples of measurable 'budget' objectives are revenue, costs, profits, average spend per head, number of customers. These objectives are used in a number of ways:

- Budget objectives are compared to actual performance and therefore help to appraise that actual performance, e.g. revenue budgets.
- Budget objectives help effect control over the operation, e.g. cost budgets.
- Budget objectives help to predict the future, e.g. cash flow and profit forecast budgets.

Operators will mainly use budgets to assist in making reasoned and objective evaluation of the performance of the operation, so that informed decisions can be made regarding their business. However, budgets can be used for other reasons.

Budgets are often thought to act as a motivator. Sometimes the ability to achieve the budget is related to remuneration and bonuses, or if budgets are not met employment of those thought to be responsible may be terminated. This 'stick and carrot' use of budgets can act as a motivator if the budgets are perceived to be achievable. Conversely they can act as a demotivator if they are perceived to be unobtainable.

In order for budgets to be perceived as a motivating factor, they should be set with the agreement of all the participating parties. In large organisations, budgets are agreed between layers of the organisation, for example between the board of directors and the operations director, then the operations director and the regional managers, and so on until agreement between the unit managers and the department heads. In smaller and owner-operated food and beverage operations this agreement between the parties is potentially easier to achieve.

Even with such a consultative approach to budget setting it is still possible for there to be conflict, with one side wishing to increase budget sales and reduce budget costs (often the position of the higher-layer manager, the budget setter), while the other party is trying to reduce budget sales and increase budget costs (often the position of the lower-layer manager, the budget taker).

Nevertheless, however they are set, it is still possible that budgets may be ill conceived and badly or falsely communicated. If the desired operational objective is to be identified through the budget, then the setting of the budget itself should be examined for its possible limitations, and how these limitations might affect the use of budgets as an appraisal or valuation of the actual achievement.

In summary then:

- Budgets which are set in measurable and achievable terms and which need to be achieved in order that the organisation can realise its goals are true objectives.
- Budgets, which are set as intentions for the organisation with little relationship with the goals of the organisation, are not true objectives. These are merely broad intentions, which are being used for other purposes, such as being the basis for determining bonus payments for managers.

In measuring performance against budgets, it is worth first considering the true nature of the budgets as this will then determine the extent to which the performance appraisal is in fact a measure of the effectiveness of the organisation in meeting its goals.

Standards

Other measurable objectives of a food and beverage operation are often expressed as standards. Examples of measurable standards are: portioning, purchasing specifications, staff uniform, temperature, time. These standards are seen to be useful to operators in a similar way to budgets:

■ Standards are compared to actual performance and therefore help to appraise that actual performance, e.g. portioning.

■ Standards help effect control over specific parts of the operation, e.g. staff uniform and hygiene.

■ Standards can contribute to ensuring a consistent product, e.g. the same service, meals and atmosphere, at all times and in all locations.

Some operators will write these standards down in the form of standards of performance manuals or training manuals, with many national branded foodservice operations being extremely detailed in their approaches. The manuals will attempt to prescribe precisely each task and duty to be performed, often supported by the use of diagrams, photographs and videos. These manuals are generally used for three main purposes:

■ Manuals can provide a way for management to communicate the prescribed performance of various tasks and duties necessary to produce and control their product.

■ Manuals help to ensure consistency of product throughout all the food and beverage operations in a group or chain.

■ Manuals can act as a set of objectives against which to appraise performance.

As with budgets, not all food and beverage operations will have written-down standards, and similarly, operators and managers should be proactive in trying to identify and establish what these standards are. In general terms, the existence of agreed standards make a valuable contribution to the maintenance of consistent product delivery for an operation.

We have already drawn a distinction, in Chapter 3, between different types of standards. Product quality (in terms of technical standards) and service quality (in terms of service standards) are by their very nature different. Technical standards can be identified, measured and compared. Also procedural service standards can often be usefully identified. Service though is highly varied and there is some doubt as the extent to which it is possible to prescribe useful service standards beyond defining a relaxed framework (especially for convivial standards) or whether it is in fact, for some operations, desirable at all.

9.2   Appraising revenue

Food and beverage operators view revenue as perhaps the most important measure in the operation. Revenue is also called turnover, and is often quoted as a measure of the size of a business; but high revenue does not necessarily equate with high success. Operations with high revenue can and do fail. However to be successful, revenue is a prerequisite, and most operators would put revenue achievement at the top of their list of objectives.

Revenue is a consequence of two variables: price and volume. Changes in either one or both of these variables will affect the level of revenue over time. Table 9.1 demonstrates how changes in the price and/or volume variables can affect the revenue.

Table 9.1: Effects of price and volume on revenue

Example	Covers/volume	Price/ASPH (£)	Revenue (£)
1	100	10.00	1000.00
2	120	10.00	1200.00
3	120	9.00	1080.00
4	100	12.00	1200.00
5	80	15.00	1200.00
6	120	12.00	1440.00
7	80	10.00	800.00
8	80	9.00	720.00
9	100	9.00	900.00
10	80	11.00	880.00
11	110	9.00	990.00

In the examples given in Table 9.1:

- Example 1 is the starting-point or base line.
- Examples 2–6 show revenue increasing.
- Examples 7–11 show revenue decreasing.
- Examples 3 and 5 produce increased revenue even though one of the variables has decreased.
- Examples 10 and 11 produce decreased revenue even though one of the variables has increased.

In order to appraise the revenue of an operation over time it will therefore be necessary to collect information on both the price and the volume variables.

Most food and beverage operations will measure volume by the number of customers served. In a table-service restaurant operation this is a fairly simple matter of referring to copy customer invoices, kitchen order checks or electronic data collection from the cash register. In a counter-service food and beverage operation it is not so easy to know the actual number of customers that have been served, and therefore the number of transactions may be recorded, e.g. in a fast food store. In some food and beverage operations it is not seen as necessary to know the actual number of customers or the actual number of transactions, e.g. in a bar. In this situation the revenue is still a product of the price and the volume, but it will not be possible to identify the reasons for any revenue variations so accurately.

The prices of an operation can be taken from the menus, wine and drinks lists and other methods of 'product offer' communication. However, price can also be measured by how much a customer is actually spending. Many operations use 'average spend per head' (ASPH), or 'average check', as a way of determining the price variable.

Using price and volume data

If an operation knows its total revenue and the number of customers or number of checks over a specific period, then it is possible to calculate the ASPH and the average check figures. For example:

If:

Total revenue (£)	1000
Total number of customers	500
Total number of transactions	100

Then:

ASPH	= £2.00	(total revenue divided by the number of customers)
Average check	= £10.00	(total revenue divided by the number of transactions)
Average group size	= 5	(total number of customers served divided by the number of transactions)

This example also shows the calculation used to determine the average size of a group of customers. This can be useful information. Knowing that larger or smaller groups of customers make up a significant part of the market can help in the planning of the restaurant and kitchen layout for example, or to focus advertising and promotion.

Interpreting calculations

An ASPH or average check amount can be misleading because 'averages' do not give the whole picture. An ASPH of £12.50 could be the result of all customers spending £12.50; or half the customers spending £6.25 and the other half spending £18.75. The same misinterpretation can be applied to the average group size measure, and also to for instance, the average number of customers per hour/day/ week. Infinite combinations are possible and it is therefore important to take into account the limitations of averages.

It is often useful to generate figures that show the ASPH for different quartiles. This will give information on, for instance how many customers are spending within the highest quartile (25% of spend), the bottom quartile and the middle two. This can also be useful over specific service times such as main meal times where minimum charges can be introduced to force up the level of the ASPH.

Additionally these measurements and others are seen to be more useful when they are used for cross-sectional and time-series analyses.

- **Cross-sectional analysis:** This is to (a) compare one section of an operation with another section of the same operation, or (b) compare one operation or part of an operation with another in the same or similar sector of the food and beverage operations business. For example, comparing the revenue of one steak house restaurant with another in the same chain, or comparing the revenue of one fast food chain with the revenue of another.

- **Time-series analysis:** This is to compare a measure over a period of time; for example, comparing the revenue of a unit for one week with the revenue of the same unit for the previous week or with the revenue from the same week one year ago. Comparing present with past performance helps place some value on the revenue measure, although it is important to take into account any circumstances that may have changed.

Taking account of price changes and inflation

When comparing revenue for different trading periods it is important to take account of price changes and inflation in order to get a truer picture of the performance of the operation.

For example: A restaurant that had a revenue of £100,000 in year one and a revenue of £120,000 in year two, is seen to have increased its revenue by £20,000 or 20%. Let us assume that the number of customers has remained static and that prices were increased by 10% (In this particular example we will assume that the current rate of inflation was 10%, although this by itself may not be the only reason why prices might be increased or changed.) Taking into account the price rise it might be said that the value of the increased revenue is not £20,000 but only £10,000. In general terms one would have expected the restaurant to increase its revenue to £110,000 in the second year just to remain at the same revenue level, i.e. £100,000 plus the rate of inflation/rate of price increase at 10% (£10,000) would be £110,000. Although the restaurant had an actual revenue of £120,000 taking account of the effect of inflation will mean that revenue has only increased by £10,000 or 9.1% in real terms. (To take account of inflation the revenue should have been £110,000. Actual revenue was £120,000, the percentage increase is therefore 9.1% [£10,000/£110,000 × 100].)

When comparing revenue for different time periods, it is therefore important to know if price rises and/or inflation have been taken into account.

Comparing like with like

Revenue comparisons between food and beverage units should also be made with some caution and in relation to the circumstances. Two roadside restaurants in the same chain will have identical menus and prices, and may even have the same seating capacity, but their revenues may be different. This difference in revenue will still be a product of the volume and price variables, but factors outside the control of the unit management, such as location and spending power of their market, will affect revenue levels, and therefore the revenue budgets need to allow for these differences. Revenue comparisons between food and beverage businesses also need to be made with caution because the objectives and/or costs of the two businesses may be different. The performance of any operation therefore cannot be made using revenue alone.

In order to try and make effective comparisons between food and beverage operations other forms of revenue measurements can be made. Revenue per customer/seat/square metre/staff member, etc. can be measured and compared to similar operations. These measures can also be performed over time on the same business or unit. The real question when these types of measurements and comparisons are made is: 'Are they useful?' It is not always clear if these measurements and comparisons will be useful until they are actually measured and compared. If the time and data are available to make these types of detailed measures and comparisons, then it may be worth doing.

Comparison over time

Perhaps the most useful form of revenue appraisal is over time. Average spend per head, average revenue per customer, number of customers, revenue per member of staff, revenue per square metre, etc. can all be measured on an ongoing basis and compared. It will therefore be possible to identify changes and maybe trends, and if any significant changes in these measures are noticed, remedial action can be taken.

When comparing over time, comparisons are often made between the same periods of different years for example January this year with January last year. This can have problems. The number of Sundays for instance can have an effect on the potential of the business let alone the actually achievement. The operations may be closed on a Sunday. For this reason rolling totals of 12 months are often used. Thus the total revenue and other measures at the end of January for the 12 months are compared to the total revenue and other measures for the end of December for the 12 months. This type of comparison over time gives a far better indication of actual trends than simply taking a comparison of month to month.

Key points of revenue appraisal

- Revenue is a product of price and volume. An appraisal of revenue will need to take account of changes in both of these variables.

- Averages of price, volume and revenue do not always accurately reflect the complete situation and are prone to misinterpretation.
- Inflation and/or price rises need to be taken into account when comparing different trading periods.
- Different businesses/operations/units may have different objectives and direct comparisons may not be comparing like with like.
- Comparison over time can be useful, with rolling 12-month totals providing a useful basis for determining true trends and performance.
- Revenue cannot be fully appraised without reference to other operational variables, such as cost and profit.

9.3 Appraising costs

As important as revenue is for the operation to obtain, costs are seen as the most important for the operation to control. Costs are usually divided into fixed, variable and semi-variable costs:

- **Fixed** costs remain constant over a set period of time even though the level of business fluctuates, e.g. rent, rates and insurance premiums.
- **Variable** costs are proportional to the level of business, e.g. meal ingredient costs and beverage costs.
- **Semi-variable** costs are part fixed and part variable, e.g. staff and fuel.

However, it is more important to know how and why any costs are incurred, and how to measure them accurately, than to argue if they are fixed, variable or semi-variable.

Most **fixed** costs (and some **variable** costs) can be negotiated with the supplier. Rent, insurance and even interest rates (the cost of borrowing money) are services that are supplied within a competitive market and it is therefore worth considering opportunities for alternative, and possibly cheaper, sources of these services. Once the costs of these services are established, they are then fixed for the duration of the contract period, which is usually one year (although interest rates and some other costs can fluctuate more often).

Variable costs and **semi-variable** costs can be appraised in absolute terms, but are more commonly appraised as a proportion of revenue. Putting aside the fixed part of the semi-variable costs, (e.g. standing charge for electricity), these variable costs are proportional to the volume of business and therefore revenue. A food and beverage operation will measure these costs as a percentage of revenue, usually on a weekly basis. Costs of food, beverage, staff, linen, disposables, marketing, maintenance and other variable costs can be, and commonly are, measured as a percentage of revenue.

■ Identifying and measuring costs

Appraising fixed and variable costs objectively can be performed as follows:

A cross-sectional analysis

This can be performed by comparing the costs incurred by one food and beverage operation with similar types of food and beverage operations, thereby allowing a 'value for money' appraisal to be performed. Publications such as Keynote and Mintel reports and trade magazines such as Caterer & Hotelkeeper, Restaurant Magazine and others, provide useful information in this area, so that comparisons can be made. However, the cost structures of food and beverage operations can vary in a way which makes comparisons difficult. For example, one restaurant may be owned and operated by a family partnership that owns the premises outright (the debt having been paid off over a long period of time), while another restaurant is paying high rent or interest charges. The fixed costs of these two similar restaurants will be very different, resulting in a much lower break-even point (the point at which the operation starts making a profit) for the restaurant with the lower fixed costs. These cost structures are often seen to change over the life cycles of most businesses.

Relating one cost to other costs

Costs are almost certain to increase in absolute terms year on year, due to inflation and/or the changing cost structure of the business, but by appraising costs as a proportion of total costs, or as a proportion of total revenue, a comparative measure can be established. For example, if fixed costs in year one are 25% of total costs and 7% of total sales, and in year two are 30 and 9% respectively, then a relative dimension is added to cost appraisal. These changes in costs can be calculated to provide a relative measure, which helps in their appraisal. This relative measure is sometimes miscalculated, as there may be confusion as to how percentage changes are measured. Table 9.2 gives an example of how these measurements are made.

A time-series analysis

Comparing costs over a period of time, usually year on year, is the basis for this type of analysis. The absolute and the percentage change in these costs can be measured and a comparison made with the previous year's changes. One common budget or standard objective measure in these circumstances is the current rate of inflation or retail price index. Changes in staff costs (rates of pay) are often related and calculated in this way. However, if some costs are seen to rise significantly more or less than the current rate of inflation, or significantly more or less than in previous years, consideration should be given to changing the operating systems of the food and beverage business to take advantage of, or counter, this changing cost structure. Changing from electricity to gas or changing from silver service to buffet service, in order to reduce fuel or staff costs, would be examples of changing operating systems in order to reduce these costs in real and proportional terms.

Again in this approach it is often that comparisons are made between the same periods of different years. As was considered under revenue above approaching comparisons in this way can have problems. Therefore consideration should also be given to the comparison of rolling 12-month totals over time.

Table 9.2: Calculation of change in costs and revenue

Costs / revenues	£
Last period costs	1,000
Present period costs	1,200
Last period revenue	10,000
Present period revenue	11,000
Absolute change in cost	200
Percentages	**%**
Percentage change in absolute cost	20.00
Last period costs as a percentage of revenue	10.00
Present period costs as a percentage of revenue	10.90
Change in cost as a percentage of revenue	9.00

The example given in Table 9.2 indicates how the percentage change in absolute terms is calculated by dividing the difference between the costs in this period and the period before (£1200 – £1000 = £200), by the original or last period's cost (£1000), and multiplying by 100:

$$\frac{1200 - 1000}{1000} \times 100 = 20\%$$

Costs can be said to have risen 20% in absolute terms. However, as a percentage of revenue, costs have been seen to rise from 10 to 10.9%. The percentage change in these cost percentages is calculated as follows:

$$\frac{10.9 - 10}{10} \times 100 = 9\%$$

The percentage change in costs as a percentage of revenue is 9%. The percentage change between 10 and 10.9% is not 0.9%. It is critically important to know the difference between these measurements, 20% being the absolute cost change percentage, and 9% being the relative change in the cost as a percentage of the revenue. It might perhaps be more accurate to say that costs have risen by 9% (relative to revenue) than by 20% (in absolute terms).

If the figures here were representing rolling 12-month totals the same issues would apply. However using a 12-month rolling total gives a truer indication of trends and how the operation is actually doing over time. It is a far better indicator and worth considering.

Industry norms

There is no one standard or budget percentage for the various costs. Food costs of between 20% and 60% are often quoted as acceptable for particular types of operation, as are staff costs of between 11% and 35% and marketing costs of between 1% and 2%. Some examples of food, liquor and labour costs for different types of operation are given in Table 9.3. However, these figures should only be used as a guide because the actual percentage of the cost will vary depending on the specific objectives of the food and beverage operation.

Table 9.3: Examples of food, liquor and labour cost percentages for differing types of foodservice operation

Type of operation	Example food cost (%)	Example liquor cost (%)	Example labour cost (%)
Public house	40–60	45–60	15–30
Restaurant	30–50	35–55	25–35
Banqueting	30–45	30–45	18–32
Fast food	20–35	–	11–18
Popular catering	30–45	45–60	15–35
Wine bar	50–60	45–55	12–22

It might be assumed that some sectors of the industry will share similar cost percentages, but there is no evidence to support this assumption. An up-market restaurant with an average spend per head of around £70–100 may have the same food cost percentage as a roadside food and beverage operation with an average spend per head of around £9. The two operations may also have very similar staff cost percentages. Conversely, two very similar operations may have widely differing cost percentages, e.g. staff cost percentages being low, say 15% of total revenue in an operation run and staffed by a family, and being say, 25% of total revenue in an operation which hires staff on the open market. Small family businesses like restaurants and takeaways can have low barriers to entry, and because of the family interest are willing to work long hours at rates of pay below what is acceptable to others, resulting in much lower staff cost percentages.

In some sectors of the foodservice industry, the market is becoming much more competitive and more concentrated in the hands of the large operators. For example, in retail foodservice, prime high street sites have become prohibitively expensive to all but those who can significantly reduce costs and afford the highly expensive mass advertising campaigns and premium rents. The barriers to entry in this 'retail foodservice' market are becoming higher and therefore restricting the smaller and family-run operations.

This move towards an oligopolistic industry structure is also found in 'contract', 'outside' and 'transport foodservice operations', and cost percentage comparisons between them can be made. The chain, or group, food and beverage operations place great value on reducing costs and cost percentages as this is seen as leading to greater profits, and opportunities for a greater market share than their rivals through more competitive pricing. In this highly competitive market, economies of scale, especially in distribution, purchasing and marketing costs, provide advantages over the smaller operator. A greater investment in new technology also provides opportunities to develop more efficient and cheaper operating systems. These large operators see their actual survival as dependent upon their ability to reduce and control their costs, and therefore the value placed on cost comparisons between them is high.

Apportioning costs

In order to understand the cost structure of a food and beverage operation it is necessary to know why the various costs are incurred, and which costs can, or should be, attributed to the various parts of the operation. As the product is made up from a number of variables comprising the meal experience (see Chapter 3), and is therefore not homogeneous – because different customers purchase and value different parts of the experience – apportioning costs requires the identification of the component parts of the product.

Costs are often identified as being either direct or indirect:

- **Direct costs**, by definition, can be apportioned directly to the various parts of the menu and drinks list. The ingredient costs of a meal or drink may be calculated accurately and therefore the direct cost for each item on the food and drinks list identified. The use of standard recipes and tailor-made spreadsheets is common among large operators in identifying and measuring these direct costs.

- **Indirect costs,** which comprise almost all the other costs beside the ingredient costs, are much more difficult to apportion. Examples of these indirect costs are: staff, linen, maintenance, cleaning materials, marketing, management, administration, rent, rates, fixtures, fittings, equipment, insurance, training and fuel.

An additional consideration in dealing with indirect costs is the proper apportioning of a range of costs that are often ignored; or rather simply absorbed without any proper accounting of them. Examples of these costs include: staff and management feeding costs; special promotions that reduce selling prices; 'comping' (providing food and beverages for free or at a discount); managers' allowances and entertaining of existing or potential clients. If these cost are not properly accounting for then the expected actual revenue for the departments providing the services is reduced. As a consequence this is then unfair to those departments, as the true gross profits figures for the departments will also be reduced. In all cases these types of costs should be charged to internal accounts such as, for example: employment costs; marketing and promotion costs; 'comping' costs, and managers' accounts. This process ensures that the expected revenue, and consequently the gross profits of the different departments, is accurately measured. The costs are also then recognised and recorded as costs to the business as a whole. In addition, and importantly, it ensures that the levels of these costs are properly measured and consequently are able to be properly controlled.

In order to overcome the problem of measuring how much of the indirect costs should be apportioned to the individual menu and drinks list items, the costs are commonly apportioned as a percentage of the selling price. This proportion is usually identified as the proportion of the total individual cost to total revenue, for example, for staff costs this might be:

Total food revenue	= £1000.00
Total staff costs	= £300.00
Staff cost	= 30%
Individual menu item selling price	= £1.25
Apportioned staff cost at 30%	= £0.375

All other indirect costs are often calculated and apportioned in this way, or they can be formed into groups such as overheads e.g. rent and rates, or operational expenses, e.g. linen and cleaning materials. Which costs are included in these different groupings can vary from operation to operation. Many operations will simply group all these indirect costs together under 'overheads'; such apportioning is calculated as follows:

Total food and beverage sales	= £1000.00
Total overheads	= £120.00
Overhead cost	= 12%
Individual menu or drinks list item selling price	= £1.25
Apportioned overhead cost at 12%	= £0.15

Although this is an uncomplicated way to apportion costs, it is clearly not accurate. If total staff costs are 30% of total revenue, it does not necessarily follow that all menu and wine list items have a labour element of 30% of their selling prices. It is the processes the various ingredients undergo which determine the labour cost, and as various ingredients undergo different processes – some highly skilled and time consuming, others simple and quick – the labour costs for individual menu and drinks list items are quite different. The same inaccuracy is inherent in apportioning other indirect costs. It is for these reasons that in foodservice operations only the material costs (food and drink) are directly related to revenue. This is the basis of a gross profit calculation for all foodservice operations. All other costs are treated as being incurred by the operation as a whole. This is the basis for determining net profit. The appraisal of profits is discussed further in the next section of this chapter.

9

■ Key points of cost appraisal

- ■ The cost structures of food and beverage operations vary, and change over time.
- ■ Costs can be measured in absolute terms or as percentages of total costs and revenue.
- ■ Changes in the proportional relationship between costs can be measured, helping to identify opportunities for increased efficiency through changing the operating systems.
- ■ Proportional relationships between costs and inflation also need to be taken into account.
- ■ Cross-sectional and time-series analyses can be used to appraise costs.
- ■ Rolling 12-month totals can provide a useful basis for determining true trends and performance.
- ■ Increased competition among food and beverage operators is leading towards an oligopolistic market in some sectors, creating a situation where operators with the lowest costs are perceived as having a key advantage.
- ■ Identifying and allocating direct costs is relatively straightforward, but methods for identifying and allocating indirect costs need to be considered carefully.

9.4   Appraising profits

Profits (or losses) are the difference between revenue and costs and appraising profit requires the identification of the relationship between the revenue and the costs. The profit and loss account of an operation summarises the result of this relationship. Table 9.4 gives an example of a simple profit and loss account.

Table 9.4: Example of simple profit and loss account

Item	£
Income/revenue	1000
Direct costs/ingredient costs	300
Staff costs	250
Operating costs	100
Overheads	150
Total costs	800
Profit	200

In the example given in Table 9.4 the profit is £200, but this does not necessarily tell the whole story. Because profitability is expressed in many different ways, and as food and beverage operators use these ways differently, it is important to clarify which costs have, or have not, been included in the profit measure.

■   Profitability measures

The main profitability measures are:

- **Gross profit** (GP) in food and beverage operations is the difference between the selling price or revenue, and the cost of the food or drink ingredients. Examples are given in Table 9.5.

Table 9.5: Comparison of gross profits

	Individual item examples				Whole operation example	
	Burger	£	Soup	£		£
Income	Selling price	3.50	Selling price	1.75	Food and beverage revenue	1000
Expenditure	Food cost	1.49	Food cost	0.34	Food costs	170
					Drink costs	130
Total costs		1.49		0.34		300
Gross profit		2.01		1.41		700

- **Gross profit percentage** (GP%) is the gross profit measured as a percentage of the selling price or revenue. The GP% of the beefburger example is 57.4, the GP% for the soup is 80.6, and the GP% for the operation example is 70. Food and beverage operations use this measure extensively but it is important to recognise that a higher GP% does not always mean a higher GP. The soup has a higher GP% at 80.6 than the beefburger at 57.4, but the soup is less profitable in absolute or cash terms with a lower GP – at £1.41 – than the beefburger at £2.01.

- **Operating profit** is measured in different ways by food and beverage operators, but its common usage would be that profit which has been derived solely from the operation, and excluding any profit that might have been made from selling land or buildings for example, which may have been owned by the business. Again, it is necessary to establish if any such 'non-operational' profits have been included in this measure before it can be appraised. It is also necessary to establish if overhead costs have been deducted.

- **Operating profit percentage** is the operating profit measured as a percentage of revenue. As with GP%s, a higher operating profit percentage does not always mean a higher operating profit; Table 9.6 gives two examples. Operation A has a higher operating profit percentage at 20% than operation B at 15%, but operation B has made a higher operating profit at £300 than operation A at £200.

Table 9.6: Comparison of operating profits

	Operation A	Operation B
Revenue	£ 1,000	£ 2,000
Operating costs*	£ 800	£ 1,700
Operating profit	£ 200	£ 300
Operating profit %	20%	15%

* These costs will include ingredient costs and staff costs, but might not include overheads, therefore the extent to which the other costs might have been included needs to be established

- **Net profit** is usually the measure where all costs have been deducted from the revenue, including the overheads. However, it is possible that not all costs have been deducted. Sometimes the cost of interest payments, loan repayments and dividends will not have been deducted, and again care must be taken to check this.

- **Net profit percentage** is the net profit measured as a percentage of revenue. Again a higher net profit percentage does not always mean a higher net profit. (See the operating profit percentage example above .)

- **Net operating profit, net operating profit percentage**, both before and after tax and/or dividends, are examples of other measures which are used. Again, it is necessary to check which costs have or have not been deducted, and to appreciate the difference between a percentage measure and an absolute measure.

- **Departmental and unit profit**: these are measures that are used to identify the profitability of individual departments or units within a food and beverage operation. Some costs can be directly attributed to a department or unit, such as the cost of staff who only work in that section, and food and drink costs, but other costs such as rates and rent may be more difficult to apportion accurately.

- **Yield profitability** measures are used mainly to measure the profitability of the beverage side of a food and beverage operation, although it can also be applied to the food side. Table 9.7 shows how yield is calculated.

Table 9.7: Yield comparisons

	Operation A	Operation B
Total beverage revenue or yield	£ 1,000	£ 1,000
Total selling price of beverage consumed	£ 960	£ 1,050
Yield percentage	104%	95.2%

At the end of each period, usually a week or month, the amount of beverage stock consumed is identified for each beverage item held in stock. In order to produce the yield figure, the selling price of each of the beverage items – taken from the price list/wine list – is multiplied by the units of that beverage item consumed. This yield is then measured as a percentage of the actual revenue.

In **operation A** the yield was 104%. This can happen because, for example:

☐ Drinks have been mixed, as in a cocktail, which realises a greater revenue than the sum of the parts that have been used to create the mixture.

☐ Customers have been overcharged or short-changed.

☐ Customers have been given short measures.

☐ The yield measure has been miscalculated.

☐ Wastage has not been as high as expected.

In **operation B** the yield was 95.2%. This can happen because, for example:

☐ Wastage or ullage has occurred

☐ Customers have been undercharged

☐ Customers have been given a larger measure than necessary

☐ All the revenue has not been received

☐ The measure has been miscalculated.

Measuring the yield percentage therefore allows an appraisal of that operation's efficiency in delivering the product and also receiving the correct revenue.

Whichever profitability measures are used it is critical to know which costs have been included in the calculations, how they were apportioned and which costs may still have to be deducted. When this has been established it is then possible to appraise profitability in both absolute and relative terms.

Before going on to consider the nature of profit in more detail it may be worth summarising the relationship between revenue, costs and profits for a foodservice operation. This summary is given in Figure 9.1.

Food and beverage costs	Cost of sales
Labour costs	
Overhead costs	Gross profit
Net profit	
Sales	**Revenue 100%**

Figure 9.1: Summary of the relationship between revenue, costs and profits in foodservice operations

Thus in foodservice operations:

■ **Revenue** (or sales) is most often counted as 100% and percentages for costs are always determined on this basis, i.e. as a percentage of sales.

■ **Gross profit** is total sales less cost of sales (or material costs – for food and beverages) and again the gross profit percentage[1] is determined as a percentage of sales.

■ **Net profit** is revenue less cost of sales, overheads and labour costs. Again net profit percentage and the percentage of overheads and labour are all calculated as a percentage of sales.

Examples of operational calculations, which include an illustration of the relationship between revenue, costs and profits, based on the matrix shown in Figure 9.1, are given at Appendix A.

---

1 For kitchen operations the gross profit percentage is sometimes referred to as kitchen percentage or kitchen profit.

■ Exploring gross profit

Gross Profit percentage (GP%) is widely considered to be the most important profitability measure. In most food and beverage operations this is measured weekly although it can be measured as often as is required as long as there are the resources available.

GP% is a simple measure of efficiency but it is important not to confuse efficiency with profitability. On many occasions an efficient operation is also a profitable one but this is not always the case. Food and beverage operations purchase ingredients that are processed into a consumable meal or drink. This process is in fact adding value to the raw ingredients, and the extent to which value is added is a measure of that operation's efficiency at achieving this conversion process.

An operation which converts a £2 ingredient cost into an £8 meal or drink might be said to be 400% efficient (£8 – the price, divided by £2 – the cost), and an operation which converts a £1 ingredient cost into a £5 meal or drink can be said to be 500% efficient. The second example is more efficient (500 compared to 400%) but is less profitable (£4 compared to £6).

An operation that has poor purchasing resulting in higher ingredient costs, poor storage resulting in wastage, poor security resulting in pilferage, poor production resulting in high wastage, poor portioning resulting in larger portions than specified and poor pricing resulting in lower revenue, will have a lower GP% than the same operation which improves on these poor performances. In larger foodservice organisations the unit and departmental manager is seen to have an influence over how these activities are performed and as such the GP% is thought to measure a particular manager's performance. However it is not usually the case that the unit or departmental manager has any influence over the price, this being determined higher up the organisation, and on many occasions they will not have an influence over the purchasing because specified suppliers and negotiated prices are again determined higher up the organisation.

The actual GP% figure against which a manager's performance is measured will also be set higher up the organisation. In a chain operation these GP%s will be set for each individual operation based on the sales mix of the menu and beverage lists. This sales mix – the amount sold of each menu and beverage list item – will vary from operation to operation depending on the customer profile and the selling techniques of the staff.

The manager can influence the selling techniques of the staff, but the manager usually has little influence over the customer profile. Perhaps the most influential factor over customer profile, especially in chain operations, is location. Bearing in mind these factors, an operation will be allocated a suitable GP% to obtain. Achieving this prescribed GP% is seen to be a good performance while not achieving it is seen to be a poor performance.

One way in which to decide upon the prescribed GP% is to run a particular unit or department over a period of time and take an average of the actual GP%s achieved. In reality GP%s are often set with reference to a desired efficiency level based on what is thought to be achievable (see also potential profitability, p. 000). This GP% is also seen to change as new menus are introduced.

An important factor which influences the introduction of new menus is the opportunity to increase the operation's efficiency and therefore new menus may often come with a higher GP% to obtain. In these situations a chain operation usually pilots the new menus in specifically selected units in order to obtain customer feedback and establish the new efficiency and profitability measure. This measure is then applied to the rest of the group's operations with slight variations for different customer profiles, as these will affect the sales mix of the individual units.

Having established the required GP%, the departmental or unit manager is then measured against the ability to achieve it. The dilemma with this measurement is that it measures a percentage not an absolute figure. Percentages are not cash and cannot be banked. A higher than required GP% will not necessarily realise a higher than required GP if the required revenue is not achieved (see Table 9.8).

Table 9.8: Comparison of GP in relation to revenue

	Operation A	Operation B
Required revenue (£)	1,000	1,000
Actual revenue (£)	900	1,100
GP percentage required (%)	65	65
GP percentage achieved (%)	66	64
GP required (£)	650	650
GP received (£)	594	704

- **Operation A** has a higher GP% than required at 66 (good management?) but only achieves a GP of £594, £56 below that required, because sales have not achieved their target (perhaps out of the control of the operation?).
- **Operation B** achieves a GP% below that which is required at 64 (bad management?) – but achieves a GP of £704, £54 above that required, because sales have exceeded the target (again, perhaps out of the control of the operation?).

In this example operation A could be said to be more efficient than operation B, but operation B is more profitable than operation A.

The example given in Table 9.8 indicates the reason why GP% is often more highly valued than GP itself. The GP% as a measure of efficiency will allow for variations of revenue. If operation A had achieved its GP% of 65, its actual GP would have been £584, and although this is below the required GP of £650 the operation can still be viewed as adding value or operating efficiently. The fact that the sales are £100 under that which is required may not be directly under the influence of the manager. Indeed it is normal for sales to fluctuate due to the inaccuracies of budgeting and predicting the future. Therefore by measuring GP%, allowances for these sales fluctuations are made. The same reasoning is applied to operation B. Sales are above the required or budgeted amount, but if the operation was running as efficiently as required and achieved its GP% of 65, the actual GP would have been £715, £11 more than actually achieved.

The tyranny of gross profit percentages

Many departmental and unit managers will perceive the achievement of the GP% as more important than the achievement of the budgeted revenue. As explained earlier in this chapter, revenue budgets may be seen as being too high for the unit to obtain and that even if the revenue budgets are achieved this may only mean that they are set higher next year. However, if the GP% is regularly achieved, the manager can state that the operation is being run efficiently. This thinking takes place at all the operational levels within a food and beverage operation. Regional managers and directors should be more concerned with cash profits rather than with percentage profits, but at the operational level the percentage values of the profits are more highly valued, often because more senior managers also attach to much value to them.

The reason for this anomaly is because the GP% measure is seen as a measure for controlling the efficiency of the management and staff rather than addressing profitability. As it is used as a control method, opportunities exist to exploit the system to the detriment of cash profit. Table 9.9 gives an example.

Table 9.9: Comparison of GP cash and GP percentage

Menu items	GP (£)	GP (%)	Selling price (£)
Beef	6.00	50	12.00
Fish	3.50	70	5.00
Chicken	4.50	75	6.00
Lamb	5.20	65	8.00

In the theoretical situation in Table 9.9 the two menu items that might be likely to be identified by the managers for positive selling would be the fish and chicken because they yielded a higher GP% than the beef and lamb. By selling these items the manager would be aiming to achieve as high as possible a GP% for the individual sale of a menu item, which would in turn contribute positively to the achievement of the required GP% for the whole operation. If, in this situation, the required GP% was 68%, the fish and the chicken sales would shift the balance of GP% achievement towards this goal, but any sales of beef and lamb would shift this balance away from the goal. The manager is motivated by an efficiency control mechanism towards achieving a required profit percentage.

However a more profit-focused examination of Table 9.9 reveals that it is not the fish and the chicken that are the most profitable items in cash terms. With GPs of £3.50 and £4.50 respectively they are considerably less profitable than the beef and the lamb at £6.00 and £5.20. A positive selling policy promoting the sales of the beef and the lamb would realise greater cash gross profits than the one promoting the fish and the chicken. However, because GP% is the control measure, the operation is seen to place more value on percentage profitability rather than cash profitability with the result of a decrease in cash profit. The fact that a control measure, which is so widely used in the foodservice industry, should have this effect (or at least the possibility of this effect) should be of serious concern to all foodservice operators.

■ Potential gross profit and potential gross percentage

Some food and beverage operations attempt to avoid the situation described above by the use of a further measure, which is termed potential profitability.

With the increasing introduction of computerised tills and control systems some operators calculate the cash GP and GP% that an operation should have achieved in theory for a particular time period. The ingredient cost and price of each menu or beverage item have already been entered into the till system which then automatically records the number of sales of these particular items, and thus a theoretical cash GP and GP% are calculated.

Recording such data is not new – computerised stock control systems are the main application of such systems – but not all operators are aware that this data can be converted into meaningful sales mix analysis information, of which potential cash GP and GP% are but two examples. Table 9.10 gives an example of a calculation for potential cash GP and GP%.

Table 9.10: Example of a calculation for potential cash GP and GP%

Menu items	Cost (£)	Price (£)	No. sold	Revenue (£)	GP (£)	GP (%)
Beef	6.00	12.00	100	1,200	600	50
Fish	1.50	5.00	150	750	525	70
Chicken	1.50	6.00	130	780	585	75
Lamb	2.80	8.00	70	560	364	65
Totals			450	3,290	2,074	63

Each of the four menu items in Table 9.10 is seen to be achieving a different cash GP and GP%. After totalling, the revenue is £3,290, and the potential cash GP and GP% are calculated at £2,075 and 63% respectively. This potential cash GP and GP% are what the operation should achieve with this particular sales mix. However, if the sales mix were to change from one period to another for any number of reasons (for example: changes in number of customers, increase in party bookings, changes in positive selling routines), then the potential cash GP and GP% may also change. Using the example of Table 9.10, an increase in the number of fish sold and with a decrease in the number of beef sold, while the total number of covers served remains the same, there is the a lower potential (and hence achievable) cash GP even though the GP% has increased. Table 9.11 shows the new potential measures to be £1949 and 66% respectively.

Table 9.11: Effect of changed sales mix

Menu items	Cost (£)	Price (£)	No. sold	Revenue (£)	GP (£)	GP (%)
Beef	6.00	12.00	50	600	300	50
Fish	1.50	5.00	200	1,000	700	70
Chicken	1.50	6.00	130	780	585	75
Lamb	2.80	8.00	70	560	364	65
Totals			450	2,940	1,949	66

In operations where potential case cash GP and GP% are calculated it is possible to measure the operation's performance against that which was actually achievable in relation to the sales mix for that particular period. In the two examples above it is seen that although the operation in Table 9.11 produces a potential GP% of 66 (a potential cash GP of £1949), it is not as profitable as the operation in Table 9.10, which only produces a potential GP% of 63 (but a potential cash GP of £2075, which is £126 more). Operations that calculate potential cash GP and GP% are therefore more able to measure the operation's efficiency in relation to a changing sales mix. This method of calculating potential cash GP and GP% not only continues to take account of changing sales levels but also changes in the sales mix, and as such can be seen as a much fairer way of measuring an operation's performance. More importantly, however, is the change in emphasis of this control and performance measure away from purely measuring GP% and towards measuring actual cash GP. Thus, taking potential GP% and cash GP into account shifts the appraisal of profit towards cash actually received and away from percentages.

However, in operations where potential GP% is calculated, there is evidence that there is a third GP% which is used to measure and control performance, namely a desired GP%. This desired GP% is set at a level that the operator would like to achieve, in much the same way as the GP% is set in operations where they do not calculate potential GP%. An example of how this might work in practice for a particular time period is:

Potential GP%	69
Actual GP% achieved	68.5
Desired GP%	70

In the example above the operator has set a desired GP% of 70. This is the GP% that the operator wants to achieve. From the actual sales mix for that period it was only possible to achieve a GP% of 69 – the potential GP% – and a GP% of 68.5 was actually obtained. The value placed on this performance might therefore be as follows:

- The unit was unable to achieve the GP% desired by the operator. This is a result of the sales mix and may have happened because waiting staff were unable to sell the required high GP% menu and beverage list items.

■ However, the unit was also unable to achieve the potential GP%, which is a measure of their inefficiency to add the required value.

Calculating potential GP% and cash GP, and using them to help appraise food and beverage operations, still allows for fluctuations of revenue – the reason why GP% is used as the main performance measure – but moves the consideration of value in the direction of GP cash and away from GP%. That many foodservice operators do not calculate potential GP% and cash GP, even though they already have the technology to do so, means that they are potentially reducing their ability to maximise cash profitability.

■ Sales mix analysis

Sales mix analyses methods involve identifying the sales relationship between the various menu and beverage list items. By far the most common application of these analyses is to determine the relationship of item numbers sold, i.e. a popularity index. A simple beverage list example is shown in Table 9.12.

Table 9.12: Sales mix example for beverages

Item	Number sold	Percentage of total
Champagne	20	10
Rhône wines	50	25
Loire wines	70	35
Bordeaux wines	60	30
Total	200	100

From the information shown in Table 9.12 it can be observed that Loire wines represent 35% of the total wine sales and as such are the most popular customer purchase. Bordeaux wines are the next most popular at 30%. Rhône wines at 25% are the third most popular and champagne at 10% is the least popular customer purchase.

Many operators use the identification and ranking of item popularity to assist with the compilation of new menus and beverage lists. In its most simplistic form the least popular item or items are removed from the listing although this is not always the case. In Table 9.12 it would worth retaining champagne on the wine list because customers expect to be able to purchase it when required, albeit infrequently. Champagne on the wine list will also contribute to the customers' perception of the operation's image.

However, popularity should not be confused with profitability. There is a relationship between popularity and profitability but the most popular selling item is not necessarily the most profitable. In order to examine this relationship it is important to identify which type of profit should be measured. As this is a relationship between individual menu and wine list items, the requirement is that the profit measure must also relate to these individual items. Apportioning costs to individual food and beverage items is difficult. How much of the electricity expenses should be apportioned to each item for example? The same difficulty is experienced when attempting to apportion labour costs. However, direct ingredient costs can be apportioned which will result in a measure of GP for each individual item. A relationship between popularity and GP is illustrated in Table 9.13.

Table 9.13: Example of profitability calculations

Item	GP (%)	No. Sold	Percentage of no. sold	Total GP (£)	Percentage of total GP
Standard burger	0.90	650	31.2	585.00	23.8
4oz burger	1.20	540	25.9	648.00	26.4
Standard cheeseburger	1.08	320	15.3	345.00	14.1
4oz cheeseburger	1.40	290	13.9	406.00	16.5
Double burger	1.65	285	13.7	470.25	19.2
Totals		2,085	100.00	2,454.85	100.00

From Table 9.13 it is possible to compare a popularity ranking with a profitability ranking, as shown in Table 9.14. The profitability ranking is clearly different from the popularity ranking, enabling a more focused valuation of the sales mix in relation to how much the individual menu items contribute – at a GP level – to operational profitability.

Table 9.14: Example of popularity and profitability rankings

Popularity ranking	Percentage of no. sold	Profitability ranking	Percentage of total GP
Standard burger	31.2	4oz burger	26.4
4oz burger	25.9	Standard burger	23.8
Standard cheeseburger	15.3	Double burger	19.2
4oz cheeseburger	13.9	4oz cheeseburger	16.5
Double burger	13.7	Standard cheeseburger	14.1

These techniques can have an element of sophistication; for example, linking with the amount of stock being held relative to its profitability, and consideration of a new menu item also relative to its potential profitability. All the various sales mix analysis techniques can categorise the individual menu and wine list items and suggest strategies for each category. These strategies are designed to improve profitability but there is evidence that the techniques themselves can be too complex and unproven to be assigned any value by many operations in the foodservice industry.

■ Menu engineering

One approach to sales analysis, which had gained some popularity, is the technique known as 'menu engineering'. This is a technique of menu analysis that uses two key factors of performance in the sales of individual menu items: the popularity and the GP cash contribution of each item. The analysis results in each menu item fitting into one of four categories: Stars, Plowhorses, Puzzles and Dogs. The advantage of this approach is that it provides a simple way of graphically indicating the relative cash contribution position of individual items on a matrix as illustrated in Figure 9.2.

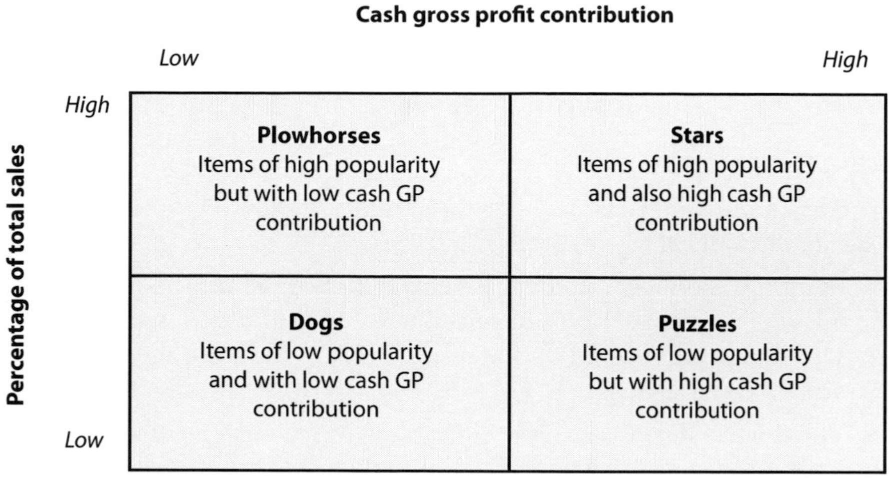

Cash gross profit contribution

Figure 9.2: Menu engineering matrix

Source: Adapted from Kasavana and Smith, 1990

There are a variety of computer-based packages that will automatically generate the categorisation, or some development of it, usually using data directly from the electronic point-of-sale control systems.

In order to determine the position of an item on the matrix two things need to be calculated. These are:

- The cash GP category
- The sales percentage category.

The cash GP category for any menu item is calculated by reference to the weighted average cash GP. Menu items with a cash GP which is the same as or higher than the average are classified as high. Those with lower than the average are classified as low cash GP items. The average also provides the axis separating Plowhorses and Dogs from Stars and Puzzles.

The sales percentage category for an item is determined in relation to the menu average taking into account an additional factor. With a menu consisting of ten items one might expect, other things being equal, that each item would account for 10% of the menu mix. Any item, which reached at least 10% of the total menu items sold, would therefore be classified as enjoying high popularity. Similarly any item, which did not achieve the rightful share of 10%, would be categorised as having a low popularity. With this approach half of the menu items would tend to be shown as being below average in terms of their popularity. This would potentially result in the frequent revision of the composition of the menu. It is for this reason that Kasavana and Smith (1982) recommended the use of a 70% formula. Under this approach, all items, which reach at least 70% of their rightful share of the menu mix, are categorised as enjoying high popularity. For example, where a menu consists of say 20 items, any item that reached 3.5% or more of the menu mix (70% of 5%) would be regarded as enjoying high popularity. While there is no convincing theoretical support for choosing the 70% figure rather than some other percentage, common sense and experience tends to suggest that there is some merit in this approach.

Interpreting the categories

There is a different basic strategy that can be considered for items that fall into each of the four categories of the matrix:

- **Stars** are the most popular items, which may be able to yield even higher GP contributions by careful price increases or through cost reduction. High visibility is maintained on the menu and standards for the dishes should be strictly controlled.

- **Plowhorses** again are solid sellers, which may also be able to yield greater cash profit contributions through marginal cost reduction. Lower menu visibility than Stars is usually recommended.

- **Puzzles** are exactly what they are called. Items such as for instance flambé dishes or a particular speciality can add an attraction in terms of drawing customers, even though the sales of these items may be low. Depending on the particular item different strategies might be considered, ranging from accepting the current position because of the added attraction that they provide to increasing the price further.

- **Dogs** are the worst items on a menu and the first reaction is to remove them. An alternative, however, is to consider adding them to another item as part of a special deal. For instance, adding them in a meal package to a Star may have the effect of lifting the sales of the Dog item and may provide a relatively low-cost way of adding special promotions to the menu.

Some potential limitations

Elasticity of demand

One of the practical difficulties with price level adjustment is not knowing enough about the 'elasticity of demand'. The effect of demand (number of covers) of any one change in the general level of menu prices is usually uncertain. Also, what applies to one menu item equally applies to the menu as a whole. There is an additional problem of 'cross-elasticity of demand' where the change in demand for one commodity is directly affected by a change in price of another. Even less is known about the cross-elasticity of demand for individual menu items than the elasticity of demand for the menu as a whole. Any benefit arising from an adjustment in the price of one item may therefore be offset by resultant changes in the demand for another item. Price level adjustments must therefore be underpinned by a lot of common sense, experience and knowledge of the particular circumstances of the operation.

Labour intensity

In menu engineering the most critical element is cash gross profit. While this may be important the aspect of labour intensity cannot be ignored. The cash GP on a flambé dish for example may be higher than on a more simple sweet, however, when the costs of labour are taken into account – especially at peak periods –it may well be that the more simple sweet is the more profitable overall.

Shelf life

The food cost of an item used to determine the cash GP may not take account of cost increases which are the result of food wastage through spoilage, especially at slack times.

Fluctuations in demand

Another factor is the consistency of the buying of the consumer. The approach assumes that changes can be made in the promotion of various items and that this will be reflected in the buying behaviour of the customer. The approach will work well where the potential buying pattern of the consumer is fairly similar over long periods. However, where the customers are continually changing, as for instance in the restaurant of an hotel, popularity and profitability can become more affected by changes in the nature of the customer and the resultant change in demand rather than as a result of the operation attempting to manipulate the sales mix.

Further applications

9

While this technique is presented here related to menu food items the same technique can also be applied to wine and drink lists. It is interesting to note, for example, that in many instances the house wine, although having the highest gross profit percentage contribution, often makes a relatively low contribution to the cash gross profit. Additionally, the principles of the technique underpin the approaches to the selling of hotel rooms and the rates that may be charged, now known as 'yield management'.

It is clear however that although there are some difficulties, benefits can arise since the menu engineering approach requires the following:

- Planning for continuous control of cash GP
- Giving prominence to, and controlling the determinants of, menu profitability; i.e. the number of items sold, the cash GP per item and the overall composition of the menu
- Application of an analytical approach recognising that menu items belong to distinctly dissimilar groups, which have different characteristics and which require different handling in the context of cash gross profit control.

■ Exploring net profit and operating profit

These profitability measures are used to evaluate more fully the efficiency of a food and beverage operation to add value, because they take account of all or most of the costs incurred by the business. The relationship between costs and revenue to produce net operating profit is not as directly proportional as the GP measure and it is more difficult therefore to identify the relationship between an individual menu and wine list item and total net operating profit.

The main relationship for total net operating profit appears to be with total sales revenue. This relationship is twofold. As a percentage measure it values an operation's efficiency at adding value. As an absolute measure it values a specific amount of residual utility – usually in cash – which has been derived from an absolute revenue. As has already been examined, a high percentage measure may be of less residual utility – cash – than a lower percentage measure. However, as long as the measures are calculated using the same criteria, i.e. they use the same revenue and costs measures, they can be compared. This comparison can help appraise an operation's performance. Table 9.15 gives examples of net operating profit measures.

Table 9.15: Comparison of net operating profit

	Year one (£ 000s)	(%)	Actual: Year two (£ 000s)	(%)	Year three (£ 000s)	(%)	Budget for: Year three (£ 000s)	(%)
Unit A								
Sales	1,500		1,600		1,700		1,800	
Net op profit	150	10	155	9.70	145	8.53	180	10
Unit B								
Sales	700		750		800		900	
Net operating profit	70	10	75	10	67.5	8.44	90	10

In the example in Table 9.15 all the measures have been made using the same criteria, year on year, and for both units. An appraisal of the operation's performance, as individual one-off food and beverage unit, might be as follows.

Unit A

- Sales have increased by £100,000 year-on-year representing a percentage increase year-on-year of 6.67% and 6.25%, and overall by 13.3%. Sales for year three are also up £100,000 but 5.55% under budget.

- Net operating profit increased 3.33% by £5000 in the year two and decreased 6.45% by £10,000 in year three. Net operating for year three is £35 000 and 19.44% under budget.

- Net operating profit as a percentage of sales has declined from 10 to 9.7 to 8.53% compared with a required level in year three of 10%.

Unit B

- Sales have increased by £50, 000 year on year representing a percentage increase year on year of 7.14 and 6.67%, and overall by 14.3%. Sales for year three are also up £50,000 but are 11.11% under budget.

- Net operating profit increased 7.14% by £5000 in year two and decreased 10% by £7,500 in year three. Net operating profit for year three is also £22,500 down and 25% under budget. From year one to year three net operating profit declined by 3.57% (£70,000 to £67,500).

- Net operating profit as a percentage of sales (10%) was maintained in year three but has declined to 8.44% in year three.

The evaluation above identifies the differences between absolute figures and the differences between percentages. This may appear at times to be fairly tortuous, especially when all the changes are presented together. In reality more value may be placed upon certain measurements than others, depending on the message to be communicated, and not all the measurements will be communicated at the same time.

Using the examples above it could be said that sales have increased in Unit A by over 6% each year, but this says nothing about net operating profit being almost 20% under budget. This is why it is so important to question the presentation of the information that is provided. When it is stated that sales have increased by over 6% each year, the immediate response should be to ask for other performance measures, in this case profit both in percentage and in cash terms. Questioning is crucial in order to fully appraise an operation. And again it is important to remember that it is only cash, and not percentages, that can be banked.

■ Industry norms

Many might argue that further value can be placed upon the information in Table 9.15 by comparing the performance of these operations with an industry norm, i.e. a measure which suggests a performance generally found and therefore expected within the industry. There are however two key difficulties in this approach:

1 Foodservice operations must be categorised into industry sectors before an average or mean net/operating profit can be calculated for that sector. It is possible to categorise foodservice operations but no two operations are the same (even chain operations differ), and each will probably have different objectives resulting in different values being placed upon their profitability.

2 The environment in which food and beverage operations operate is dynamic. This environment relates to: consumer behaviour and social/cultural changes; the financial market; the national and international economic position; and political issues and legislation. Different operations will react to these continuing changes in different ways resulting in differing valuations of profitability. The norm therefore may be seen as an arbitrary measure.

9

■ The effects of inflation

Inflation is another consideration, which may be taken into account, as it is a measure of the usually upward movement of prices across a range of commodities and services. For example, if net/operating profit had increased by 10% over the last 12 months, and inflation had been 5% over the last 12 months, it might be considered that in real terms profitability is up only 5% (10% profitability improvement minus 5% inflation). This will be an important consideration for those managing, owning and directing food and beverage operations in the appraisal of profitability. In addition, company taxation and dividends are also an important consideration and will affect profitability.

■ Stakeholder interests

As in any appraisal of performance, the important consideration in making any comparison is the value of the information to the stakeholders, i.e. those with a vested or invested interest in the business. An understanding of the stakeholder interests can make the appraisal of the operation more objective and of more value.

■ Key points of profit appraisal

- It is always necessary to be clear how any profit measure is arrived at and ensure that any comparisons made are like with like.
- Profitability measures themselves have no value, it is only when they are appraised against an objective that they may have some value attached to them.
- Setting the objective, norm and/or budget is difficult and sometimes results in subjective judgements.
- Sales mix analysis is important in determining the difference between the popularity and profitability of items.
- Gross prof it percentages are used as a measure of efficiency but this is not the same as measuring profitability.
- Profit percentages are often used, as the basis for comparison but cash profit contribution is what the operation should be seeking to achieve.
- Comparison with industry norms can be useful, if applied with caution, especially to chain operations.
- Comparison over time can be useful with rolling 12-month totals providing a useful basis for determining true trends and performance.
- Considering profitability must take account of the needs and interests of the operation's various stakeholders.

For further information on profit planning see, for example, Harris (2011).

9.5   Appraising the product

It is clearly good business sense to monitor level of satisfaction that customers have with the current customer service specification. This is especially important in relation to changing customer needs. Objective product appraisal will help in determining the extent to which the customer service specification is matching, and continuing to match, both the operator's and the customers' expectations.

We saw, in Chapter 3, a six-stage process for an integrated approach to service quality management. This process was summarised in the Figure 3.4. Stages four and five of the process require the monitoring of the operational aspects (technical and procedural standards) and the monitoring of customer satisfaction. The undertaking of these two stages in tandem will provide the information on the product of the operation, which will identify the need for changes that might be necessary to the customer service specification.

Single unit and/or owner-operated food and beverage operations often adopt a fairly subjective and intuitive approach to product appraisal. However this does not mean that it cannot be as, or even more, effective than a structured and objective one. This subjective and intuitive approach may be more efficient for a single operation that does not have to appraise and control its product over a multi-unit structure. Also, although it is highly dependent on the integrity and skills of its management and staff, there is really no problem if the customers also have the same subjective values and perceptions. It is this intuitive response to customer needs that enables some single food and beverage operations to be highly successful.

Chain operations usually lead the field in this area. With their branded products it is necessary to effect tight control over the customer service specification. Appraising and controlling revenue and costs are systemised through budgeting, and standardised procedures. Appraising and controlling the product are also effected through the use of standardised procedures, including the use of standards of performance manuals. Many of these approaches are also adaptable and useful to a single foodservice operation.

■   Approaches to product appraisal

Customer satisfaction questionnaires

Customer satisfaction questionnaires are often found in hospitality operations and/or sent to customers after they have experienced the product. The forms usually ask for some rating of the experience with details ranging from factors such as warmth of greeting to value for menu and also likelihood of recommending the operation to someone else. Whilst these types of forms can be very useful from a public relations point of view they often provide little in the way of useful objective measurement of the achievement of the customer service specification.

Complaint monitoring

The monitoring of complaints (and compliments) can assist in measuring the achievement of customer satisfaction and the achievement of various aspects of the customer service specification. The effectiveness of this process though is very dependent on being able to determine if the complaint is in fact a result of not meeting the customer service specification. It is quite possible that complaints will come from those whose expectations are higher than the intended customer service specification or that the complaints are unjustified or the result of some other dissatisfaction, which is not in the control of the operation in the first place.

Staff focus group sessions

The running of staff focus groups can provide a valuable review process for operations, especially when independent people lead these sessions. Opportunities can be taken to review the customer service specification against the experience of the staff who have to operate as part of it. Reports from the service staff can provide a springboard from which to go back through the design of the original customer service specification and to identify where changes can and need to be made.

Mystery shopper

A mystery shopper is an unidentified customer who tests the services of the organisation. This individual will check that standards are maintained. The mystery shopper will work to a brief and check list (basically a diagnostic tool). Some mystery shoppers will also be involved in benchmarking competitors. Mystery shoppers are not expert; they need by necessity to remain customers. The individual shoppers tend then not to be professionals, although the companies behind them are professional.

Process reviewer

The process reviewer differs from a mystery shopper in that the process review is employed to identify problems and also opportunities for improvement. This approach can also be adapted for use in making comparisons with competitors. The process reviewer will more than likely be an internal reviewer (a member of staff) who will also signal training needs. Reviews are primarily concerned with checking if the right things are being done.

Quality auditor

Quality auditors are usually independent people who are concerned with checking on the standards at every stage to ensure conformance to procedures. An audit can also test hypotheses or substantiate hunches about organisational service efficiency and effectiveness. The auditor offers independent evaluation of facility and service quality to determine fitness for use and conformance to customer service specifications. The auditor will both observe and participate in the customer experience. Audits tend to be consumer oriented and usually provide a wealth of detail on the operation as well as comparisons with competitor achievement.

Quality standards analyst

The quality standards analyst (QSA) is a professional, with hospitality industry experience, generally brought in by senior management. The analyst will undertake a planned and systematic examination of the quality system and its implementation and determine the adequacy of the system and conformance to it. This individual will also look at all quality related aspects of the business. As well as producing a standard report, the analyst will ensure that the report is more qualitative in nature, than a quality auditor's report, which is usually more quantitative. This is also similar to the *Hospitality Assured* programme of the Institute of Hospitality (previously referred to in Chapter 3, page 57).

The basis of many of these approaches is often a checklist of aspects, with some operations having identified and specified over 150 aspects. This list will contain aspects covering such areas as:

- The words, demeanour and body language of the welcome
- The information and selling routine
- The time taken to deliver each menu and beverage list item ordered
- The taste, colour, texture, temperature and presentation of menu and beverage items
- The presentation of the bill and concluding routine.

Once the customer service specification has been evaluated both in terms of the operational aspects (technical and procedural standards) and the level of customer satisfaction, an appraisal can also take place in non-customer areas. This part of the appraisal can cover such areas as:

- Temperature and stocking levels in the fridges and freezers
- Cleanliness, security and safety of all areas
- Current data collection and collation up to date.

Once this product audit has been completed the results are often calculated as a percentage of the possible achievement. Each operation will, or should have, already determined the level of achievement required. Where the level of achievement is unacceptable this then leads to resources being concentrated to rectify specific underperformances (or non-compliance with the customer service specification). This process is dynamic, and as changes are made to the product, so the customer service specification is modified.

■ Using product appraisal data

The various processes outlined above will produce a variety of data about the operation. This can be used to review, and alter where necessary, the customer service specification.

However within the data there will also be information that may provide for a broader range of possibilities. Better use of the data can provide for a far more qualitative, and therefore richer, analysis of the information, which leads to be better understanding of the operation.

The data can be used to generate information on what is important to the customer and how the operation is achieving those things, is capable of achieving those things and also if the staff share the same view on what is important. Considering these various aspects is the basis of some of the thinking behind the 'SERVQUAL' approaches (as discussed in, for instance, in Bowie and Buttle, 2004 and Johnston and Clark, 2008). Three other examples of useful comparison matrices, which apply and extend some of the approaches, are presented and explained below:

Customer importance/Operational achievement

This two-by-two matrix considers all the aspects of the customer service specification and is used to indicate the level of importance the customer attaches to them, against the level of the achievement of the operation in meeting these requirements. Placing the various aspects on the matrix can be useful in determining and planning what action should be taken. The matrix, which has four positions, is shown in Figure 9.3.

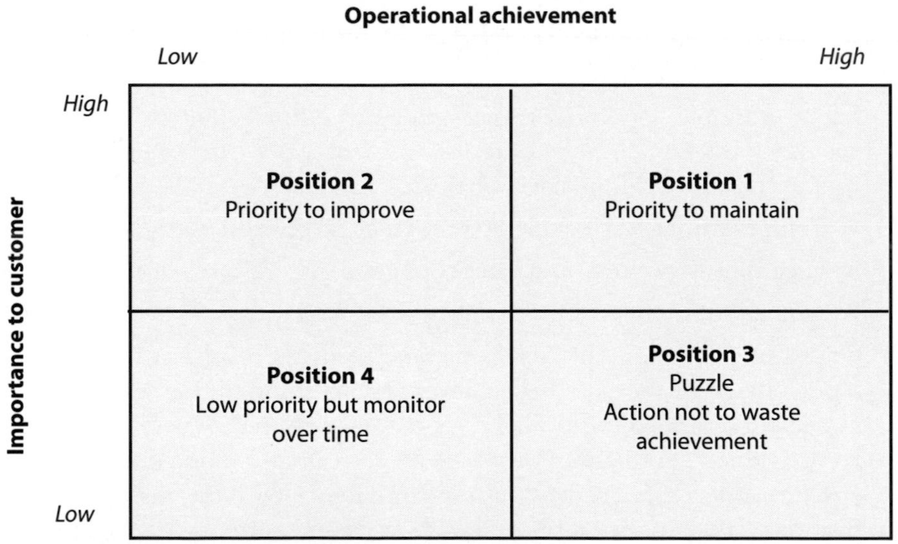

Figure 9.3: Customer importance/Operational achievement matrix

- **Position 1 – High Importance and High Achievement**

    The first priority of any operation is to maintain these aspects. This is always true as taking action on other positions before these are attended to could potentially endanger achievements in this position. Action should only be taken in the remaining three positions if the operation can be sure that aspects already in this position can be maintained.

■ **Position 2 – High Importance and Low Achievement**

The second priority is to examine and take action on these aspects. It is clear that the customer places a high importance on these aspects and therefore action taken on them can lead to quick returns in improved customer satisfaction levels. Action to be taken here can be a mixture of reviewing equipment appropriateness and stock levels as well as staff training and development.

■ **Position 3 – Low Importance and High Achievement**

Aspects that appear in this position are always a puzzle. There is something being achieved but it is not of great importance to the customer. Aspects here can be combined with aspects in box 2 above so that possible trade-offs can be achieved. Offering the customer high achievement in something else could in some way compensate for things, which are of high importance, but which are not currently being fully achieved. Offering a fast business lunch option could, for instance, potentially compensate for a limited range menu.

■ **Position 4 – Low Importance and Low Achievement**

The initial response to aspects that appear here is to leave them. Yes they are of low priority but customer needs change and these factors do need to be monitored. Long-term lack of achievement could lead to possible future customer dissatisfaction with another aspect of the service.

Customer importance/Operational capability

This two by two matrix considers aspects of the customer service specification and is used to indicate the level of importance that the customers attach to them against the extent to which the operation is actually capable of achieving them. Placing the various aspects on the matrix can be useful in determining and planning what action should be taken. The matrix, which has four positions, is shown in Figure 9.4

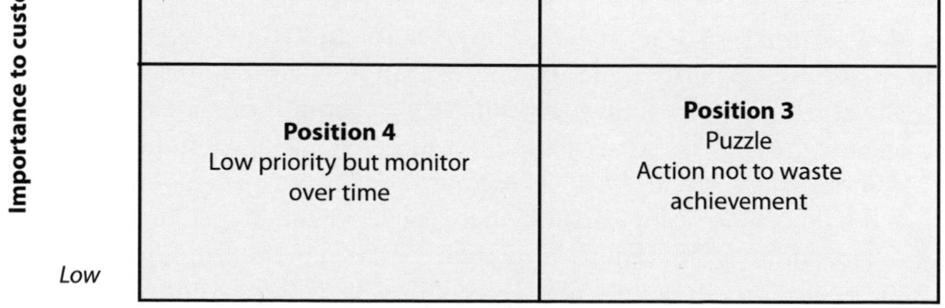

Figure 9.4: Customer importance/Operational capability matrix

- **Position 1 – High Importance and High Capability**

  Again the first priority for action in any operation is to maintain these aspects. This is always true. Taking action to improve capability elsewhere could potentially endanger achievements in this position. Action should only be taken in the remaining three positions if the operation can be sure that aspects already in this position can be maintained.

- **Position 2 – High Importance and Low Capability**

  The second priority is to examine and take action on these aspects. It is clear that the customer places a high impotence on these aspects and therefore again action taken on them will lead to quick returns in improved customer satisfaction levels. The action taken however may also mean that the customer service specification is changed and that the customer is advised more clearly that the operation is not able to offer particular aspect.

- **Position 3 – Low Importance and High Capability**

  Aspects that appear in this position are again a puzzle. There is something that the operation is capable of achieving but it is not currently of great importance to the customer. Again aspects here can be combined with aspects in box 2 above so that possible trade offs can be achieved. Additionally a feature and benefit can be made of this particular aspect so that customer satisfaction can be improved through an impression being given of greater added value.

- **Position 4 – Low Importance and Low Capability**

  The initial response to aspects that appear here is again to leave them. The priority for action planning may be low but again customer needs change and these factors do need to be monitored. Long-term lack of capability could lead to possible future customer dissatisfaction either with another aspect of the service or with the operation not being able to respond to future priorities that customers may have.

Customer importance/Staff importance

This matrix considers aspects of the customer service specification and the level of importance the customer attaches to them against the extent to which the same aspects are important to the staff. Again placing the various aspects on the matrix can be useful in determining and planning what action should be taken. The matrix has four positions and is shown in Figure 9.5.

- **Position 1 – High Customer Importance and High Staff Importance**

  The first priority again of any operation is to maintain these aspects. This is again always true. Strengthening the capability of staff and rewarding their achievement of these aspects will reinforce their importance for staff and the operation as a whole. Again it is important to focus on these aspects first as taking action to balance things up elsewhere could potentially endanger achievements in this position. Again action should only be taken in the remaining three positions if the operation can be sure that aspects already in this position can be maintained.

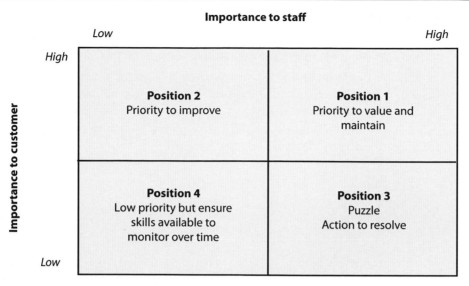

Importance to staff

Figure 9.5: Customer Importance/Staff Importance matrix

- **Position 2 – High Customer Importance and Low Staff Importance**

  The second priority is to examine and take action on these aspects. It is clear that the customer places a high impotence on these aspects and therefore again action taken on them will lead to quick returns in improved customer satisfaction levels. However there could be a variety of reasons why staff may not consider these aspects as important. These may range from difficulties that the staff encounter in providing a particular type of service, such as equipment shortages, to a lack of competence or confidence. Action taken here then should be well considered, although clearly the intention is that the staff should share the same value as the customers in the importance attached to a particular aspect of the customer service specification.

- **Position 3 – Low Customer Importance and High Staff Importance**

  Aspects that appear in this position are again a puzzle. These are things that the staff think are important to achieve but which are not currently of great importance to the customer. This can have serious consequences for an operation. If the members of staff believe that they have capabilities that the customer and the establishment do not value, or that they do not in effect share the same values as the customer in relation to the customer service specification, then it does raise obvious questions about the suitability of the staff in the first place. Difficulties here can also be affecting the problems being identified by aspects in box 2 above. Trade-offs are not really possible. The aspects that are of importance to the customers must be reflected in the importance attached to them by staff, otherwise the customer service specification cannot be achieved.

- **Position 4 – Low Customer Importance and Low Staff Importance**

  The initial response to aspects that appear here is again to leave them. The priority, for action planning purposes, may be low but again customer needs change and these factors do need to be monitored. Therefore there is some merit in increasing the awareness of staff about these aspects so that they are able to monitor possible changes over time in the customers' priorities.

The use of the three approaches exampled above can be complex and sophisticated, using well-designed questionnaires and external consultants to provide greater objectivity. However these approaches can also be used simply and productively as, for example, a basis for conducting staff focus groups or as a basis for team development sessions.

10 Making strategic decisions

Aim

This chapter aims to consider and apply approaches to strategic decision-making.

Objectives

This chapter is intended to support you in:

- Identifying the components of strategic planning as a systematic process

- Developing skills in the application of a range of performance measures and appraisal techniques

- Identifying and applying approaches to business analysis and evaluation

- Selecting and applying strategic planning models and approaches appropriate to foodservice operations.

10.1 The origins of strategy

Assessing the achievement of an organisation against its aims and within the business environment leads to the requirement to consider making strategic decisions about the current operation and the future of the organisation.

Strategy is the means by which organisations attempt to achieve their objectives. In most organisations there is likely to be a complex set of stakeholders concerned to influence the objectives and hence the strategy of the organisation. Rather than be too concerned about the right definition of strategy it is useful to develop an understanding of what different writers or speakers mean by strategy, i.e. what are the underlying concepts that they are trying to get across?

As a working definition for the purposes of this book, let us propose that strategic decisions are:

- Major decisions that affect the direction that an organisation, or part of an organisation, is committed to for the next few years
- Decisions which involve a commitment of resources
- Decisions which involve complex situations at corporate, business unit and operational level which may affect and be affected by many parts of the organisation.

Within this context there are then a number of terms often used in relation to strategic decision-making. These include:

- **Vision**: conceptual or imagined view of the organisation as it might be in the future.
- **Mission**: fundamental purpose of an organisation, which is intended to lead it towards its vision.
- **Policy**: set of ground rules and criteria to be applied when making decisions.
- **Goals/Aims**: broad intentions of the organisation.
- **Strategy**: means by which the organisation tries to fulfil its mission.
- **Objectives**: measurable statements of what must be achieved as part of the strategy in order for the goals/aims to be realised.
- **Tactics**: decisions and actions intended to achieve short-term objectives.

These terms may also be see as being presented in a hierarchy. Thus **policies** are derived from thinking about the **vision** and the **mission** of the organisation, and **objectives** are determined in order to ensure that the **goals/aims** of the organisation are achieved. The establishment of goals and objectives for an operation have previously been discussed in Chapter 2. The interpretation of these terms can however vary depending on where and how they are being used.

■   Levels of strategy

It is now widely recognised that strategy making should take place at different levels of the organisation. It is also common practice to identify three levels of strategy: corporate, business unit and operational levels:

1   **Corporate strategy** includes the plans for the strategic direction of the enterprise and how this is to be achieved.

2   **Business strategy** is developed for the business unit whether this be a single establishment or a division of a company.

3   **Operations strategy** includes the product, market, and functional and departmental plans.

The part of the organisation where the responsibility will lie for these different levels will vary from organisation to organisation. In a small company the business unit will also be the corporate level and operational level; but in a larger organisation the levels can be separated with different managers at each level. How the three levels of strategy relate can be indicated as in Figure 10.1.

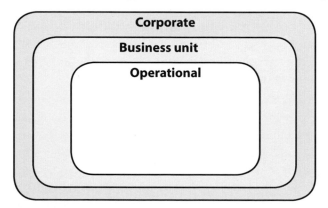

Figure 10.1: The three levels of strategy and the relationship between them

10

The strategies at the various levels in an organisation clearly need to be consistent. However this does not mean that they have to be common or the same. The appropriate business and operational strategies for a national foodservice company may not need to be the same in each of the locations it is operating in (for example, resort, city centre, tourist area, transportation). It is also worth reminding ourselves that any foodservice operation is not necessarily in one market. The same unit could, for instance, be in the restaurant, licensed trade, banqueting, conference, business and leisure markets. In short, different approaches may be required for different customer groups or more appropriately the different types of demand, which the operation is designed to satisfy.

10.2 Assessing current performance

In the same way as we identified three levels for considering strategy it is also common to use the same three levels when considering the performance of the current operation as a whole. These levels are:

1 **Operational** – which includes day-to-day sales and the way the product is provided and promoted

2 **Business** – which is considering the performance of the enterprise in terms of profitability, competitiveness and other business measures

3 **Corporate** – which is considering the strategic direction of the operation and how this is being achieved.

In a single business unit these three levels are operating together. In a larger enterprise different members of staff and management may undertake the responsibilities for each of these levels separately.

It can be useful though, to consider any enterprise having these three levels. It makes for the consideration of any matters at any of the three levels not as independent issues but within the context of the organisation as a whole. Thus operational issues and decisions made about them are set within the business requirements and also then within the contribution that is being made to the corporate direction of the enterprise.

Operations are not an end in themselves: decisions made to correct underperformance or over performance at the operational level have to take account of the business implications and the strategic direction required. It may well be that operational underperformance or over-performance is a result of changes in the business environment and this should be identified before any corrective action is taken, otherwise this can lead to an effort potentially frustrated and at worst, resources wasted. Equally corporate and business decisions must take account of the operational capability of the operation in achieving them.

■ When and how

Decisions need to be made on when the appraisal of the whole operation should take place and how such an appraisal should be performed.

When the appraisal takes place will be dependent upon the constraints and opportunities perceived by the enterprise, and the rate of change in these issues. Although formal performance appraisal can normally be undertaken half-yearly or yearly, it is often the case, especially within a fast-changing business environment, that the process would be more organic with the formal processes being used to confirm the action, which may have already been taken.

How such an appraisal is structured will affect the outcome of the appraisal process and the value placed upon it. It can be helpful to separate the appraisal of the whole operation into three main activities:

- Quantitative analysis
- Business environment appraisal
- Qualitative evaluation.

These three areas are interdependent, but it can be useful to consider them separately before considering the interrelationship between them and subsequently the processes for making strategic decisions.

Quantitative analysis

An analysis of financial and other quantitative data relating to a specific foodservice organisation is useful because undertaking it can:

- Enable a study of trends and progress over a number of years
- Enable comparisons with the competition and the industry as a whole
- Reveal lost profit and growth potential
- Point the way forward by identifying areas needing improvement. This is especially the case when the organisation is not performing well compared to major competitors and/or within the industry as a whole
- Identify and emphasise possible danger areas.

Much of the Chapter 9 was concerned with identifying techniques for quantitative operational appraisal. Alongside the operational ratios should also be considered other financial ratios. Ratio analysis is extensively used to assess the financial position of a company. It is aimed at characterising the company in a few basic areas affecting its financial standing.

There are many ways of grouping operational and financial ratios and formulae. The following are the main categories for most of the common formulae:

- Operational ratios
- Activity ratios
- Profitability ratios
- Liquidity ratio
- Gearing ratios
- Stock market ratios.

Each of the common ratios, and the formulas and explanations of what the individual ratio can indicate, are detailed under these six headings in Appendix B. As there are several formulae in each category, this can make this type of analysis seem complicated. However the operational ratios summarised in Appendix B have already been considered in depth in Chapter 9. Many of the rest of these ratios are calculated at either the business or corporate level in the organisation.

In order to interpret fully the meaning of a ratio, it is necessary to have some basis of comparison. For operational ratios, there will usually be internal budgets and objectives against which to measure them. To illustrate this further an

10

examples of budget and trading results comparison and evaluation is detailed in Appendix C.

Operational ratios can also have more general values based on traditional experience and industry norms. Many of the rest of the ratios also have such values. For instance generally desirable figures for liquidity are a liquidity ratio of 2 and an acid test of 1. Such absolute figures are difficult to justify completely and relative figures are therefore often used with respect to the industry average or close competitors. When considering the share prices of a company, for example, it is usual to compare the company's share price with other companies' share prices within the sector and to compare it against the Stock Market FTSE 100.

No single figure provides sufficient information for evaluating the operational and business performance and also the financial health of the enterprise. Reasoned judgements as to the financial standing of the company will involve groups of calculations being undertaken. The important point is that this analysis taken as a whole is what needs to be considered not any particular figure.

Skills in quantitative analysis and evaluation are an essential part of food and beverage management. This is because quantitative analysis and evaluation of the operation:

■ Are essential parts of performance appraisal, alongside other analytical tools

■ Need to be considered over time in order to compare how they vary year on year and where possible how they compare with the average of the industry.

Generating quantitative data provides a useful background for appraising the performance of the organisation; but care needs to be taken when the results are being interpreted:

■ The view that is being provided is based on historical data. It does not automatically imply that the trend identified will continue into the future.

■ At best, average ratios provide a guideline to existing proportions that are representative in a given industry.

Additionally a number of different ratios need to be calculated before any conclusions should be drawn:

■ Ratios should be used as an additional tool to back up issues identified in another area of analysis.

■ The evaluation of the ratios is more important than the figures themselves.

■ Business environment appraisal

Appraising the business environment enables a food and beverage operation to understand how it relates to the current business environment, how the business environment is changing, and facilitates an objective view of the future. Appraising the business environment also includes an examination of the competition and the threats to the operation, which competitors may pose.

The range of resources apportioned to this activity can vary, with large operators employing economists and strategic directors, and small operators often relying on instinct and intuition. For the hospitality industry there are a range of professional sources of information that regularly provide opportunities for sharing information and gaining insights into changes in the business environment. These include the professional and trade bodies and the trade press.

There are also several techniques available to assist in the appraisal of the business environments, which are covered in detail in a variety of texts and publications. We have previously considered two of these in Chapter 1. These two approaches to analysing the business environment are: PESTLE analysis (pages 16 to 18) for considering the macro-environment, and Porter's Five Forces (pages 18 to 21) for considering the industry environment. In Chapter 2, we have also considered the basis for determining aims and objectives and the concept development. Chapter 3 continued then to examine how the food and beverage product can be developed to ensure a consumer-product relationship as a dynamic process.

The PESTLE (Political, Economic, Social, Technological, Legal and Ecological) analysis, when carried out well, is a sophisticated approach, which provides for a fairly wide and deep evaluation of the current and potential business environment.

Porter's Five Forces model helps in considering the competitiveness of a particular industry. The approach takes account of the rivalry amongst existing firms competing in the industry, the threat of new entrants, the strength of buyers, the strength of industry suppliers and the extent to which substitute products can affect the demand for particular foodservice products.

Using these, amongst other, analysis techniques is a learning process, which will strengthen the organisation by making possible a more focused appraisal of how the food and beverage operation complements and matches the business environment in which it operates.

The value placed upon any of the analysis tools by foodservice operators will be dependent upon their skills and objectives. To ignore these approaches is unwise; to include them in appraising an operation's performance, no matter how modestly, is good business sense.

Qualitative evaluation

In many ways the qualitative evaluation of an operation is on the one hand the hardest to achieve well but on the other hand potentially the most rewarding. It is about getting to the heart of the reasons for the success of the operation and for considering how to maintain and develop it further.

Section 9.5, *Appraising the product*, details various approaches to qualitative analysis on which to make judgements about the extent to which the organisation is achieving its customer service specification. We have also considered above the various approaches to quantitative analysis and approaches to appraising the business environment. In all cases any qualitative evaluation needs to be considered taking account of the current and future business needs as well as being supported by data. We have already identified that:

- Quantitative assessment should be used as an additional tool to back up issues identified in another area of analysis
- The evaluation of the quantitative analysis is more important than the figures themselves.

Qualitative evaluation takes account of the quantitative analysis and also the appraisal of the external business environment. The outcomes of qualitative evaluation are informed views being taken on, for example, the extent to which:

- The customer service specification is appropriate to meet the current and intended customer demand, or are some parts of the specification higher than required and others insufficient
- The customer service specification can be simplified to make it easier to provide, or to make it more cost effective and reliable
- The service is consistent and reliable and whether that is a major selling point
- Processes and procedures are competitive with those of competitors and if not knowing why not
- All the aspects of quality control and quality assurance of the food and beverages being sold and the service of them are being controlled
- The equipment is at the standard required (both in capability and stock level terms) to meet the customer service specification and what equipment will have to be improved or replaced
- Members of staff are well selected, up to the job and supported by sufficient training
- Members of staff are paid well enough and are motivated to contribute to the fulfilment of the customer service specification
- Staff suggestions are listened to in order to consider changes to the range of products on offer
- The organisation has the ability to maintain the current customer service specification and the ability to respond to change.

Attempting to develop views on these types of issues can illuminate other issues such as the effectiveness of the customer service specification in meeting what the customer wants, and also what staff and managers understand the competitors are about to do.

The data that will be generated from the quantitative analysis, and the appraisal of the business environment will have already generated a variety of possible actions to be taken. Action will be as much dependent on the needs of the operation as it will on determining the effectiveness of the operation in meeting current and future business demands.

■ Using the foodservice cycle as an analysis tool

A systematic way of approaching the appraisal of the operation is to use the foodservice cycle as an analysis tool. The cycle can be used as a dynamic model. Figure 10.2 gives the eight stages of the cycle (which we first saw in Chapter 1) and indicates the issues that could be considered under each stage.

The foodservice cycle	Issues to be considered in appraising the operation
1 The consumer and the market	Changes in the markets served by the operation and changes in the consumer needs.
2 Formulation of policy	The level of achievement in meeting the objectives of the operation and the extent to which the goals and the vision are being realised.
3 Interpretation of demand	The appropriateness of the existing menu and beverage lists and other services in meeting the customer needs, and the extent to which the existing customer service specification is sustainable.
4 Convergence of facilities	The effectiveness of the planning and design and operational capability of the facilities, plant and equipment to support the customer service specification.
5 Provisioning	The effectiveness of the purchasing, storage and control methods to meet the operational requirements.
6 Production and distribution	The effectiveness of the food production and food and beverage service methods, and the efficiency and appropriateness in the use of the resources being applied to them (including staffing), in order to support the customer service specification.
7 Control of costs and revenue	The extent to which revenue and the costs of materials, labour and overheads have been controlled, and the appropriateness of the methods adopted to meet operational requirements.
8 Monitoring of customer satisfaction	The effectiveness of the methods used to monitor the level of customer satisfaction and the extent to which the customer satisfaction has been achieved.

Figure 10.2: The foodservice cycle as an analysis tool

There are two dimensions to using the foodservice cycle in this way:

■ By using the foodservice cycle to present the information that has been generated, it will help to organise what is known about the operation and its performance, but more importantly it will also help to identify where there are gaps in the information and where additional information might be required to make the evaluation more complete.

- Viewing the operation within the cycle will help to identify operational strength and weaknesses. Within the cycle any difficulties, which are identified in one area of the cycle, will cause difficulties in the elements of the cycle that follow. For instance, difficulties with purchasing will then have had effects on production and service, and control. Similarly the difficulties experienced under one stage of the cycle will often have their causes in the stages that precede it.

The foodservice cycle helps in considering the operation as a whole i.e. as an operating system. Approaching the analysis and evaluation of the operation using the foodservice cycle will also help to determine the limitations of the information that is known, which will then lead to better evaluation of the operation and its performance.

The true causes of difficulties in any of the eight stages and the implications of them can be more easily and accurately identified. In operations the causes of difficulties in one stage are often one or two stages before that stage, rather than necessarily being in that stage it self. For instance difficulties with food and beverage service can often be because of equipment shortages, stock outs, incorrect pricing information etc. rather than being a result of difficulties directly associated with the service. Similarly difficulties identified in one stage will also have knock on effects on the stages that follow. Being able to identify and understand these various interrelationships will mean that decisions on operational changes will only be considered after finding the true cause of any difficulties, and taking account of the effects of any proposed changes might have throughout the operation as a whole.

External comparison

The current performance of the operation will have been compared with performance in the past and also against the current goals and objectives of the organisation. This can then also be extended to making comparisons with other organisations. This is sometimes called **benchmarking**.

Benchmarking is a process of making comparisons with the performance indicators of other foodservice operations, and then also making comparisons with the performance indicators of organisations in similar types of operations, but in different industries, to see the how the organisation compares with best practice. This process could involve undertaking comparisons using many of the ratios which are given in Appendix B as well as, for instance, complaint levels, or stock handling, or energy saving, or staff turnover in other service operations. For foodservice operators, there is also the Best Practice Forum – further information can be obtained at http://www.bestpracticeforum.org).

In the same way as the foodservice cycle can used as a basis for investigating the internal operation (see Figure 10.2), it can also be used as a basis for comparisons with other operations. Information gathered about competitors' operations can be organised and examined in a similar way to the internal operation. This helps to make the comparison more systematic and objective.

Additionally in the past few years there has been an increased interest in **performance indicators** in both the public and private sectors. These are often fairly simple quantitative measures such as:

- Time to answer the telephone
- Time to respond to a 999 call
- Percentage of trains arriving on time, or
- Percentage of patients on a hospital waiting list for more than two years.

They might also be more specific or detailed, such as those widely used in hospitality industry. The industry uses quantitative measures such as:

- Average sales per sales person
- Gross profit percentages
- Occupancy levels, or
- Energy efficiency measures.

Whilst few people would disagree with the need to try and improve efficiency whilst maintaining standards, and to assess efficiency and effectiveness, the use of performance indicators can have drawbacks such as:

- The concentration on quantitative measures tends to draw too much attention to that which can easily be measured, rather than considering the much richer concepts of service and quality that are much more difficult to measure.

- Performance indicators measure behaviour, but they also have the tendency to change behaviour; people start to work to satisfy the indicator rather than the requirements of the customers.

- Some of the indicators are prone to being manipulated in order to give the impression of a higher quality than is actually being achieved.

More recently however, for the hospitality industry in the UK, under the aegis of the Institute of Hospitality, an accreditation programme has been developed which is based on quality management assessment systems that do take into account a measure of the reality of customer service. This is the Hospitality Assured programme. You can find more information on this from the website at http://www.hospitalityassured.com.

Whatever approaches are considered and used, the question always needs to be asked as to whether any organisation should actually be doing the things that the performance indicators are measuring. Many people work extremely hard doing jobs that either do not need doing or do not need doing in that way. Instead of asking questions such as how can things be done better, at lower cost or faster, it is often better to first ask 'Why do we do what we do at all?'

Effective qualitative evaluation is the essence of successful food and beverage management. It is systematic, in that it is supported by data, but it also allows for appropriate professional judgement to be applied. Well done it can ensure that valuable resources are not wasted on making the operation comply with a

10

customer service specification that either is no longer relevant to customer demand or no longer able to be achieved by the physical capabilities of the operation, by its staff or both. Overall, the food and beverage manager's job is to ensure that the right questions are being asked, not to provide all the right answers.

10.3 Assessing organisational capability

Any foodservice organisation should be in a position to assess its strengths and weaknesses and determine what it sees as its core competencies. Many of the existing strengths and weaknesses, which already exist within the operation, are as result of linkages between different activities and the consistency of the operational strategies. It can therefore often be shown that:

- Better training of staff tends to result in better service
- Early attention to problems may avoid expensive compensation later
- Greater prevention of problems reduces unexpected demands
- Better design leads to lower service costs
- Liaison between departments allows for better planning, reduced costs and improved customer service.

One way of exploring these issues further is to consider **resource analysis**. This is concerned with:

- Identifying the strengths and weaknesses of the organisation's resources in meeting the requirements of the current strategies
- Identifying how the current resources could meet the needs of possible changes in the business environment and therefore customer demand
- Identifying what changes would need to be made to the current resources in order for the organisation to meet future and competitive demands.

There are a variety of methods for carrying out a resource analysis. Some organisations go through very formal processes, whilst others have a more informal approach. Whichever way it is done, it is important that, once carried out, it is continuously updated. One approach to resources analysis, based on approaches to resource audit put forward by Johnson *et al.* (2008), is outlined as follows:

1 Carry out a value chain analysis:
   - ☐ To look at how effectively and efficiently all the resources are being used in each stage of the operation.
   - ☐ To look at how effectively the resources are contributing to meeting the goals and objectives of the organisation
   - ☐ To develop and use measures for the control of resources.

(The value chain includes all the stages of the operation. For foodservice operations the various stages and interrelationships are indicated in Chapter 1, Figure 1.3).

2 Draw comparisons:

☐ With past performance of the organisation

☐ With norms in the industry

☐ With best practice in similar activities in other types of organisation.

3 Assess balance within the organisation:

☐ Analyse the range of products that are offered and make decisions about the appropriateness of them in meeting current demand

☐ Analyse the skills/personalities of the staff involved in order to determine to extent to which they complement the requirements of the customer service specification

☐ Analyse the flexibility of the organisation in meeting the range of current demand

☐ Analyse the capability of the resources of the operation in order to determine the extent to which the operation is able to meet the demands of potential future demand.

Undertaking these activities should lead to the identification of key issues which will enable the identification of the:

■ Strengths and weaknesses of the operation

■ Core competencies of the operation (what do we do and how good at it are we? And then: what could we do and how good at it could we be?).

Such an audit should enable the organisation to assess its current and potential strategic capability.

■ The development of the strategies for the organisation can then take into account:

■ The current and potential strategic capability of the organisation

■ The opportunities and threats it faces

■ An identification of the future resources and capabilities required to implement an adopted strategy successfully.

Strategic analysis, planning and implementation are a continuum, not as a sequence. Therefore equally there may need to be modifications to the existing strategies to take account of the strengths and weaknesses of the existing resources, as well as also ensuring that plans are considered which will develop the resources so as to be able to implement future strategies.

10

10.4 Strategic analysis and planning

Strategic analysis and planning of the organisation is concerned with attempting to identify:

- Its strengths and weaknesses
- The opportunities and threats facing it at the time.

Most writers on strategic management argue that the task of managers is to develop strategies which:

- Use the organisation's strengths to capitalise on external opportunities or counter threats.
- Seek to alleviate the organisation's weaknesses.

This is in an effort to achieve the organisation's goals and objectives and hence satisfy its stakeholders. Strategy formulation is thus an interplay between internal strengths and weaknesses, external opportunities and threats, and stakeholders' expectations.

SWOT analysis is useful to the food and beverage operator because it allows a focused identification and evaluation of the issues that affect the operation. Strengths and weaknesses are usually internal to the operation and might include such items as the product, staffing, management and the effectiveness of the operating systems. Opportunities and threats are usually external to the business and might include such items as the existing and potential customer needs, interest rates, demographic changes, infrastructure developments and national and local economic outlooks.

Strategic management then can be considered to be a process aimed at managing the interface between the external environment (the opportunities and threats) and the internal capabilities (the strengths and weaknesses) of the organisation.

■   Using SWOT analysis

SWOT analysis can be used in considering the organisation and the business environment in which it operates and as a basis for developing strategy in line with its mission. It can be a very powerful and effective tool because it has the great benefit of conceptual simplicity. The idea of identifying what you are good at, and where you are weak, is very simple. But in practice different managers have different perceptions of the strengths and weaknesses of the same organisation. The same is true of opportunities and threats.

However, the conceptual simplicity of SWOT allows it to be used very creatively. It can bring into the open conflicts of perception and test assumptions. Used well, it can cut through internal politics and its use and application need not be threatening.

Using SWOT analysis in practice

Strategy should be related to the external environment and the internal resources and capabilities of the organisation, not made in a vacuum. Similarly, the separate components of a SWOT analysis should not be considered in isolation as can be seen in the extended SWOT matrix shown in Figure 10.3.

		Strengths	Weaknesses
		List of strengths	List of weaknesses
Opportunities	List of opportunities	**Box 1** Strengths to make use of opportunities	**Box 2** Weaknesses which prevent the exploitation of opportunities
Threats	List of threats	**Box 3** Strengths to counter threats	**Box 4** Weaknesses which prevent the countering of threats

Figure 10.3: SWOT Matrix

An organisation may have resources that give it strengths to take advantage of opportunities in the external environment (Box 1) or that can be used to reduce the effect of the threats (Box 3). Alternatively, external opportunities and threats may cause an organisation to examine current weaknesses (Boxes 2 and 4) and eradicate these so that it can take advantage of opportunities or counter potential threats. In some situations, an organisation can use existing or newly developed strengths to benefit from new opportunities (Box 1).

To use this as a process tool, specific opportunities and threats need to be listed to see how each of these links to the strengths and weaknesses of the organisation. This helps in making decisions on the actions that need to be taken. Similarly, an organisation can list individual strengths and weaknesses and see how these relate to the potential opportunities and threats. It is also useful to match these against the needs of the existing markets, the potential markets and also to those of competitors.

■ The need for constant monitoring

Business generally is going through a period of rapid change, which is turbulent and uncertain, not developmental or evolutionary. In this situation, it is not enough simply to monitor periodically the factors that in the past have indicated opportunities and threats. Rather, foodservice organisations need to be constantly on the lookout for new issues and new developments, which may have a radical effect on the business environment, and on the actions of competitors both of which may have an affect on the business that the foodservice organisation is in.

10

The annual event of monitoring 'key variables' in readiness for an update of the annual plan, or budget, may be too infrequent; an important opportunity may be missed or a dangerous threat may become a reality. Even if a threat is recognised, the organisation may not be able to adapt in time.

Monitoring can also be more difficult because many opportunities and threats are not easily recognisable. A development in an obscure area of technology may have effects on a wide variety of sectors of the economy that few, if any, people recognise at the outset. The developments, which may ultimately have a high impact on a business, do not often happen in an area that directly affects a particular organisation, but to businesses three or four positions up or downstream. For example changes in the use of specific packaging materials not only affect the manufacturers of the packaging materials but also the wholesalers and then the foodservice operation, which subsequently retails the products.

In such a situation there can be an in-built pressure to collect more and more data on an ever-increasing number of factors to try to make the future more certain. This can be counter-productive and cause data overload or 'paralysis by analysis'. There are more data available but less information than before.

■ Assessing for now and the future

The assessment of strengths and weaknesses cannot stand still. It is a continuous process. Strategic capability needs to be assessed, not just for now but also for the future. As time passes the current strategy will have developed and been modified and also the external business environment is likely to have changed. This in turn will lead to the need to modify strategies in the light of these changes.

There is then a continuous interplay between formulation, implementation and assessment of SWOT analysis now and in the future. The process of assessing current strengths and weaknesses should be part of this process. They should be assessed not only in terms of their appropriateness now but also for the future. It works in many ways:

- What possible external changes might make a current strength into a weakness or vice versa?

- How can a current strength be used to explore a future opportunity?

- How can strength be developed further to be of greater benefit in the future?

The other issue that needs to be faced is where changes are required and where the resource capabilities of the operation are unable to meet them.

As the market, competition and the business environment change over time, so there will need to be changes in the core competencies of the organisation. A current core competence that gives a foodservice operation an edge over competitors may become commonplace amongst competitors in a few years. Thus any organisation need to be continually developing its core competencies so as to be better prepared to face the future.

10.5 The basis of strategy

One of the most influential concepts in the development of strategic thinking in the last decade has been that of generic strategies. Michael Porter (2004a) proposes that there are three basic ways by which organisations can achieve a 'sustainable competitive advantage' over its rivals. These are the 'generic strategies' of:

- **Cost leadership**: whereby the organisation sets out to be the lowest cost producer in its industry.

- **Differentiation**: a strategy based on enhancements to products which are valued by customers and for which the customer will be prepared to pay higher prices in order to obtain unique benefits.

- **Focus**: where the organisation chooses a narrow competitive scope; that is, it selects a particular segment or group of segments of the market that it can serve exclusively well. There are two variants of this strategy:

  ☐ A focus based on cost whereby the organisation seeks a cost advantage in its chosen segment

  ☐ A focus which is based on achieving differentiation in that segment.

Porter argues that for an organisation to be successful over the long term it must be very clear which of the generic strategies it is following. Such a choice then informs all strategic decisions that must be made.

A development of Porter's approaches has been the **Strategy Clock** (as detailed in Johnson *et al.*, 2008). This has eight different strategy options (rather than Porter's four) and these are based on combinations of price (low to high) and perceived added value (low to high). It attempts to ensure coherence of strategy across different resources in the organisation, and links the use of resources to customer requirements.

The Strategy Clock takes a customer perspective on strategy by plotting perceived added value against price. These are both factors external to the organisation that relate to how customers make their purchasing decisions. However a modification to this model is proposed in that the horizontal axis should more appropriately be the 'cost to the customer' rather than simply being the price (in cash terms), as in the Johnson *et al.* model. This issue has been discussed (in Chapter 2, pages 42 to 43), where we indicated that value in a foodservice operation is more likely to be measured by the customer as the relationship between worth and the total cost to the customer. This 'cost to the customer' included, for instance, the lost opportunity of being somewhere else, travel costs, the possibility of disagreeable company, poor service, poor food, etc.

Taking account of this modification, the Strategy Clock, as shown in Figure 10.4, illustrates that the strategic routes indicated by the positions 1 to 5 inclusive, can be sustainable strategies and that the strategic routes indicated by positions 6, 7 and 8 are destined for failure.

10

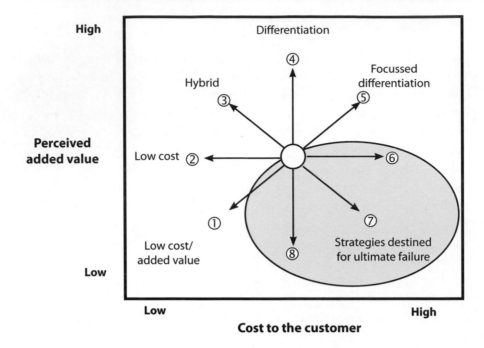

Figure 10.4: The strategy clock

Source: Based on Johnson *et al.*, 2008

	Needs/risks	
1 Low cost to the customer/ low added value	Likely to be segment specific	
2 Low cost to the customer	Risk of price war and low margins/need to be low operating cost leader	
3 Hybrid	Low cost base and reinvestment in low cost and differentiation	Differentiation
4 Differentiation - without price premium - with price premium	Perceived added value by user, yielding market share benefits / Perceived added value sufficient to bear price premium	Differentiation
5 Focussed differentiation	Perceived added value to a particular segment, warranting price premium	Differentiation
6 Increased cost/standard value	Higher margins if competitors do not follow/ risk of losing market share	Likely failure
7 Increased cost/low value	Only feasible in monopoly situation	Likely failure
8 Low value/standard cost	Loss of market share	Likely failure

Developing this further, the strategic basis of each of the eight routes may be summarised as in Figure 10.5. From this figure it can be seen that:

■ Strategic routes 1 and 2 are strategies that are aimed at achieving sales through being of low cost to the customer.

■ Strategic route 3 is a hybrid.

■ Strategic Route 4 and 5 are about being different from competitors.

■ Strategic routes 6, 7 and 8 offer a mixture of high cost to the customer and low perceived added value and therefore all of these are likely to be unsuccessful strategies, which will ultimately lead to the failure of the business.

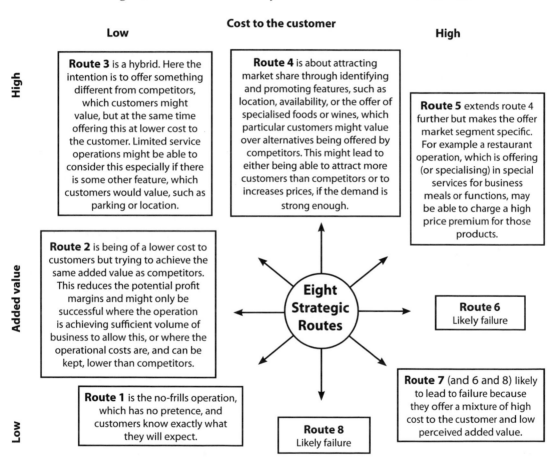

Figure 10.5: Eight possible strategic routes for foodservice operations

Source: Developed from Johnson *et al.*, Strategy Clock, 2008

Using this application of the Strategy Clock for considering the strategic route for foodservice operations may at first appear simple. However the nature of any food and beverage product is that it may simultaneously be aimed at meeting a wide variety of different types of demand. This is both in terms of the types of demand being met by one particular part of the product as well as by the nature of a foodservice operation, for instance, offering a range of products, e.g. breakfast service, morning coffee, business lunches, afternoon teas, family meals, special diet provision, pre-theatre meals, evenings out, post-theatre meals, special parties, functions and also retail merchandise and parking services. It is therefore quite likely that any operation will need to split the product(s) down and consider the types of demand being met and then place each of these products separately on the Strategy Clock.

10.6 Strategic options

Various approaches exist to assist in determining strategic choices for an organisation. These include the Growth Share (BCG) Matrix, which considers various aspects of market share against market growth, or the Directional Policy (GE-McKinsey) Matrix, which considers business strength against industry attractiveness (both detailed and discussed in Johnson *et al.*, 2008).

■ Ansoff Growth Matrix

The Ansoff Growth Matrix (1988 and also discussed in Johnson *et al.*, 2008) inter-relates the product and the market, each of which will vary depending upon whether we are dealing with new or old products or markets or both, as illustrated in Figure 10.6. So, for example, if the current product range is being provided within existing markets the organisation needs to have a clear market penetration strategy. If the products are current, but are being offered within the new markets, then a market development strategy will be required. If the organisation has developed new products that it aims to sell within a new market the strategy needed will be diversification orientated.

		Products	
		Present	New
Markets	Present	Do nothing Withdraw Consolidate Market penetration	Product development
	New	Market development	Related diversification Unrelated diversification

Figure 10.6: Ansoff's growth matrix with alternative strategies/directions

The strategic options identified within the matrix are explained below:

■ **Do nothing**: a 'no change' strategy can be wrongly perceived as 'no strategy'. If there are no foreseen internal and external environmental changes the organisation may choose to take a conscious step to continue with the strategies currently being undertaken. A positive decision to retain the business in its present market is a perfectly logical one. To stand still in a dynamic environment however is to move backward, but changing strategies in an unchanging environment may be quite inappropriate. Generally though, unless an organisation's environment is very stable, this is unlikely to be a viable option, but it can serve as a useful comparison when considering other different options.

■ **Withdrawal**: there may be circumstances in which it might make sense to withdraw from a particular activity in a particular market, especially if continuation is no longer profitable or viable. For a single foodservice operator this is often that hardest decision to have to make.

■ **Consolidate**: this implies taking action to retain existing market shares. In growth markets this will lead to increased sales. In mature or declining markets actions such as improved service or quality, or reduced costs may be required.

■ **Market penetration**: this is a strategy of attempting to increase market share. This is likely to be easier in growth markets. In mature or declining markets, competitors are likely to react to competitive moves (for example, lowering prices, increasing advertising, improving quality and so on) to steal their business.

■ **Product development**: this involves offering new products to existing markets. A decision to develop new products may be based on an identified customer need, which is currently not being met, or be derived from technological advancements. New product development always carries an element of risk as many new products do not achieve required levels of profitability and may loose money.

■ **Market development**: this involves taking existing products into new markets. These may be new market segments, new uses of existing products, or new geographic markets. Penetrating new markets is risky as it represents a move into the unknown.

■ **Diversification**; although this term is often used fairly loosely, here it is used in the sense of offering new products to new markets. There are two types of diversification: related and unrelated.

■ **Related diversification**: where the development is broadly within the same industry. This can further be classified as:

☐ **Backward integration**, which is a move into an activity that is already an input into the foodservice organisation's existing operations (i.e. backwards in the supply chain, further away from the customers, such as a restaurant having interests in a farm).

☐ **Forward integration**, which is a move into an activity which is an output of the organisation's existing operations (that is, forward in the supply chain, nearer to the consumer. This is difficult as many foodservice operations are already at the end of the supply chain. However it can include activities such as joining marketing consortia).

☐ **Horizontal integration**, which is a move into a competitive or complementary activity, such as a restaurant linking with leisure attraction or being located within an hotel.

■ **Unrelated diversification**: where the development is outside the industry in which the organisation currently operates. This can be for instance a foodservice operation also being in the car trade.

Diversification in any form is doubly risky as it involves both products and markets of which the organisation has no experience. Nonetheless, the attraction of diversification is often irresistible for organisations apparently offering possible opportunities to control supply (backwards integration), control markets (forward integration), spread risk (particularly in unrelated diversification), utilise underemployed capacity or cash, and so on.

Particularly alluring is the prospect of synergy whereby two or more activities complement each other to the extent that the whole is greater than the sum of the parts. This simple concept that 2 + 2 = 5 is often put forward as the reason for diversification, but in many cases it has proved very difficult to achieve in practice.

When applying this matrix – or more importantly the thinking behind it – an organisation can consider possible options it could adopt in each of the four segments of the alternative strategies directions matrix in Figure 10.6 and then appraise each of these for suitability, for and against.

This approach requires the process to be undertaken systematically in order to answer a variety of questions as follows:

Present market, present products

■ What would be the implications of doing nothing? Is withdrawal feasible? What would consolidation or market penetration mean for the organisation?

Present market, new product

■ This presents much scope for creative powers. What sort of new product could be developed for the present market? The environmental analysis (see page 268) and SWOT analysis (see page 276) could give some clues here.

New market, present products

■ This requires a reassessment of the strengths of the products. Has the organisation really considered fully the scope for entering into new markets?

New markets, new products

- Here there is a need to control imagination. Diversification may look superficially attractive, but there are a host of potential dangers and risks. Decisions of this nature tend to involve a considerable outlay. This is particularly true of unrelated diversification. What special skills can the organisation bring which will promise success in new and unfamiliar markets? Unless these can be identified then it would be better to forget it.

Life cycle analysis

Life cycle analysis is an approach that attempts to consider what strategies might be appropriate taking account of the position of the product in the product life cycle and also the competitive position of an organisation. The approach can be used to identify possible strategies that might be considered. Thus for instance a strong competitive position in a mature market indicates that possible strategies might be to aim to attain cost leadership, to renew the product, to aim for a focussed strategy or to seek to differentiate the product (see, for example, Bowie and Buttle, 2004 and Kotler *et al.*, 2009).

The main usefulness of this approach is that it can be used to establish the suitability of particular strategies in relation to the stage of industry maturity and the organisation's competitive position. In the life cycle analysis, as in the other approaches, determining the stage in the product life cycle of the particular hospitality product is necessary in order to consider appropriateness of current strategies or to consider future ones. However identifying the position of the various hospitality products can be difficult.

The hospitality industry provides products that are already well established alongside some products that are newly launched and others that are at the end of their life cycle. Bowie and Buttle (2004) identify four stages of the product life cycle: **introduction**, **growth**, **maturity** and **decline**. As well as presenting this classic view of the product life cycle they also identify two specific, and for the foodservice industry very important, variants:

- The first is the **fad product** life cycle, which is characterised by rapid growth matched by equally dramatic collapse. Certain types of restaurants or discos might fall into this type of life cycle.

- The second variant is the **long or extended product** life cycle. This cycle is characterised by an extended maturity phase, which implies high consumer repurchase levels, with little loss of sales to other competitors. Some products of the hospitality industry can fall into this type of life cycle. Examples are some fashionable luxury restaurants and five star hotels, essential function foodservice outlets, life style products such as holidays and a wide variety of other products that have been revamped and re-launched.

10

In many cases the foodservice product being considered will be positioned in the extended life cycle phase. Therefore the main strategies required are primarily those that are mainly aimed at:

■ Increasing customer loyalty

■ Investing to maintain customer service and improve perceived value

■ Developing and extending existing sales through repackaging and re-launching the product.

When considering the complexity of the foodservice product and endeavouring to determine the position of the particular product in the product life cycle and within the various standard strategic direction models, it is worth taking account of these two variants in particular, as these will significantly change the interpretation of some of the more standard strategic direction models.

10.7 Strategic direction

Through the use of the various approaches put forward by Johnson *et al.* (2008) and Ansoff (1988), various strategic options can be identified. Strategic direction can be implemented through three basic means: internal development, acquisition (external) development and through joint ventures. Each of these three options is considered below:

■ Internal development

This is also referred to as 'organic growth'. It depends on the organisation using its own competencies and resources to put its strategy into effect. The advantages are that the organisation can build and develop the required skills and knowledge without encountering the cultural problems often associated with developments involving other organisations. Internal development also enables developmental costs to be spread over a longer period. In many foodservice operations internal development is the only realistic option. Its major disadvantage is the length of time that may be required, to develop new products, acquire new skills and gain access to the new markets, which a particular strategic direction might imply.

■ Mergers and acquisitions

Acquisition has proved a particularly attractive means of moving quickly in a chosen strategic direction although this has mainly been related to larger organisations. The ownership structures of UK and American companies have made this a common means of achieving fast and very visible strategic action for many organisations.

The reasons for acquisition vary. Rapid entry to particular markets, immediately increased market share, cost savings through rationalisation, balance sheet improvements or other financial reasons including more favourable tax treatment, may all play a part. Potential problems for acquiring firms usually arise from not knowing exactly what is being bought. Many factors do not emerge until after acquisition.

Mergers differ from acquisitions only in the sense that the coming together is voluntary, although it may be as a result of competitive pressures. Mergers and acquisitions are often justified on grounds of potential synergies although these often prove difficult to actually realise. However, the biggest problems usually arise post merger or acquisition when cultural differences between the two organisations emerge. When combined with political activity these often cost more in terms of time and resource to resolve than originally envisaged.

■ Joint development

These are becoming both increasingly varied and popular. They arise where an organisation recognises the need to work with one or more outside organisations to achieve its strategy. It may be a need to share costs, or scarce resources, knowledge or skills or regulatory or legal constraints, which lead to the need for joint development. Such arrangements include joint ventures, marketing consortia, franchising, business networks, strategic alliances, subcontracting and so on. Issues to be considered include how to manage relationships between the organisations, and identifying when the arrangement should be ended and how.

10.8 Evaluation criteria

Clearly it is possible to think of many different options for any foodservice organisation given its position in the business environment at a particular point in time. Making choices about which of these alternatives will best help the organisation to achieve its strategic objectives requires some criteria against which to evaluate the various possible alternatives. What specific criteria will be used will depend on how success is to be measured in the organisation. However Johnson *et al.* (2008) suggest that it can be helpful to consider the **suitability**, **feasibility** and **acceptability** of any given option.

10

■ Strategy assessment

Assessing suitability

Consideration of suitability can be based on assessments of whether the option:

Exploits the core competencies of the foodservice organisation

■ Seizes opportunities presented to the foodservice organisation by changes in the business environmental and counters any threats which the organisation may be facing, or

■ Meets the expectations of key organisational stakeholders.

These considerations are not necessarily mutually exclusive but there may be conflict within and between them. This goes back to the previous discussion in this chapter on the basis of strategy.

It may be useful to consider the issues, which can arise, using three different approaches. Again these are not mutually exclusive, and each one may offer new insights into the options being evaluated:

- **Strategic logic:** this is the rational/economic approach primarily concerned with matching an organisation's core competencies with the business environment (and in particular the market) it faces. Such an approach draws heavily on the various models of strategic analysis mentioned here and elsewhere (for example, Porter's competitive advantage concepts, Johnson *et al.*, Strategy Clock, Ansoff's matrix, life cycle analysis, synergy, and so on).

- **Cultural fit:** this approach attempts to assess the extent to which an option fits the prevailing culture and the political realities in the organisation. If a proposed strategy is likely to be rejected by key players in the organisation or runs counter to the prevalent organisational thinking, it is likely to run into difficulties during implementation no matter how logical it may appear from an economic perspective. This raises the issue of whether an organisational culture can be changed to suit an apparently desirable strategy or whether strategy should be driven from the existing culture.

- **Research evidence:** it may be quite reasonable to ask why, with so much research being carried out by businesses and academics over many years, it is necessary to approach each strategic decision as if it were unique. It can be argued that any such decision will indeed be unique, but any decision-making can be usefully informed by past experience of other such similar decisions. Monitoring the trade and business press, networking through professional trade bodies and associations, taking the advice of consultants and generally reading the business literature, can prove very rewarding.

Assessing feasibility

Feasibility is concerned with whether the foodservice organisation can actually put the strategy into operation. In other words: does the foodservice organisation have the resources, such as finance, skills, equipment and the technology, to support the strategic choices being made? Of particular concern should be the assessment of:

- **Funding:** any strategy is likely to require capital investment. A cash flow forecast is vital to assess both the amounts and timing of the investment and the returns from the project.

- **Break even:** it is essential to assess the volume of sales required to achieve the required return from any strategy. It is then possible to assess the resource implications of such a volume and whether in fact it is possible to achieve such a level of sales.

- **Resource implications**: this is a detailed assessment of the physical and human resources required to achieve the strategy. If there is a shortfall between existing and required resources the organisation will need to determine how this can be met in the time-scales and within the costs assumed by the proposal.

Assessing acceptability

The key issue in assessing acceptability is an understanding of stakeholder expectations. These may well vary between different stakeholder groups. Of particular interest to many key stakeholders (particularly managers, owners and providers of finance) will be an assessment of the potential financial returns and risks from any particular proposal.

Financial return can be assessed using payback or discounted cash flow (DCF) investment appraisal methods. Cost/benefit analysis is widely used in the public sector, where the analyses of profit is inappropriate or too narrow a measure. Cost/benefit analysis attempts to put a financial value on all costs and benefits including intangibles.

Financial risk can also be assessed through calculating the projected financial ratios that adopting a specific strategy would imply. Important factors are gearing ratios (increased gearing through increased borrowing exposes a company to greater risk) and liquidity ratios (lowering the liquidity ratios increases financial risk). (See Appendix B page 297 for a listing of key financial ratios). Another useful approach is to use sensitivity analysis, particularly by using spreadsheet packages, to pose various 'what if?' questions. These approaches enable owners and managers to assess the impact of changes in interest rates, capacity, utilisation, market shares and so on, on the financial projection for a possible strategy.

■ Strategy and organisational types

If the approaches to strategic management were (or could be) undertaken in a wholly scientific way, decisions would only be rational and objective. But organisations are complex and the culture and power that exists in and around an organisation will substantially affect the actual decisions that are made. Some of this will be reflected in, and thus determined by, the nature of the objectives of the organisation.

We saw in Chapter 2 that organisational goals will tend to be derived from a mixture of economic, managerial and social factors. It can also be useful to consider the type of organisation that the foodservice operation might be, as this will substantially affect the specific approaches that will be adopted and the nature of the strategic decisions that will be made.

The nature of any organisation is created through a complex interplay between the various stakeholders involved and the level of power that they can exert. Individual owner-operated foodservice businesses will often predominately reflect the nature of the owner, as the owner is likely to hold the most power. In larger organisations the number of stakeholders that are involved will increase, and with this the predominance of power may shift to, for instance, shareholders, or strong groups of customers.

Considering organisations from this perspective can help to indicate why, for instance, similar foodservice businesses facing similar business environments, might make quite different strategic decisions. The actual decisions about the strategic approaches adopted, the strategic direction of an organisation, the basis of strategy and the ways in which strategies will be achieved, are likely to be largely dependent on the predominant organisational characteristics of the individual enterprise.

The reality of strategic decision-making

In this chapter we have considered some essential elements of the process of strategic decision-making. The intention has been to encourage the consideration of strategic issues in a systematic way through the application of a range of approaches, only some of which have been identified here. However, although it may appear from this presentation of the material that strategic management is a linear process starting at the establishment of a mission and ending with implementation, these elements in fact often run in parallel. Any operation will fail if it attempts to sets out its mission without knowing what its resources are or without considering the practicalities of implementation.

In reality strategic management is largely organic in nature and affected by a range of factors, such as organisational culture, which will mitigate against viewing the process as being simply scientific. The process of strategy that enables successful strategic management to be achieved certainly includes the need for some formal planning, but there is also a need for all managers to be involved in the continuous strategic management of the enterprise. In addition, no matter how well planned a strategy may seem to be, there will be many forces that will affect the extent to which the planned course of action will be achieved, and the possibility of this must always be taken into account in the strategy process. Strategic management therefore needs to be:

■ Recognised as being complex and judgemental

■ Continuous, rather than a once a year process

■ Developed using a combination of a variety of different approaches and techniques

■ Carried out by managers not planners

■ Based on a continuum of formulation and implementation, and be

■ Flexible enough to cope with an uncertain future.

Appendices

A: Operational calculations

Being able to interpret operational data is an essential skill for the food and beverage manager. In order to be able to do that well it is necessary to have a sound understanding of the basis for operational calculations.

Chapter 9 details the appraisal of revenue, costs and profits. This appendix provides examples of operational figures and calculations.

Example figures

Below are examples of the figures that can be generated in a foodservice operation and how these can be used to create operational data.

The following information is based on a 120-seat café restaurant:

Operational hours

The restaurant is open six days a week all year

Opening hours

Lunch Service 12 noon to 2pm

Dinner Service 7pm to 10pm

Average customer numbers

Lunch – 40

Dinner – 75

Average customer spending

	Food	Beverage
Lunch	£12 per head	£6 per head
Dinner	£20 per head	£10 per head

Staffing establishment

Lunch – a daily average of one member of staff per 10 customers

Dinner – a daily average of one member of staff per 15 customers

All members of staff are employed for the entire service period plus one hour prior to the service and one hour after the service

Costs

The food costs are 40% of the annual food revenue

The beverage costs are 50% of the annual beverage revenue

The staff (labour) costs are averaged at £15.50 per hour per member of staff

The total overhead cost for one year is estimated at 20% of the total annual revenue (food and beverage)

Possible calculations

Using the information above it is possible to calculate all of the following:

a. Annual revenues

The annual food revenue

The annual beverage revenue

The annual lunch revenue

The annual dinner revenue

The total annual revenue

b. The total number of staff needed each day for the service of:

lunch

dinner

c. The total annual labour costs

d. The percentage of labour costs in relation to the total annual revenue

e. The average daily percentage seat occupancy during the year for:

lunch

dinner

f. The average daily overhead costs for each day of operation

g. The gross profit cash and percentage for the year for:

food

beverage

total (food and beverage)

h. The total amount of money left over at the end of the year (net profit) after all costs have been deducted and its percentage of the total revenue.

Example calculations

The calculations are as follows:

a. Annual revenues

The annual food revenue

Lunch food revenue = spend per head x No. of covers x No. of days x No. of weeks

= £12 × 40 covers x 6 days x 52 weeks

= £149,760

Dinner food revenue	= spend per head x No. of covers x No. of days x No. of weeks
	= £20 x 75 covers x 6 days x 52 weeks
	= £468,000
Total annual food revenue	= lunch food revenue + dinner food revenue
	= £149,760 + £468,000
	= £617,760

The annual beverage revenue

Lunch beverage revenue	= spend per head x No. of covers x No. of days x No. of weeks
	= £6 x 40 covers x 6 days x 52 weeks
	= £74,880
Dinner beverage revenue	= spend per head x No. of covers x No. of days x No. of weeks
	= £10 x 75 covers x 6 days x 52 weeks
	=£234,000
Total beverage revenue	= lunch beverage revenue + dinner beverage revenue
	= £74,880 + £234,000
	= £308,880
Total annual lunch revenue	= annual lunch food revenue + annual lunch beverage revenue
	= £149,760 + £74,880
	= £224,640
Total annual dinner revenue	= annual dinner food revenue + annual dinner beverage revenue
	= £468,000 + £234,000
	= £702,000
The total annual revenue	= annual lunch revenue + annual dinner revenue
	= £224.640 + £702,000
	= £926,640
OR	
	= annual food revenue + annual beverage revenue
	= £617,760 + £308,880
	= £926,640

A

b. **The total average number of staff needed for each day for the service of:**

Lunch

one member of staff is required for ten customers

the average number of customers per day = 40

therefore the average number of staff for lunch = 40/10 = 4

Dinner

one member of staff is required for 15 customers

the average number of customers per day = 75

therefore the average number of staff for dinner = 75/15 = 5

c. **Total annual labour costs**

Lunch labour costs per day	= No. of staff x working hours x rate per hour
	= 4 staff x 4 hours x £15.50
	= £248.00
Dinner labour costs per day	= No. of staff x working hours x rate per hour
	= 5 staff x 5 hours x £15.50
	= £387.50
Total labour costs per day	= lunch labour costs + dinner labour costs
	= £248.00 + £387.50
	= £635.50
Total annual labour costs	= total labour costs per day x No. of days x No. of weeks
	= £635.50 x 6 x 52
	= £198,276

d. **Percentage of labour cost in relation to total revenue**

$$\text{Labour cost percentage} = \frac{\text{Labour costs} \times 100}{\text{Revenue}}$$

$$= \frac{£198,276 \times 100}{£926,640}$$

$$= 21.4\%$$

e. **The average daily percentage seat occupancy during the year for:**

Lunch

$$\text{Percentage seat occupancy} = \frac{\text{covers actual} \times 100}{\text{covers available}}$$

$$= \frac{40 \times 100}{120}$$

$$= 33.33\%$$

Dinner

Percentage seat occupancy $= \dfrac{\text{covers actual} \times 100}{\text{covers available}}$

$$= \dfrac{75 \times 100}{120}$$

$$= 62.50\%$$

f. The average daily overhead cost

Overheads = 20% of revenue

Total annual overheads $= \dfrac{20 \times £926{,}640}{100}$

$$= £185{,}328$$

daily overheads costs $= \dfrac{\text{annual cost}}{6 \text{ days} \times 52 \text{ weeks}}$

$$= \dfrac{£185{,}328}{312}$$

$$= £594 \text{ per day}$$

g. The gross profit cash and percentage for the year for:

Food cash gross profit and percentage

Food cost   = 40% of total food revenue

therefore gross profit   = 60% of total food revenue

gross profit on food $= \dfrac{60 \times £617{,}760}{100}$

$$= £370{,}656 \text{ cash, } 60\%$$

Beverage cash gross profit and percentage

Beverage cost   = 50% of total beverage revenue

therefore gross profit   = 50% of total beverage revenue

gross profit on beverage $= \dfrac{50 \times £308{,}880}{100}$

$$= £154{,}440 \text{ cash, } 50\%$$

Total cash gross profit and percentage

Total cash gross profit = food gross profit + beverage gross profit

$$= £370{,}656 + £154{,}440$$

$$= £525{,}096$$

Percentage gross profit $= \dfrac{\text{cash gross profit} \times 100}{\text{revenue}}$

$$= \dfrac{£525{,}096 \times 100}{£926{,}640}$$

$$= 56.67\%$$

A

h. Net profit – the total amount of money left over at the end of the year after all costs have been deducted and its percentage of total revenue

Net profit $= $ gross profit $-$ (labour costs $+$ overhead costs)

$= £525,096 - (£198,276 + £185,328)$

$= £141,492$

As a percentage of revenue $= \dfrac{\text{net profit} \times 100}{\text{revenue}}$

$= \dfrac{£141,492 \times 100}{£926,640}$

$= 15.27\%$

Check matrix

In foodservice operations there is an established relationship between revenue, costs and profits. In order to check that all the cash and percentages figures are correct, a matrix can be constructed. This matrix is based on Figure 9.1, which summarises the relationship between revenue, costs and profits. The check matrix, for the figures used in the example above, is given in Table A.1.

Table A.1 Calculations Check Matrix

Check matrix	£	%		£	%
Material costs	401,544	43.33	Material costs	401,544	43.33
Labour cost	198,276	21.40			
Overheads	185,328	20.00	Gross profit	525,096	56.67
Net profit	141,492	15.27			
Revenue/sales	926,640	100.00	Revenue/sales	926,640	100.00

(Material costs = costs of food and beverages)

B: Operational and financial ratios

The most of the common quantitative performance measures for a foodservice operation (as identified in Chapter 9 page 000) are the operational ratios and (as identified in Chapter 10) the financial ratios. These may be grouped under six main categories:

- Operational ratios
- Activity ratios
- Profitability ratios
- Liquidity ratio
- Gearing ratios
- Stock market ratios.

The most common operational and financial ratios, the formulas for them and explanations of what the individual ratio can indicate, are grouped together under these six headings below:

Ratio	Formula	Meaning
Operational ratios		
Gross profit %	$\dfrac{\text{Sales revenue} - \text{cost of sales} \times 100}{\text{Sales}}$	A measure of operational efficiency (not profitability). Shows the gross profit i.e. the sales less the costs of materials (food or beverage) as a percentage of sales. Conversely can be used to indicate the percentage of material costs. Can be used over time for budgeting and comparison purposes and for comparison with industry norms.
Net profit %	$\dfrac{\text{Sales revenue} - \text{total costs} \times 100}{\text{Sales}}$	Shows overall net profit percentage i.e. the sales less the total costs as a percentage of sales. Conversely can be used to indicate the percentage of costs. Can also be used over time for budgeting and comparison purposes and for comparison with industry norms.
Average check	$\dfrac{\text{Sales}}{\text{Number of bill transactions}}$	Measures the average amount spent per bill transaction. Usually calculated for a specific service period in order to compare spending power of customers and average customer group sizes over time. Useful when interpreting and comparing sales figures.

B

Spend per head	$\dfrac{\text{Sales}}{\text{Number of customers}}$	Measures the average amount spent per person served. Usually calculated for a specific service periods in order to compare spending power of individual customers. Can be broken down further to indicate spend on food or beverages. Useful when interpreting and comparing sales figures over time.
Material costs %	$\dfrac{\text{Cost of materials x 100}}{\text{Sales}}$	Identifies the cost of materials (either food or beverage) as a percentage of the sales revenue. Usually calculated separately for food and beverages and also then down to individual or groups of menu or beverage items. Useful for comparison over different service periods and for comparison against industry norms.
Labour costs %	$\dfrac{\text{Cost of labour x 100}}{\text{Sales}}$	Identifies the cost of labour as a percentage of the sales revenue. Useful for comparison over different periods and for comparison against industry norms.
Productivity index	$\dfrac{\text{Sales}}{\text{Cost of labour}}$	Alternative method for showing labour costs in relation to sales. Low index would be where there is a high labour cost in relation to sales. Can be used as budget measure and also for comparison with industry norms.
Revenue per employee	$\dfrac{\text{Sales}}{\text{No. of staff employed}}$	Gives sales revenue per member of staff. Can also be calculated for full time equivalent. Used as a measure of efficiency. Usually calculated for specific service periods and comparison made over time.
Sales per seat available	$\dfrac{\text{Sales}}{\text{No. of seats available}}$	Indicates the amount of sales that are generated per seat available. Usually calculated for given service periods and compared over time. Can also be calculated on the sales per seat actually used. Comparison between these two figures can indicate efficiency of operation.
Seat turnover	$\dfrac{\text{No. of seats used}}{\text{No. of seats available}}$	Indicates the occupancy efficiency of the seating in a foodservice area. Usually calculated for specific service periods and compared over time.
Sales per square metre	$\dfrac{\text{Sales}}{\text{Total area of operation in m}^2}$	Can also be calculated per square foot. Commonly used in retail operations. Can be useful in bar areas or for takeaway operations where earnings per seat cannot be calculated.

Activity ratios

Net asset turnover	$$\frac{\text{Sales}}{\text{Net assets}}$$	Measures how effectively the net assets are used to generate sales; measures how many sales are generated by each pound of net assets.
Fixed asset turnover	$$\frac{\text{Sales}}{\text{Fixed assets}}$$	Measures the utilisation of the company's fixed assets (i.e. plant and equipment); measures how many sales are generated by each pound of fixed assets.
Stock turnover (rate)	$$\frac{\text{Cost of sales}}{\text{Average value of stock}}$$	Measures the number of times the stocks of food or beverage items were turned over during the year. Indicates management's ability to control investment in stocks.
Stock turnover (period)	$$\frac{\text{Average value of stocks} \times 365}{\text{Cost of sales}}$$	Indicates the stock level being held as shown by the number of days it takes to use and replace it.
Debt turnover	$$\frac{\text{Sales}}{\text{Average level of debtors}}$$	Indicates the number of times that debtors are cycled during the year.
Average collection period	$$\frac{\text{Average level of debtors} \times 365}{\text{Sales}}$$	The number of day's credit the firm gives to customers. The longer the period the more cost to the firm in outstanding debts.

Profitability ratios

Return on capital employed	$$\frac{\text{Profit before interest and tax} \times 100}{\text{Capital employed}}$$	Measures the performance of the firm regardless of the method of financing.
Return of equity	$$\frac{\text{Profit after tax} \times 100}{\text{Shareholder' funds}}$$	Measures the rate of return or profitability of the shareholders' investment in the company.
Gross profit margin	$$\frac{\text{Profit before interest and tax}}{\text{Sales}}$$	Shows the total margin available to cover operating expenses and still yield a profit. Useful for comparison over time and with industry norms.
Net profit margin	$$\frac{\text{Net profit after tax}}{\text{Sales}}$$	Shows how much after-tax profits are generated by each pound of sales. Also useful for comparison over time and with industry norms.

B

Liquidity ratios

Current ratio	$$\frac{\text{Current assets}}{\text{Current liabilities}}$$	Indicates the extent to which a firm can meet its short-term liabilities from short-term assets. This should be in the region of 2:1 or 1:1 to reflect a health proportion of current assets (stock, debtors and cash) to current liabilities (overdraft, creditors).
Acid test or quick ratio	$$\frac{\text{Current assets} - \text{stocks}}{\text{Current liabilities}}$$	Measures the firm's ability to pay off short-term liabilities from current assets without relying upon the sale of its stock. A stricter test of liquidity because it compares only money assets (cash and debtors) to current liabilities.

Gearing ratios

Debt ratio	$$\frac{\text{Long-term debt}}{\text{Capital employed (net assets)}}$$	Measures the extent to which borrowed funds have been used to finance the company's net assets. The more long-term debt the higher is the gearing and the greater the risk incurred. Gearing is generally considered to be high above 1:1.
Debt-to-equity ratio	$$\frac{\text{Long-term debt}}{\text{Share capital}}$$	Measures the funds provided by long-term creditors against the funds provided by shareholders.
Interest cover	$$\frac{\text{Profit before interest and tax}}{\text{Interest payable}}$$	Indicates the ability of the company to meet its annual interest costs. The higher the ratio the less risk is involved, as the interest being paid becomes a smaller proportion of the profit generated.

Stock market ratios

Earnings per share	$$\frac{\text{Profit after tax}}{\text{No. of ordinary shares in issue}}$$	Shows the after-tax earnings generated for each ordinary share. High earning per share can encourage new investors and promote investor loyalty.
Price/earnings	$$\frac{\text{Market price per share}}{\text{Earnings per share}}$$	Shows the esteem in which the market holds the company, the higher the ratio the more popular the share.
Net dividend yield	$$\frac{\text{Dividend per share}}{\text{Market price per share}}$$	Indicates the dividend rate of return to ordinary shareholders.
Dividend cover	$$\frac{\text{Earnings per share}}{\text{Dividend per share}}$$ or $$\frac{\text{Profit to pay ordinary dividends}}{\text{Ordinary dividends}}$$	Measures the extent to which the company pays dividends from earnings. High dividend cover is healthy provided that investors judge the gross dividend on ordinary shares to be adequate. Low dividend cover may indicate that gross dividends to ordinary shares have been set too high.

C: Budget and trading results: comparison and evaluation

Being able to interpret trading results is an essential skill for the food and beverage manager. In order to be able to do that well is necessary to have a sound understanding of the basis of operational ratios. The various operation ratios are detailed in Appendix B. In addition Chapter 9 identifies that in order to interpret fully the meaning of operational ratios, it is necessary to have some basis of comparison. For operational ratios, there will usually be internal budgets and objectives against which to measure them.

Below is an example of the budget and trading results for a foodservice operation followed by an analysis and evaluation of the data.

The budget and trading figures

The figures presented in Table C.1 are for a 62-seat, plated table service, café style restaurant. The restaurant holds a restaurant licence and is open from 8.30 a.m. to 9.30 p.m., Monday to Saturday.

Table C.1: Budget and trading results for 3 months

	Budget		1st month		2nd month		3rd month	
	(£)	(£)	(£)	(£)	(£)	(£)	(£)	(£)
Food								
Sales	40,575		40,109		41,003		39,624	
Food costs	14,201		14,711		15,200		13,824	
Gross profit		26,374		25,398		25,803		25,800
Beverage								
Sales	10,279		10,019		10,990		10,410	
Liquor costs	4,008		4,020		4,230		4,040	
Gross profit		6,271		5,999		6,760		6,370
Total sales	50,854		50,128		51,993		50,034	
Total cost of sales	18,209		18,731		19,430		17,864	
Total gross profit		32,645		31,397		32,563		32,170
Unallocated costs								
Labour costs	12,500		12,906		12,992		13,111	
Overheads	8,200		8,410		8,717		8,315	
Total costs		20,700		21,316		21,709		21,426
Net profit		11,945		10,081		10,854		10,744
Stockholding								
Food	7,710		8,010		7,924		7,999	
Beverage	1,520		1,670		1,910		1,710	
No. of customers	5,410		5,340		5,420		5,430	

C

Analysis

For the data provided in Table C.1, operational ratios can be calculated as the basis for comparison. Table C.2 gives the trading figures together with a variety of performance measures. Table C.3 looks at the percentage variance against budget.

Table C.2: Analysis of the budget and trading results for 3 months

	Budget			1st month			2nd month			3rd month		
	(£)	(£)	(%)	(£)	(£)	(%)	(£)	(£)	(%)	(£)	(£)	(%)
Food												
Sales	40,575			40,109			41,003			39,624		
Food costs	14,201		35	14,711		37	15,200		37	13,824		35
Gross profit		**26,374**	**65**		**25,398**	**63**		**25,803**	**63**		**25,800**	**65**
Beverage												
Sales	10,279			10,019			10,990			10,410		
Liquor costs	4,008		39	4,020		40	4,230		38	4,040		39
Gross profit		**6,271**	**61**		**5,999**	**60**		**6,760**	**61**		**6,370**	**61**
Total sales	50,854			50,128			51,993			50,034		
Total cost of sales	18,209			18 731			19,430			17,864		
Total gross profit		**32,645**	**64**		**31,397**	**63**		**32,563**	**63**		**32,170**	**64**
Unallocated costs												
Labour costs	12,500		24	12,906		26	12,992		25	13,111		26
Overheads	8,200		16	8,410		17	8,717		17	8,315		17
Total costs		**20,700**	**41**		**21,316**	**42**		**21,709**	**42**		**21,426**	**43**
Net profit		**11,945**	**23**		**10,081**	**20**		**10,854**	**21**		**10,744**	**21**
Stockholding		STO*			STO			STO			STO	
Food	7,710	1.84		8,010	1.83		7,924	1.91		7,999	1.72	
Beverage	1,520	2.63		1,670	2.40		1,910	2.21		1,710	2.36	

*STO: Stock turnover.

Table C.3: Variance percentage against budget

	1st month	2nd month	3rd month	To date
Food sales	−1.14	1.05	−2.34	−0.81
Food costs	3.59	7.03	−2.65	+2.65
Gross profit	−3.70	−2.16	−2.17	−2.68
Liquor sales	−2.52	6.91	1.27	+1.88
Liquor costs	0.29	5.53	0.79	+2.21
Gross profit	−4.33	7.79	1.57	+1.67
Total sales	−1.42	2.24	−1.61	−0.26
Total cost of sales	2.86	6.70	−1.89	+2.55
Total gross profit	−3.82	−0.25	−1.45	−1.84
Wage and staff	3.24	3.93	4.88	+4.02
Overheads	2.56	6.30	1.40	+3.42
Total costs	2.97	4.87	3.50	3.78
Net profit	−15.60	−9.13	−10.05	11.59
Net profit under budget	−£1 864	−£1 091	−£1201	−£4 156

Notes: Variance percentage = [(actual − budget) / budget] x 100

Variance percentage to date = [(actual to date − budget to date)/budget to date] x 100

Table C.4 gives the percentage for food and drink sales of the total sales; Table C.5 shows the average spend per head on food and drink; Table C.6 shows the average seat turnover.

Table C.4: Percentages of food and beverage sales of total sales

	Budget (£)	(%)	1st month (£)	(%)	2nd month (£)	(%)	3rd month (£)	(%)
Food	40,575	80.0	40,109	80.0	41,003	78.8	39,624	79.1
Beverage	10,279	20.0	10,019	20.0	10,990	21.1	10,410	20.8
Total	50,854	100	50,128	100	51 993	100	50,034	100

Table C.5: Average spend per head

	Budget	1st month	2nd month	3rd month
Food	7.50	7.51	7.56	7.29
Beverage	1.90	1.87	2.02	1.91
Total	9.40	9.38	9.58	9.20

Note: average spend per head = sales (food or/and beverages) ÷ number of customers

Table C.6: Average seat turnover

Budget	1st month	2nd month	3rd month
3.64	3.58	3.64	3.64

Note: seat turnover = No. of customers served ÷ No. of seats available
(Figures assume that establishment is open for 24 trading days per month (4 x 6 days)

Evaluation

Evaluation of the operational data which has been generated might be as follows:

Apparent strengths:

- Conservative budget (given the number of seats) and targets for sales are being met.
- Reasonable match between spend and number of customers and budget with the principal problem being costs.

Areas for concern:

- Food costs are higher in variance than sales resulting in the gross profit running under budget at £2,121 to date (–2.68%).
- Although liquor sales were slightly above budget the costs were higher than forecasted.
- Stock turnover in food is slightly lower than budgeted possibly suggesting a problem with purchasing not matching usage.
- Wage costs are between 3.24 and 4.88% over budget (+4.02% or £1509 to date) with upward trend indicating possible overstaffing.
- Overheads are increasing from 1.40 to 6.30% over budget (£842, or +3.42% to date).
- Overall performance of restaurant is poor against budget. Net profit is between –9.13 and –15.60% under budget and –11.59% under budget to date (£4156). The reduction in the net profit is mainly as a result of increasing labour costs but there are also increases in the food cost and overhead costs, which are contributing to this reduction in the net profit.

General overview:

- Sales on food are more or less static on budget while drink sales are slightly over budget. Also the main problems are seen to be costs: staff costs along with food costs are over budget and overhead costs are increasing.
- Overall there is a need to reduce costs to budget or increase sales to achieve targeted net profit.
- Assuming the budget to be accurate, and that costs can be brought under control, there may be little need for change. However without information on the nature of the customer demand being met, and the business environment in which this restaurant is operating, no further judgment can be made.

Additional information

Additional information required to make evaluation more complete will include:

- Basis of budget formulation including investigation of budgeting procedures to identify their appropriateness and accuracy.
- Previous trading information for comparison and to consider trends over the longer term.

- Analysis service period breakdown to show types of customer demand being met and analysis of sales mix date to determine popularity of menu and beverage items.

- Examination of food costs, purchasing and control system including pricing of food items. As well as possible problems with the relationship between demand and purchasing, which may lead to waste, there may also be difficulties with increases in prices of food.

- Identification of reason for drink sales increase and higher gross profit in order to determine cause (overages can indicate problems as much as shortages).

- Staffing information and breakdown of wage costs including investigation of staffing costs with a view to reducing them in line with budget.

- Examination of reasons for the high variance in actual overhead costs against budget.

- Assessment of the business environment.

C

Augmented bibliography

This bibliography contains all the references made within the text together with selected further information sources.

ACORN Classification at http://www.caci.co.uk/acorn-classification.aspx (accessed April 2011).

Ansoff, H.I. (1988) *Corporate Strategy*, London: Penguin.

Armstrong, G., Kotler, P., Harker, M. and Brennan, R. (2009) *Marketing an Introduction*, Harlow: Pearson.

Barth, S.C. (2008) *Hospitality Law: Managing Legal Issues in the Hospitality Industry*, 3rd edn, Oxford: John Wiley and Sons.

Best Practice Forum at http://www.bestpracticeforum.org (accessed June 2011).

Bissell, T. and Bissell, F. (1999) *A–Z of Food and Wine in Plain English*, London: Macmillan.

Boella, M..J and Goss-Turner, S. (2005) *Human Resource Management in the Hospitality Industry: An Introductory Guide*, 8th edn, Oxford: Butterworth-Heinemann.

Booty, F. (ed.) (2008) *Facilities Management Handbook*, 4th edn, Oxford: Butterworth-Heinemann.

Bowdin, G., Allen, J., O'Toole, W., Harris, R. and McDonnell, I. (2006) *Events Management*, 2nd edn, New York: Butterworth-Heinemann.

Bowie, D. and Buttle, F. (2004) *Hospitality Marketing, An Introduction*, Oxford: Butterworth Heinemann.

Bowie, D. and Buttle, F. (2011) *Hospitality Marketing, Principles and Practice*, 2nd edn, Oxford: Butterworth Heinemann.

British Standards Institution (BSI) at http://www.bsigroup.com (accessed March 2011).

Brotherton, B. (2003) *International Hospitality Management*, Oxford: Butterworth Heinemann.

Burill, C.W. and Ledolter, J. (1999) *Achieving Quality Through Continual Improvement*, New York: Wiley.

Caterer & Hotelkeeper at http://www.reedbusiness.co.uk/rb2_products/rb2_products_caterer_hotelkeeper.htm (accessed March 2011).

CESA (2009) *Introduction to Food Service*, (training manual), London: Catering Equipment Suppliers Association.

Chon, K.S., Kandampully, J. and Mok, C. (eds) (2001) *Service Quality Management in Hospitality, Tourism, and Leisure*, New York: Routledge.

Cousins, J. (1988) 'Curriculum development in operational management teaching in catering education', in R. Johnson (ed.), *The Management of Service Operations*, Bedford: IFS Publications, pp. 437–459.

Cousins, J. (1994) 'Managing capacity', in P. Jones (ed.), *The Management of Foodservice Operations*, London: Cassell, pp. 174–187.

Cousins, J. and Lillicrap, D. (2010) *Essential Food and Beverage Service*, London: Hodder Education.

Cousins, J., O'Gorman, K. and Stierand, M. (2010) 'Molecular gastronomy: basis for a new culinary movement or modern day alchemy?', *International Journal of Contemporary Hospitality Management*, 22 (3), 399–415.

Cracknell, H.L. and Kaufmann, R.J. (2002) *Practical Professional Catering Management*, 2nd edn, Andover: Thomson Learning Vocational.

Croner's Catering (1999) Reference guide and updating service, London: Croner Publications.

Cvent at http://www.cvent.com (accessed June 2011)

David, F. (2009) *Strategic Management: Concepts and Cases*, 12th edn, London: Pearson.

Davis, M.M. and Heineke, J. (1994) 'Understanding the roles of the customer and the operation for better queue management', *International Journal of Operations and Production Management* 14 (5), 21–34.

Debrett's Correct Form (2010) Surrey: Debrett.

Debrett's New Guide to Etiquette and Modern Manners (1999), edited by J. Morgon, London: Headline.

Debrett's Wedding Guide (2007) Surrey: Debrett.

Drink Aware at http://www.drinkaware.co.uk (accessed March 2011).

EFQM (European Foundation for Quality Management) at http://www.efqm.org (accessed March 2011).

Foskett, D., Paskins, P., Rippington, N. and Ceserani, V. (2011) *The Theory of Hospitality and Catering*, 12th edn, London: Hodder Education.

Getz, D. (2007) *Event Studies: Theory, Research and Policy for Planned Events*, Oxford: Butterworth-Heinemann.

Harris, P. (2011) *Profit Planning*, 3rd edn, Oxford: Goodfellow Publishers.

Harrington, D. and Lenehan, T. (1998) *Managing Quality in Tourism*, Dublin: Oaktree Press.

Hartman, L. (2008) *Business Ethics: Decision-making for Personal Integrity and Social Responsibility*, Boston, MA: McGraw-Hill International.

Hospitality Assured at http://www.hospitalityassured.com (accessed March 2011).

HotelPlanner at http://www.hotelplanner.com (accessed June 2011).

Jeston, J. and Nelis, J. (2006) *Business Process Management: Practical Guidelines to Successful Implementations*, Oxford: Butterworth Heinemann.

Johns, N. and Jones, P. (2000) 'Systems and management: understanding the real world', *Hospitality Review*, January, pp. 47–52.

Johnson, G., Scholes, K. and Whittington, R. (2008) *Exploring Corporate Strategy, Text and Cases*, 8th edn, Harlow: Prentice Hall.

Johnston, R. and Clark, G. (2008) *Service Operations Management*, 3rd edn, Harlow: Prentice Hall.

Jones, C. and Jowett, V. (1998) *Managing Facilities*, Oxford: Butterworth Heinemann.

Jones, P. (ed.) (1988) *Food Service Operations*, London: Cassell.

Jones, P. (ed.) (1994) *The Management of Foodservice Operations*, London: Cassell.

Jones, P. and Peppiatt, E. (1996) 'Managing perceptions of waiting times in service queues', *International Journal of Service Industry Management*, 7 (5), 47–61.

Jones, P., Ball, S., Kirk, D. and Lockwood, A. (2003) *Hospitality Operations: a Systems Approach*, London: Continuum.

Kasavana, M. and Smith, D. (1990) *Menu Engineering: a Practical Guide to Menu Analysis*, Lansing, MI: Hospitality Publications.

Katsigris, C. and Thomas, C. (2009) *Design and Equipment for Restaurants and Foodservice: a Management View*, Institute of Hospitality ebook held in the Institute's Online Catalogue (accessed March 2011).

Keynote Market Research Reports at http://www.keynote.co.uk (accessed March 2011).

Knowles, T. (1996) *Corporate Strategy for Hospitality*, Harlow: Longman.

Kotler, P., Keller, K., Brady, M., Goodman, M. and Hanser, T. (2009) *Marketing Management*, Harlow: Pearson Education.

Kotler, P., Bowen, J. and Makens, J. (2010) *Marketing for Hospitality and Tourism*, Harlow: Pearson Education.

Laloganes, J. (2008) *The Essentials of Wine: With Food Pairing Techniques*, London: Prentice Hall.

Larousse Encyclopaedia of Wine (2001), C. Foulkes (ed.), London: Hamlin.

Lascelles, O. and Peacock, R. (1996) *Self-assessment for Business Excellence,* Maidenhead: McGraw-Hill.

Lawson, F. (1995) *Restaurants, Clubs and Bars: Planning, Design and Investment in Food Service Facilities*, 2nd edn, Oxford: Architectural Press.

Lillicarp, D. and Cousins, J. (2010) *Food and Beverage Service*, 8th edn, London: Hodder Education.

Lockwood, A. (1994) 'Developing operating standards', in P. Jones (ed.), *The Management of Foodservice Operations*, London: Cassell.

Maister, D.H. (1985) 'The psychology of waiting lines', in J.A. Czepiel, M.R. Soloman and C.F. Surprenant (eds), *The Service Encounter*, Lexington Books, Washington,Heath and Company, Lexington, MA, pp. 113 – 123

Malouf, L. (1999) *Behind the Scenes at Special Events: Flowers, Props, and Design*, New York: Wiley.

Martin, W. (1986) 'Defining what quality service is for you', *Cornell Hotel and Restaurant Administration Quarterly*, 27(1) February, 32–38.

McDonough, B., Hill, J., Glazier, R., Lindsay, W. and Sykes, T. (2001) *Building Type Basics for Hospitality Facilities*, Oxford: John Wiley & Sons.

Meetings Industry Association at http://www.mia-uk.org (accessed April 2011).

Millar, J.E. and Pavesic, D.V. (1996) *Menu: Pricing & Strategy*, 4th edn, New York: Wiley.

Mintel Global Consumer, Product and Market Research at http://www.mintel.com (accessed March 2011).

Monroe, J.C. (2005) *Art of the Event, Complete Guide to Designing and Decorating Special Events*, New York: Wiley.

Morris, B. and Johnston, R. (1987) 'Dealing with the inherent variability – the difference between manufacturing and service', paper presented at the Operations Management Association International Conference, Warwick University.

Mullins, L.J. (2007) *Management and Organisational Behaviour*, 8th edn, Harlow: Financial Times Prentice Hall.

New Larousse Gastronomique (2009) London: Hamlin.

Ninemeier, J. and Hayes, O. (2006) *Restaurant Operations Management*, Upper Saddle River, NJ: Prentice Hall.

Nickson, D. (2006) *Human Resource Management for the Hospitality and Tourism Industries*, Oxford: Butterworth-Heinemann.

O'Gorman, K. (2010) *The Origins of Hospitality and Tourism*, Oxford: Goodfellow Publishers.

Palmer, A. (2007) *Principles of Services Marketing*, 5th edn, London: McGraw Hill.

Pavesic, D. and Magnant, P. (2005) *Fundamental Principles of Restaurant Cost Control*, 2nd edn, Upper Saddle River, NJ: Prentice Hall.

Porter, L. and Tanner, S.J. (2004) *Assessing Business Excellence: a Guide to Business Excellence and Self-assessment*, Oxford: Butterworth-Heinemann.

Porter, M. (2004a) *Competitive Advantage*, New York: Free Press.

Porter, M. (2004b) *Competitive Strategy: Techniques for Analyzing Industries and Competitors*, New York: Free Press.

Qualman, E. (2011) *Socialnomics: How Social Media Transforms the Way we Live and do Business*, New Jersey: Wiley and Sons.

Records, H. and Clennie, M. (1991) 'Service management and quality assurance', *Cornell HRA Quarterly*, 32 (1) May, 26–35.

Restaurant Magazine at http://www.bighospitality.co.uk/Info/Restaurant (accessed March 2011).

Riley, M. (2005) *Managing People: A Guide for Managers in the Hotel and Catering Industry*, 2nd edn, Oxford: Butterworth Heinemann.

Robinson, J. (2006) *The Oxford Companion to Wine*, Oxford: Oxford University Press.

Roger, T. (2003) *Conferences and Conventions: a Global Industry*, Oxford: Butterworth-Heinemann.

Saulnier, L. (1982) *Le Répertoire de la Cuisine*, translated by E. Brunet, 17th edn, London: Leon Jaeggi & Sons.

Simon, J. (1999) *Wine with Food: the Ultimate Guide to Matching Wine with Food for Every Occasion*, London: Mitchell Beazley.

Sink, E. (2006) *The Business of Software*, New York: Apress.

Slack, N., Chambers, S. and Johnston, R. (2004) *Operations Management*, 4th edn, Harlow: FT Prentice Hall.

Spears, M. and Gregoire, M. (2007) *Foodservice Organizations*, 6th edn, Upper Saddle River, NJ: Prentice Hall.

Starcite at http://www2.starcite.com/starcite (accessed June 2011).

Stipanuck, D.M. (2006) *Hospitality Facilities Management and Design,* 3rd edn, MI: American Hotel and Motel Association.

Tabs FM at http://www.tabsfm.com (accessed March 2011).

The Loyalty Guide 4. at http://www.theloyaltyguide.com/executive-summary.asp (accessed June 2011).

Thyne, M. and Laws, E. (2005) *Hospitality, Tourism, and Lifestyle Concepts: Implications for Quality Management and Customer Satisfaction*, New York: Haworth PR.

Toptable at http://www.toptable.com (accessed May 2011).

Walker, J. (2006) *Introduction to Hospitality*, 4th edn, Upper Saddle River, NJ: Prentice Hall.

William, A. (2002) *Understanding the Hospitality Consumer*, Oxford: Butterworth-Heinemann.

Yukl, G. (2005) *Leadership in Organisations*, 6th edn, Harlow: FT Prentice Hall.

Index

I

I

I